John Main
By Those Who Knew Him

John Main
By Those Who Knew Him

edited by
PAUL HARRIS

Introduction by Laurence Freeman OSB

Darton, Longman and Todd
London

First published in 1991 by
Darton, Longman and Todd Ltd
89 Lillie Road, London SW6 1UD

© 1991 Paul T. Harris
Introduction © 1991 Laurence Freeman OSB

British Library Cataloguing in Publication Data
John Main by those who knew him.
1. Christianity. Meditation
I. Main, John *d.1982*   II. Harris, Paul
248.34092

ISBN 0–232–51927–7

The portrait of John Main on the
cover is by Brenda Bury

Phototypeset by
Input Typesetting Ltd, London SW19 8DR
Printed and bound in Great Britain by
Courier International Ltd, Tiptree, Essex

Contents

Illustrations

The Contributors

TOM ABRAHAM was a lay member of John Main's meditation community at Ealing Abbey, London and also became a member of Father John's Benedictine community at the first foundation in Canada at Vendome Avenue, Montreal. Now married with two children, he is a staff scientist with Northern Telecom Electronics Ltd in Ottawa.

JOHN BOLAND is Public Trustee for England and Wales and was a Trinity College, Dublin classmate of John Main. He is an oblate of the Benedictine Abbey of Quarr of the French Solesmes congregation.

FATHER MARTIN BOLER is the Prior of Mount Saviour Benedictine Monastery, Elmira, New York. The Priory in Montreal became affiliated to Mount Saviour shortly after Father John Main went to Canada.

FATHER PAUL BOWE OP lives in Dublin where he has recently retired from teaching at University College. He studied theology with John Main in Rome in 1949–50.

SUE BRITTON of Montreal assisted John Main with her palliative care nursing skills in the month prior to his death, December 1982.

BRENDA BURY was born and educated in the north of England and took an honours degree in Fine Arts at the University of Reading. She began to establish herself as a portrait painter by painting people in widely different spheres of influence.

In 1965 she did her first English royal portrait, of Lord Mountbatten of Burma, and in 1969 was invited to paint the Queen at Buckingham Palace. She now works in Toronto where she went to live in 1983. Before his death she painted a portrait of John Main which now hangs at the Benedictine Priory, Montreal.

SISTER CAMILLE CAMPBELL is a sister of Notre Dame stationed in Drayton Valley, Alberta, Canada. She writes, 'I experienced a conversion when I first heard John Main speak. That conversion deepened when for a reason known only to God, I witnessed and shared in his death. For me it was in his death that his message became alive.'

LEONARD J. CROWLEY VG is auxiliary bishop of Montreal and was instrumental in bringing John Main to Montreal to found the Benedictine Priory.

MOLLY CURRAN is married with six children and lives in Toronto. She was a neighbour of the Main family in Muswell Hill, North London before the war, and shared in the activities of the family.

JACK DAVITT is a Washington DC lawyer, and worked for the US Justice Department. John Main visited the Davitts at their Cape Cod home shortly before his death in 1982.

FATHER BERNARD DEEGAN, a Servite priest in London, is a Christian Meditation group leader. He met John Main in 1975 in Manchester.

WILLIAM DONAHUE, now retired in Montastrue, France, was a confrère and fellow monk with John Main at St Anselm's Abbey in Washington DC. After leaving St Anselm's he worked as an editor on the daily *Ottawa Journal*.

FATHER JOHN FARRELLY is a Benedictine monk of St Anselm's Abbey in Washington DC. He teaches systematic theology at De Sales School of Theology and conducts workshops on spirituality at the Abbey. He is author of many theological works including *God's Work in a Changing World*.

MONSIGNOR TOM FEHILY is a well known Irish priest and pastor and was chairman of the Dublin Committee for the papal visit. As a friend of John Main and a meditator, he chairs the Christian Meditation co-ordinating committee in the Irish Republic, which has seen the growth of forty-five meditation groups in recent years.

GERALD FITZGERALD is a retired orthodontist living in Dublin. He is the husband of Yvonne (Main) Fitzgerald, sister of John Main.

YVONNE (MAIN) FITZGERALD, sister to John Main, lives in Dublin with her husband Gerald, where she helps to co-ordinate the forty-five Christian Meditation groups that have developed in the Republic of Ireland and follow John Main's teaching on prayer.

FATHER EDMUND FLOOD is a Benedictine monk of Ealing Abbey in London, and a prolific writer on spirituality and theological topics. He knew John Main at Ealing, Washington and Montreal.

FATHER LAURENCE FREEMAN OSB succeeded John Main as Prior of the Benedictine Monastery in Montreal. Born in London, he read English Literature at Oxford University before pursuing careers in journalism and banking. In 1975 he joined Ealing Abbey as a Benedictine monk and in 1977 went with John Main to found the Montreal Priory, which has subsequently become the centre of a remarkable revival of contemplative prayer. He is author of two books on Christian meditation: *Light Within* and *The Selfless Self*; and editor of *Monastic Studies*, a publication addressed to Christian as well as non-Christian monastic life.

FATHER ANTHONY GEE, a Benedictine monk of Ealing Abbey, knew John Main in Rome as a student and in Ealing Abbey as a fellow member of the community.

FRANÇOIS C. GÉRARD is principal of St Paul's United College, University of Waterloo, Ontario, where he teaches Reformation history and theology. He is an ordained minister of the United Church of Canada.

FATHER ELTIN GRIFFIN is Retreat Director at Gort Muir Carmelite retreat house in Dublin. He was a fellow student with John Main in 1969 at the Catholic University of America, Washington DC.

FATHER BEDE GRIFFITHS is a Benedictine monk who founded the ashram of Shantivanum, Tamil Nadu, Southern India. He is widely known for his many books on the advaitic experience and the integration of the spiritual values of East and West. His remarks here formed the introduction to John Main's book, *The Inner Christ*.

PATRICIA GUY was raised in the Anglican Church and was married to a United Church minister for fifteen years. She has two children, Mark and Rebecca. She spent ten years (1963–73) in a Yoga ashram in the Laurentians near Montreal, under the guidance of Swami Vishnu Devananda. In 1980 she became an oblate of the Benedictine Priory, Montreal and in 1981 was received into the Catholic Church by Dom John Main.

HENRY HILL was Bishop of the Anglican diocese of Ontario 1975–81; he lived as an oblate at the Benedictine Priory of Montreal for three years; and has been Anglican chairman of the Anglican–Eastern Orthodox Joint Doctrinal Commission; and episcopal liaison with the Oriental Orthodox Churches. He travels worldwide for ecumenical concerns.

ROBERT KIELY is Loker Professor of English and American Literature at Harvard University. He teaches nineteenth- and twentieth-century fiction, Christian Literature and the English Bible. He is author of *The Romantic Novel in England* and *Beyond Egotism: the fiction of James Joyce, Virginia Woolf and D. H. Lawrence*. In his contribution he looks at John Main's teaching on meditation through two books, *Moment of Christ*, and *Community of Love*.

PAUL LAFONTAINE of Montreal knew John Main in the early days of the Benedictine Priory at Vendome Avenue and for a time was a frequent visitor at the monastery.

FATHER WALTER LALLEMAND has been a parish priest in the archdiocese of Montreal for many years and was one of the first priests to welcome John Main on his arrival in Montreal from England.

LUCY MCDONALD, a widow, mother of three and a Benedictine oblate of the Montreal Priory, has been active in Dublin since 1978 in supporting Father John Main's teaching on Christian meditation. In 1987 she participated in the second meditation group leaders' meeting held in Montreal. She is currently on the executive of the Dublin Christian Meditation co-ordinating committee.

SISTER GERTRUDE MCLAUGHLIN SNJM, who died in 1988, received a Magisterium in Sacred Sciences from the Pontifical Institute Regina Mundi in Rome in 1957. She was a founding member of the World Catholic Federation for the Biblical Apostolate and Vice-President of the Canadian Bible Society.

SISTER PATRICIA MCLAUGHLIN is a Daughter of Charity of St Vincent de Paul and a former Superior of Glenmaroon Convent, Dublin. She is currently working in Dublin's inner city where the Daughters run two schools and a variety of social programmes.

IAN AND JUDITH MAIN. Judith is married to John Main's elder brother Ian, and they live on the Greek island of Karpathos.

MOTHER ABBESS MARY MECHTILDE, Superior of Benedictine Kylemore Abbey, Co. Galway, wrote her tribute to John Main in January 1983, shortly after his death. It is addressed to the Prior and community of the Montreal Priory.

CONNIE MOORE, an oblate of the Montreal Benedictine Priory, is a wife, mother and college teacher.

TERESA MORTON, a cousin of John Main, lives in Dublin.

BALFOUR M. MOUNT is a professor of surgery at McGill University and founder and first director of the Palliative Care Unit, Royal Victoria Hospital, Montreal. One of Canada's best known specialists in pain control, he assisted the medical team during John Main's last illness. In 1988 he conducted the John Main seminar at the Benedictine Priory on the subject of Human Wholeness.

FATHER SEAN MULLIN is an Irish Redemptorist. He met John Main when they were both studying at the Catholic University of America in 1969.

AGNES MURPHY was a friend of John Main and with his encouragement started the first Christian Meditation group in Liverpool. She has visited the Benedictine Priory in Montreal three times.

FATHER PATRICK MURRAY, an Irish Pallotine priest, has been a missionary in Africa, a parish priest in Canada and today with Sister Consilio Fitzgerald runs Galilee House in Athy, Co. Kildare, Ireland. Galilee House is a unique experiment aimed at rehabilitating the most wounded in Irish society, including alcoholics and drug addicts. He spent six months at the Benedictine Priory in Montreal with John Main in 1982. His rehabilitation programme at Athy includes three daily periods of Christian meditation with both staff and patients. His memoir was recorded in a conversation at the Christian Meditation Centre in London.

DON MYRICK, along with his wife Therese and two children, lives in Ottawa. He is a Benedictine oblate, and works for the government of Canada. For nine years he was co-ordinator of the Christian Meditation groups in Ottawa.

DIANE (MAIN) O'NEILL, youngest sister to John Main, lives with her husband Hugh in Co. Wicklow, Ireland where they run a commercial fruit orchard.

SISTER MIRIAM O'QUIGLEY, an Irish Medical Missionary of Mary, met John Main at Ealing Abbey in London in 1976. Her commitment to Christian meditation has led her to a recent assignment as a staff member at the Christian Meditation Centre in London.

FATHER BERNARD ORCHARD was a fellow Benedictine monk with John Main at Ealing Abbey, London. His homily was given at the requiem mass for John Main at Ealing Abbey on 8 January 1983.

JACK PEFFERS attended St Benedict's School, Ealing, 1964–8, where he was a student of Dom John Main. He studied Comparative Government and Politics before he entered teaching. He is currently national co-ordinator of the School Curriculum Industry Partnership (SCIP), a curriculum development organisation whose basic principles draw heavily on John Main's philosophy of life.

NEIL PORTER, now retired in Dublin, taught physics at University College, Dublin.

JEAN R. PRIEUR of Montreal was a warden of the Ascension of Our Lord parish as well as a car dealer. He recounts his friendship in Montreal with Father John.

DOREEN ROMANDINI is an oblate of the Benedictine Priory of Montreal and assists in the administrative work and teaching at the monastery.

GREGORY J. RYAN is a husband, teacher, meditation group leader and an oblate of the Benedictine Priory, Montreal. In his contribution he examines John Main's teaching on Christian meditation as well as the common bond that links the American Cistercian monk Thomas Merton and the Benedictine monk John Main.

FATHER THOMAS RYAN is a Paulist priest, author and lecturer, who directs the Canadian Centre for Ecumenism in Montreal.

JAMES SCARLETT, a circuit judge in Kent, was a young cadet in the Malayan Civil Service at the same time as John Main. He writes of his friendship with him at that time.

SISTER MARIAN SCENA MMM was born in Stamford, Conn. She grew up in Denver, Colorado and entered the Medical Missionaries of Mary in 1963 at Winchester, Mass. She qualified with an MB from National University of Ireland in June 1975 and then worked for two years at the International Missionary Training Hospital, Drogheda, Co. Louth. Her mission experience includes six years in Tanzania, working in two Medical Missionaries of Mary hospitals.

THOMAS F. SCHLAFLY, a teacher at St Anselm's Benedictine Abbey School in Washington DC, 1972–4, worked closely with John Main and in August 1980 invited him to his family's holiday home, Rainbow Springs in southern Missouri, to do some white water canoeing.

POLLY SCHOFIELD, her husband Mark, and their three children Julian, Dominic and Adrian became friends of John Main and Laurence Freeman shortly after the monks moved to Vendome Avenue in the west end of Montreal. All the family began to meditate at the Vendome House. Today, as Benedictine oblates, Polly and Mark continue as long time special friends and supporters of the Priory. Polly is curator of the Priory's antiquities. The interview between the editor and Polly Schofield was taped at the Christian Meditation Centre, London.

FATHER BROCARD SEWELL, a Carmelite of the ancient observance, knew John Main during his 1946–50 stint with the Canons Regular of the Lateran.

SISTER MADELEINE SIMON is a religious of the Sacred Heart and has been involved as a sister in teaching and parish work. In 1986 she founded the Christian Meditation Centre, London, dedicated to promoting John Main's teaching on Christian meditation. She recently founded a second Christian Meditation Centre in Royston near Cambridge.

SISTER CARLA SIMMONS is a Medical Missionary of Mary now stationed in Detroit, Michigan. She spent a month in retreat in 1980 at the Montreal Priory.

FATHER JOHN SMITH is a diocesan priest of St Andrews and Edinburgh and a former missionary in South America. He met John Main in Montreal shortly before Father John's death in 1982.

CEDRIC M. SPEYER is a Montreal psychotherapist, a writer and a Benedictine oblate of the Montreal Priory.

KITTY (MAIN) STANLEY, eldest of the six Main children and John Main's sister, lives on Valentia Island, Co. Kerry, Ireland.

BRUCE TODD, a cousin of John Main, lives in West Sussex.

JOHN TODD, a co-founder of the English publishing house Darton, Longman and Todd, was the publisher of John Main's first books on the subject of Christian meditation. His article, specifically written for this book, first appeared in the *Tablet*, 27 May 1989.

FATHER GERARD P. WEBER, a seventy-two-year-old priest of the Archdiocese of Chicago and ordained forty-five years, met John Main in Washington DC. Father Weber presently lives in Los Angeles where he works in the field of education.

FATHER JOHN WINGFIELD is a priest in Tolworth, Surrey. Since meeting John Main in a seminary in 1977 he has started five meditation groups in Tolworth and gives conferences and retreats on John Main's teaching.

Preface

Since his death on 30 December 1982 at the age of fifty-six Dom John Main's teaching on Christian meditation has spread from the Benedictine monastery he founded in Montreal to embrace a worldwide fellowship of meditators. People of various faiths, ages and occupations, from executives to housewives, from teachers to taxi drivers, have felt the call to follow the path of silence, stillness, simplicity, and the use of a mantra in prayer. Meditation groups are now flourishing in North America and around the world from New York to Dublin, from London to Melbourne, from Singapore to Manila.

Many people noticing this rebirth of traditional contemplative prayer have begun to ask more about the career and the spiritual development of this extraordinary teacher. This book attempts to answer that need and includes reminiscences and memories of Dom John Main from those who knew him. It also supplements our knowledge not only of the man himself but of his teaching on prayer.

As Father Laurence Freeman points out in his introduction, in the short span of fifty-six years John Main was journalist, soldier, law student, diplomat, university lecturer and finally a Benedictine monk. His journeys took him from London to Ballinskelligs, Co. Kerry, to Dublin, Rome, Malaya, Washington DC, back to London and finally to Montreal.

Ballinskelligs may have had a mysterious but hidden influence on John Main's future life. Close to Ballinskelligs is the famous island site of Skellig Michael, a rocky promontory rising 700 feet, eight miles out in the Atlantic off the Kerry coast. Irish monks built a monastic hermitage at the summit of Skellig Michael in the sixth century and monastic life continued there for over 400 years.

There is an even deeper question and a more intriguing conjecture. To Benedictine John Main is given credit for recognising and rediscovering the teachings of John Cassian (360–435) and the early Egyptian Desert Fathers on the use of a short phrase in prayer to bring one to an interior silence. St Benedict was deeply influenced by Cassian's teachings. The writings of Cassian also played a decisive role in the life of John Main.

Cassian came to Provence in Gaul and brought a new influx of spiritual traditions from the Desert Fathers with the avowed aim of reforming Gallic monasticism. It was by way of Gaul that monasticism spread to settlements such as Skellig Michael off the west coast of Ireland. Was the 'mantra' tradition of John Cassian and the Desert Fathers implanted on Skellig Michael from Gaul? Did John Main ever make this connection? Whether he did or not, it is an intriguing hypothesis that the teaching of the mantra came from Egypt to Gaul to Ireland's Skellig Michael and that John Main, who spent part of his youth in sight of Skellig Michael, rediscovered in the twentieth century this ancient prayer tradition.

But John Main's greatest journey was a journey 'inwards' towards the centre. He understood fully the words of Jesus in Luke 17:20–21, 'The kingdom of God does not come in such a way, as to be seen. No one will say, "look here it is" or "there it is", because the kingdom of God is within you.' This became John Main's final journey leading thousands of people around the world to the discovery of this 'kingdom within' through the path of interior silence in prayer.

The range of his thought and experience, the number of his books, the 160 cassette talks on meditation, the founding of a Benedictine monastery, the diverse variety of friends and people he reached, make John Main one of the spiritual giants of the twentieth century. But John Main taught, as all great teachers do, by example. He never tried to persuade anyone to meditate. Rather he hoped *you* would enter into the experience itself. In the final analysis it was the authenticity of his life that instructs us. As United Church theologian François Gérard says (p. 185), 'If one were to characterise the spiritual pilgrimage and teaching of Dom John Main in one sentence or phrase, one could suggest that he rediscovered and lived the simplicity of the gospel.' But John Main was always pointing to the teacher beyond himself – Jesus. All this becomes very clear in this book as people who knew Dom John Main give us not only a deeper insight into his life and personality but also into his teaching.

But to understand the fully mature Benedictine monk we must first see that person in the context of early family life and take a look not only at the various points of growth but also at the vicissitudes and changes of direction that mark John Main's pilgrimage. The experiences and memories of those who knew him shed a revealing light on John Main's inner growth from early childhood to Benedictine Prior.

From the contributors we begin to get a multi-faceted portrait of a remarkable man. But in many respects he also becomes a sign of contradiction; deeply spiritual while wise in the ways of the world; cultivating privacy yet always at centre stage; speaking with conviction and authority while never foisting his teaching on anyone; the funniest man in the world yet intensely serious; truly a man who fitted Thomas Merton's description of a person 'born under the sign of contradiction'.

Perhaps the central theme of John Main's life and his timeless teaching on Christian meditation could be summed up in the following story. In Japan for an international conference on religion, an American delegate, a social philosopher from New York, said to a Shinto priest, 'We've been now to a good many ceremonies and have seen quite a few of your shrines. But I don't grasp your ideology, I don't understand your theology.' The Japanese paused as though in deep thought and then slowly shook his head, 'I think we don't have ideology,' he said. 'We don't have theology. We dance.'

John Main would have loved that story. How often he asked listeners to stop intellectualising and stop being so cerebral about prayer. He urged everyone 'to enter into the experience of silence itself'. 'Just do it, just say your mantra,' was John Main's final gift to all of us.

His influence as a teacher continues to spread as more and more people around the world hear his call to enter 'the country beyond words and beyond names'. This book gives us a better understanding of the man, the teacher and the teaching.

PAUL T. HARRIS

Acknowledgements

I would like to acknowledge a special debt of gratitude to Father Laurence Freeman OSB, former Prior of the Benedictine Monastery, Montreal. When I first broached the idea of this book he offered his enthusiasm and encouragement and for the past three years has urged me to persevere in tracking down the personal memories of people who knew Dom John Main OSB. In addition to writing the introduction, Father Laurence gave permission to reprint a number of articles which originally appeared in the Christmas 1984 and 1988 issues of the Priory periodical, *Monastic Studies*.

To all the contributors my grateful thanks for sharing their personal memories of Dom John Main along with their incisive observations and insights. My particular thanks to two Benedictine oblates, Jean Lee and Anita Finnigan of Dorset, as well as Gabriella Stables of Hertfordshire, who gave their time, effort and professional expertise in typing the draft manuscript. Jean Lee died in August 1989 and this book is a fitting memorial to her dedication.

Special thanks must also go to members of the Main family, Yvonne, Diane, Kitty and Ian, and to John Main's nephews William and David, who gave unsparingly of their time and have contributed greatly to a better understanding of the early Main family life.

Thanks also to the many people around the world who sent me over 180 photographs of Dom John Main; and to Yvonne (Main) Fitzgerald for assistance in identifying them. My gratefulness also to Sister Madeleine Simon, Director of the Christian Meditation Centre, Hertfordshire, who gave unstintingly of her hospitality, enabling me to spend an additional two months in England in research and editing this book.

Acknowledgements

My gratitude also to the English Catholic weekly the *Tablet* for permission to reprint John Todd's contribution in Chapter 9.

I would like to pay special tribute to Bill Long, writer and presenter of the 1990 RTE (Irish) radio documentary on John Main, *Inward Towards the Self*; and to John MacKenna, its producer. Some of the insights from this programme I have included in my preface; as well as excerpts of Yvonne (Main) Fitzgerald in Chapters 1, 3 and 8.

My sincere thanks also to Neil and Catharine McKenty for their encouragement and assistance; and for the invaluable research Neil provides in his biography of John Main, *In the Stillness Dancing* (Darton, Longman and Todd, 1986).

Finally this book is dedicated with thanks to a worldwide group of meditators, 'this motley crew', as John Main once described them, whose lives have been transformed through the gentle teaching of the mantra and who seek to know more about their teacher and the teaching.

PAUL T. HARRIS

Introduction

LAURENCE FREEMAN OSB

John Main said he became a monk because he wanted to be free. To many his life, up to his entering the Benedictine monastery where his monastic adventure began, seemed already to express a very free spirit. It was a life that had moved freely through several cultures, English, Irish, European and Oriental, through war and peace, through Church and state, through love in its human and divine manifestations. Despite the variety of his pre-monastic experience, however, one senses, as he did himself, not a restless wandering but a passionate, directed search for his vocation. It was a search that so expanded his native capacity for freedom and spontaneity that when he became a monk he was already superbly confident in his own identity. By the time he took the habit he had *done* a lot. He was now concerned to *be* more. 'The real freedom,' he would write shortly before his death, 'is not the freedom to do but to be.' This was the spirit of freedom he breathed in from the beginning of his life, from the family he was born into.

Preparation

Douglas William Victor Main, born in Hendon, London on 21 January 1926, was the second son and third child of David and Eileen Main. A sister and brother followed into what became and still is a closely-knit and intensely vital family. David Main was born in 1893 in Ballinskelligs, Co. Kerry. His father had moved there from Scotland to establish the first transatlantic cable station. Douglas loved Ballinskelligs, where some of the family still live. He felt it to be his *home* in

1

an atavistic sense, a place where he belonged through blood and ancestral consciousness, the *topos* where he was *known*. He was moved and impressed when Kenneth Clark started his story of *Civilisation* at the Celtic monastic settlement of the Skellig Rocks that rear up grandly from the Atlantic, seven miles off the coast of his beloved Ballinskelligs.

Eileen Hurley was a nurse who met her future husband during the terrible flu epidemic of 1919. David fell in love with her and persevered in his intentions even when she had told him of her engagement to another man. He swept her off her feet and gave her his ring before she had time to return her fiancé's. Douglas inherited his father's passion and determination. David and Eileen were married in Cork city on 7 February 1920 but moved to London after the birth of their first child.

Family life was colourful, entertaining and often dramatic, dominated by David's strong temper and flamboyant but generous hospitality, moderated by Eileen's equally strong but steadier will and quieter spirit. The fun and humour of his childhood shaped Douglas's expectation of life wherever he was. His most disparaging epithet for people, communities or events was 'dull' or 'boring'. He was criticised later for equating dullness with lack of goodness. He did not. But he felt it must be a rare exception, and one to be pitied, to be good and dull. Goodness for him meant vitality and vitality was for him a way to goodness. The words of Jesus that he loved especially, and often quoted to describe meditation, were those describing his mission: 'I have come that men may have life, life in all its fullness.' John Main also understood D. H. Lawrence's exciting words, 'What I want is life and the pure contact with life.' For less exuberant spirits his intense vitality could easily become threatening. This optimistic pattern of response in such a personality could easily be seen as ambition. The strong, protective and caring concern for others could be seen as domination. In fact John Main, like his father, was too ambitious for pure contact with life to be satisfied by fame or success. Their freedom from materialism lies behind David Main's bankruptcies and his son's major uprootings. They both knew that the person unable to renounce success or wealth would be possessed by them.

2

Every summer the Main family went on special holidays. One year David hired a truck and driver to transport the eight members of the family on a tour of Sussex. The highlight occurred when they were parked near a travelling circus and a giraffe poked its head into the back of the truck, to the delight of all the children. Sunday evenings in the Main house were times of visitors and family entertainment. David Main sang well and there were games like the 'One-Minute Speech'. Topics were drawn from a hat and Douglas's topic for his brother Ian on one occasion was 'Early Byzantine Architecture'. Even at the age of seven or eight people were not certain how seriously to take him. Even then he had a serious air but a quick wit and took pleasure in confounding people's expectations of him, as he did throughout his life. While playing 'Doctors and Nurses' he calmed his sister Yvonne, whose leg he was supposed to amputate, by saying, 'Don't worry madam, the knife is quite blunt.' He liked to sit and talk with his mother's tea guests and once, at the age of eight, he startled a London matron by walking into the room, sitting beside her and asking her intently, 'What do you think of the Abyssinian question?'

The Main home was a religious one of deep Catholic faith (although Eileen Main would confidently overlook Friday abstinence if it meant good food going bad). Their faith was human and uncompromising. Waifs and strays, unwed mothers turned away from rectories, abandoned wives or alcoholics were not only welcomed into the family for their stay but often given the room of one of the family who would return to find himself assigned to the sofa. The children played ecclesiastical games in which Douglas usually assumed the role of bishop. His sisters were dragooned into serving his 'mass' and scolded for not lighting the candles or ringing the bells on time.

In 1932 Douglas spent several months in Ballinskelligs. He was regarded as a delicate child and the country food and healthy air, it was hoped, would build him up. He did not like school work and was always up to pranks or persuading fishermen to take him out to the islands. When he returned to England his parents moved to Highgate and he spent an intensely unhappy time at a council school where his refined

3

manners drew the opprobrium of the class. He always had an aversion to crowds and street-life. But in 1937 he was accepted into Westminster Cathedral Choir School where he found the life and companions more congenial. He was groomed to serve mass for Cardinal Hinsley in the private chapel of Archbishop's House, a special privilege. Douglas was not good at sports but learned to dance, enjoyed the tea-dances and wore an Eton suit with panache. He was academically successful and caught the attention of the head-master who wrote in a prophetic moment: 'Pleasing boy – smart – very good mimic – tendency to Benedictines.'

In 1939 because of the war Douglas was moved to a Jesuit school which was then evacuated to the country. Douglas and his brother Ian stayed with a family who were friends of the Mains. Douglas was thirteen, and Diana, the only daughter of the family, was six. It was the beginning of an important friendship in his life.

Douglas was not happy with the Jesuits whom he found rigid teachers. He was glad to leave school and returned to London where he worked as a reporter for a local newspaper and volunteered as a fire-watcher during the Blitz. In 1943 he trained privately as a wireless operator and enlisted with the Royal Corps of Signals whose records described him as '6 foot 1¾ inches in height, weighing 145 pounds, blue eyes and light brown hair'. He was assigned to SCU3, a special communications unit whose secret and highly sensitive work was to detect enemy espionage signals, and Douglas was actively involved in it in Belgium by January 1945. Working sometimes behind the retreating enemy lines, Douglas experi-enced physical danger but also the camaraderie of warfare. An exploding shell gave him a lifelong back problem. His older colleagues were protective but respectful. He wrote love poems for some of them to send home to their girlfriends. They taught him to swim. He visited most of the churches that his unit passed *en route*.

After serving for nearly three years in England, Belgium and Germany, Douglas was restored to civilian life but with a stronger sense of his calling to the priesthood. While work-ing as a journalist he had met the Canons Regular of the Lateran, a religious order whose community life was shaped by the Rules of St Augustine and St Benedict. The novitiate was held in Bodmin Moor, Cornwall, stark surroundings which could not depress his enthusiasm or good spirits. When his sisters visited him with a birthday cake he amused them by mimicking the members of the community. He took simple vows a year later and began studies at the diocesan seminary of St Edmund's, Ware. His superiors at this time remember him as an attractive personality interested in the eremitical life. He was chosen for special studies in Rome and went to study theology at the Angelicum. He was soon to have doubts about his vocation, however, and eventually decided to leave. It was a difficult time and he later remembered receiving little sympathetic support. Over twenty years later, however, while visiting the Canons' church in Rome, the Lateran Basilica, he ran into his former novice master, now the superior-general. The recognition was mutual and immediately warm and they spent an hour in the general's room catching up on their life stories. Douglas did not speak much about this early attempt at his vocation except to praise the Canons for teaching him how to study. He was young and had been deeply affected by the war when he entered but this attempt only strengthened his sense of having a vocation.

There had been a monastic flavour to the life of the Canons to which he had been attracted, but not monastic enough to satisfy his need for an absolute commitment to God. Nor was he yet temperamentally mature enough to express this commitment with balance and moderation. His humour and good spirits never expressed lack of true reverence but were his way of keeping his intense spiritual life both private and down to earth. The stories of those first student days in Rome show his characteristic blend of religious idealism and iconoclasm. In his childhood and adolescence the seeds of his later prophetic vision of monasticism and the Church were sown. He would say that seriousness leads to joy, solemnity to triviality. Though he could laugh at ecclesiastical self-importance and pomposity, there was also anger in his rejection of such attitudes because he saw them to be not only humanly destructive but belittling to the mysteries of the sacred. These mysteries he reverenced in his heart silently, shyly, and at this stage of his life even with a certain embarrassment.

There was never much delay in making decisions in John Main's life. He could also, if necessary, wait long and patiently. But he could not be depressed for very long. He felt the tide of life pulling him too strongly. After leaving Rome he went to Dublin, where his family now lived, and began to study law. The Catholic university would not accredit him for his previous studies but Trinity College was eager to receive him and did. Special permission was reluctantly granted by the Archbishop to allow Douglas as a Catholic to enter Trinity.

He loved Trinity and his years of academic law. His professor applauded his intelligence and style. His fellow-students found him the best of company, imaginative, lively and often disconcertingly honest in his reaction to others. He lived a disciplined life, reading extensively in literature, theology and history. Most of his studying was done very early, thus leaving the day free for the Dublin social life that he loved and would transplant to other locations in later life. He went to parties, gained a reputation as a dancer and developed a highly profitable betting system at the races. In 1954 he graduated but was already looking beyond Dublin for his next adventure.

Outward pilgrimage

Douglas was politically a socialist. His Irish roots and his own intellectual formation as well as his personal temperament also made him, if not a complete republican (he liked ceremonial both liturgical and constitutional), at least pragmatically anti-imperialist. When he joined the British Colonial Service in the autumn of 1954 many countries in the British Commonwealth were gaining their independence. Douglas joined, eager to be involved in this momentous period of history. It was also to be a decision of eternal moment in his own life. He was assigned to Malaya, and first studied Chinese in London at the School of Oriental and African Studies. He was to remember the motto inscribed over its front door when writing on meditation years later: 'Knowledge is power'. He rejected that claim. The only *real* power, he wrote, is love. But in 1954 he was eagerly absorbing knowledge and new skills to train him for the exercise of civil power over large numbers of people. In January 1955 he sailed to Malaya. On the boat out he broke with convention and offended some of his superior officers by throwing a party on a grand scale, assuming a custom usually reserved for the senior members of the service. On arrival at Kuala Lumpur he continued his study of Chinese (Hokkien dialect) at a language school housed in a Confucian temple and assisted in the preparation of the first elections for an independent Malaya. His life was that which English imperialists had cultivated overseas for several generations and, though he lived it energetically, it was clear both to his closer friends and himself that it was not his life. A friend asked him why he did not go into the Church. Douglas replied that he had not given up the idea. The director of his language school wrote of him:

> He was exceptional. In that large body he had the gentleness of a child. His intelligence was keen, quick and vibrant. He was out of place in a brash society emerging from colonial rule which was crude compared with the intellectual and spiritual realm which was later to be the home of Douglas Main.

One of his duties was that of Protocol Officer and one day it sent him on an apparently trivial mission. He was to deliver a photograph of the Governor to a Hindu monk who ran an orphanage of the Pure Life Society on the outskirts of Kuala Lumpur. Father John thought he would quickly despatch the assignment and be free for the rest of the day. In fact it was a mission that changed his life and gradually revealed to him his own vocation.

Swami Satyananda, the Hindu monk, was born in India in 1909. He was educated in a Roman Catholic mission and had often considered baptism. At the age of seventeen he entered the Malayan government service, which he left in 1936 to become a monk in India where he spent several years of study and discipleship with spiritual masters, including Ramana Maharshi. He was sent back to Malaya in 1940 and, through the Pure Life Society, founded in 1949, expressed his life's goal to 'restore the consciousness of the kingdom of God among his fellow-men'. His school, orphanage, Temple of the Universal Spirit, adult education classes and regular group meditation classes all aimed to harmonise the diverse communities and races living in Malaya. In 1954 he was made a Justice of the Peace. But he was pre-eminently a monk, a meditator since the age of eighteen, a teacher and disciple, a man of the spirit whose faith was alive in love and service. Douglas Main recognised these qualities at their first meeting. In retrospect their lives seem a strangely similar blend of experiences. Both died at a relatively early age. He later described how this encounter led him to the pilgrimage of meditation.[1] He returned each week to the ashram to meditate with his teacher and thirty years later remembered the importance of that experience of holy presence. John Main's own confident openness to the religions of the East can be traced back to the openness of the Hindu monk who had accepted him as a Christian disciple and taught him to meditate as the way to deepen his discipleship to Christ. It was the experience of this human relationship and its underlying spiritual courage that formed John Main's later attitude to teaching meditation himself, to 'all who come to pray with us'.[2]

Douglas Main returned to Dublin in the summer of 1956 and for the next four years taught Administration and Roman and International Law at Trinity College. He was popular with colleagues and students. He was still outspoken. Questioning the controversial appointment of a new lecturer considered by many to be unqualified, junior Professor Main said in the senior common room that he could not see why a third-rate intelligence should be appointed when there were already so many second-rate ones around. It was an example of his realistic and mischievously iconoclastic wit that won him friends and disciples as well as rejection and misunderstanding. To a few of his more perceptive acquaintances he appeared, as he was, a 'deeply religious man possessing peace and tranquillity'. He went to mass daily and meditated twice a day. His academic career was bright and promising. 'Had he remained with Law, Douglas would have been a national authority,' said a colleague.[3] His friends from this period went on to become the country's leaders, such as Garret FitzGerald, a former Prime Minister and his lifelong friend.

Douglas Main's friendship with the daughter of the family he had lived with during the war had continued and in 1957 blossomed into love. They would meet when Douglas came to London to eat his dinners at Gray's Inn where he would later be called to the Bar. In their long talks and walks through the city they discussed socialism and especially Douglas's idea of a society of people living in community – a community of love.[4]

The most intense emotional period of their twenty-year-old relationship was to begin at a restaurant in London where Douglas entertained her with some Malayan friends and two Buddhist monks of his acquaintance. During the next few days Douglas and Diana talked about marriage. She broke off her engagement to another man but neither she nor Douglas felt really confident of the fulfilment of their plans. Praying together in a church in London on one of their long walks she experienced a sense that their relationship could not be fulfilled in marriage. They both recognised that two intense forms of love, human and divine, were interacting in two strong, passionate personalities. Shortly after their time together in London she wrote to him saying she had become re-engaged and some months later she married.

This trauma of detachment (they remained friends for the rest of his life) was immediately followed by another – the trauma of death. His eldest sister's son, eleven-year-old David, developed an inoperable brain tumour. Douglas took him to the doctor for the diagnosis while his sister was out of the country as he had become a second father to all his sister's children since her husband's early death. David and the other children worshipped him. He always had a marvellous rapport with children, telling stories (acting every part), taking them for walks and mystery tours, playing all sorts of magical tricks. He sat beside the bed of his dying nephew for weeks. David died in September 1958. A year later Douglas Main was a monk.

He told his sister he did not want to become a monk but

knew that he had to. He compressed his reasons into a few words in *The Gethsemani Talks*:

> About this time, 1958, a nephew of mine, one of my sister's children, became seriously ill and died. The death of this child had an enormous effect on me and brought me face to face with the question of life and death and the whole purpose of existence. As I reviewed my life at this time, I was forcibly struck by the fact that the most important thing in my entire existence was my daily meditation. I decided, therefore, to structure my life on my meditation and sought to do so by becoming a monk.[5]

He carried his suffering lightly as he did his learning and, later, his spiritual experience. But he did not dissimulate his feelings and was usually disconcertingly frank in replying to direct questions. He avoided depression and nostalgia with characteristic Irish zeal. He drove up for his interview at Ealing Abbey in his shiny new red MG. The abbot accepted him. The novice master predicted he would last only a month.

Why England? Why Ealing and not Downside or Ample-forth? He said that if he had entered the Church in Ireland he would probably have given up religion altogether. Another reason was that, as a true Irishman, he could love his country best only in self-imposed exile. He felt too old for Downside, and Ealing attracted him for two reasons. He knew of another Dublin professor who had recently joined there and on visiting Ealing it seemed to him, under Abbot Rupert Hall, 'a very civilised and relaxed place'.[6] More importantly it seemed to him a place of potential in the new Church, a monastic community in the city with a strong apostolate in school and parish work, a place of growth. Becoming a monk was not an escape but rather the discovery of a new and more ultimate path of growth. He always had and he always would respond to misfortune by expansion of heart. He took the name of John, the disciple of love. John Main loved Ealing because of his faithful commitment to the community and to his vows, which to him were sacred and inalienable events of his life.

Early in his novitiate he met his novice master to discuss prayer. Father John remembered this meeting differently from the novice master, no doubt because it was such a turning point in his own life. The description of the meditation he had been practising since his meeting with the Hindu monk struck the Benedictine novice master as non-Christian and he advised Brother John to desist and return to a way of prayer employing words and images. It seemed a cruel stroke of irony, a final and decisive impoverishment. Much later, when he had been led back to the mantra through the very English Benedictine tradition that had diverted him from it, he saw this spiritual detachment as a preparatory *ascesis* enabling him to return to the pilgrimage entirely on God's terms, 'not on my own'.[7] His own absolutist temperament, his tendency to balanced extremism, enabled him to see the same qualities in the way God directed a human life. 'In retrospect I regard this period in my life as one of great grace.'[8]

He stopped saying the mantra. But the 'spiritual desert' he now entered was not without human friendship and laughter. Father John's impulse was always to absorb the inevitable and make it his own. His novitiate was a happy and joyful time largely because of sharing it with a fellow-Celt. Those were still the days when novices were given the cast-off habits of the community and the novice master's used razor-blades. Father John often said, though, that it was one of the simplest years of his life. He was then sent to Rome to study at the Benedictine University of St Anselmo and for these years was immersed in the milieu of European monasticism, visiting monasteries in Italy, France and Germany on his annual return home and making friends for life in monasteries around the world. Perhaps even more decisive was his sharing in the extraordinary renaissance of Catholic Christianity that began with the Second Vatican Council. They were stirring years to be at Rome: to see seminarians blocked by Swiss Guards as they moved out of St Peter's in protest at a papal pronouncement, to see Holy Office agents expelled from lectures by suspect professors, but above all and most positively to feel the new waves of hope and the energies of both intellectual and pastoral growth that were re-forming the Church he had always loved but never feared to criticise.

The record of Father John's Rome years shows the many simultaneously active parts of his character. He relished his studies, especially the Trinitarian theology and contemplative-liturgical approach of Dom Cipriano Vagaggini. He held in some contempt the more childish insistence of some lecturers on learning names and dates by heart. He loved the cultural atmosphere of an international community, his holidays and hiking trips with fellow-students. He enjoyed the fun of organising a tour of Roman fountains for the German monks, which carefully avoided all fountains.

Shortly before his ordination on 21 December 1963, Father John's younger brother was killed in a car accident in Australia and his father died of cancer in Ballinskelligs. His mother was unable to attend the ordination but a large family contingent did. He left soon afterwards for Dublin where an appointment with the Irish President had been arranged and Eamon de Valera knelt one January night in 1964 to receive the first blessing of Dom John Main.

For the next three years he taught in the Ealing school. As the youngest professed monk he was the porter at the 1967 abbatial election and fetched the monks for their interview with the abbot president. He was also one of the candidates in the election. Another monk was elected, however, and Father John was appointed his replacement as deputy headmaster. Headmaster Bernard Orchard and John Main made for strong and imaginative leadership in the school. As a result there was soon a major clash of policy within the community, about whether or not to expand the school. Obviously personalities and larger issues of monastic life were also involved. The outcome was the resignation of the headmaster. John Main, who did not need to resign and who would have been his obvious successor, felt honour-bound to do so in the spring of 1969. The community was divided and its internal divisions were common knowledge in the school and parish. Fathers Main and Orchard as the epicentres of the storm were to go away. Father Bernard went to Rome where he used the opportunity for research to earn a prominent place in international biblical scholarship. Father John was offered a position at the University of Oxford which he was not allowed to accept. A plan to establish a Benedictine chaplaincy at the University of Sydney, Australia also fell through. In the end he was sent on what was for a man of his credentials a less than flattering assignment, to do a doctorate at the Catholic University of America.

He felt hurt by the decision and the manner of its implementation. But as usual he accepted the given and made it his own. Academic theology in Washington he found narrow and frustrating. But by September 1970 the Abbot of Washington asked the Abbot of Ealing if John Main could be their new headmaster at St Anselm's. By the autumn of 1970 therefore Father John was on a new part of his monastic adventure. He took over an American school with severe administrative and personnel problems at a time of general student rebellion. But he rebuilt morale, reassured parents of their religious doubts by his powerful and evident vision of Christian education and also by his Irish charm and English urbanity. He took charge. He got people to work together towards a common goal. He began to raise a million dollars for a new science wing. He drove his old friend Garret Fitz-Gerald, then Foreign Secretary, around Washington and was drawn into the social round of the diplomatic world. He was successful and life had a glitter. 'It was the busiest period of my monastic life,' he wrote later.[9] Another abrupt change in direction was imminent and entirely unexpected.

Return pilgrimage

The turning point of John Main's life occupies an ontological rather than a chronological centre. This point is historically visible in his life and he describes it in the persuasive simplicity of *The Gethsemani Talks*. A young man who wanted to learn about Christian mysticism came to stay in the monastery from the ashrams of California. Father John gave him Augustine Baker's *Holy Wisdom* to read, the quintessence of English Benedictine spirituality. Written in the seventeenth century, it is now little read and certainly cannot rival the 'Cloud' for popular appeal. Father John was all the more surprised therefore to see the young man return aglow with enthusiasm. Father John was moved to re-read Baker. Baker sent him to the Cloud of Unknowing and then back to John Cassian. He rediscovered the mantra and started to meditate again.

He read Cassian not with the eye of a historian or a textual scholar but as a monk guided by grace towards a deepening of his life in the spirit. He recognised, by reference to his own earlier experience, exactly what Cassian and the 'Cloud' were saying. When he came, as he did very shortly, to teach others, it was by expressing the same teaching in contemporary terms. It was not Cassian or the 'Cloud' that needed to be communicated. They were themselves communicators. The message was not the letter but the spirit. John Main was concerned not with mere scholarship but with a living tradition, a tradition that had come alive again in his own life of service.

Shortly before he left for Montreal a community meeting was held at Ealing to discuss who would go with him. One monk rather naïvely asked if it would be necessary for anyone else going to pray 'in John's way'. Father John was amused and disappointed at the implication. He responded strongly by saying that meditation was no invention of his own but it was the tradition that, consciously or unconsciously, had shaped them all. He reacted in a similar way if people later thought his teaching an 'eastern form' of prayer. It is no more eastern than western, he would say, and what makes meditation Christian is precisely the faith in Christ that we bring to it. When he taught meditation John Main used almost exclusively the western tradition and the Christian scriptures. There was no doubt in his mind that this teaching went back in direct line to the apostolic community of the primitive church and to the Master himself.

He began to meditate three times a day, coming back to the monastery from the school across the campus to meditate at midday. He taught meditation at this time only to those individuals who had come to him for personal advice. Interiorly his life was undergoing an accelerated re-formation, a catching up of an interrupted pilgrimage, while external events were shaping his life to harmonise with the interior world. In 1974 he left Washington and returned to London by way of Australia where he visited his brother's grave and discussed again the establishing of a Benedictine chaplaincy in Sydney. The deepening of his prayer was changing his views on what constituted an appropriate monastic life in the twentieth century.[10] What special Christian formation was given to graduates of the Benedictine school he had worked in? What were the real needs of parishes and society at large? These were no longer academic questions, the material for articles, but matters of integrity. The response he found to them in 1975 was to be the pattern of the rest of his life: meditation and the community that silence creates.

Most of his brethren were sceptical about Father John's proposal for a lay community living alongside the monastic community, sharing its work and worship and in addition meditating together. However he went ahead to restore an old, run-down house on the property – the sort of project he relished – even though there was no sign of anyone coming to join a community with as yet no members. He set up a meditation room with floor cushions, meditated there himself and waited. Before long a group of six young men had come. The form which the rest of his life was to take had come into being.

The inner journey

The events of the remaining seven years can be found described in his own words. The decision of the Ealing community to allow him to respond to the invitation from Bishop Crowley of Montreal and establish a contemplative monastery in the city allowed him to realise the form of the new monasticism he had envisioned since the Vatican Council. In 1975 he was almost elected abbot to two monasteries. He would have undertaken the office energetically but he knew it would not have enabled him to live the radically single-minded monastic life he was able to create in Montreal. He longed for a new, simpler, more truly traditional and so also more contemporary monastic community. He was able to see it beginning before he died.

The events of this venture were an integral part of the teaching which flowered in those years and bore such extraordinary fruit in so many hearts. In *Letters from the Heart* and in the sequel which appeared in 1985, *The Present Christ*, one can see the spiritual and theological growth that occurred in Father John simultaneously with the growth of the Montreal

Priory he founded in 1977 with one other monk from Ealing. His faith worked a monastic miracle which served the Church and the secular world of which it was and remains a part. 'A monastery does not exist for itself,' wrote Father John, 'but for the kingdom.' It was the secret of his monastic freedom and courage.

A definitive turn in his monastic pilgrimage took place during a few days spent at the Abbey of Gethsemani in 1976. One might say his public teaching on meditation began in the three now famous conferences given to the monks. But it was in the time of silence spent in Thomas Merton's hermitage that the Spirit moved so deeply in his heart and pointed him towards the work for the kingdom to which he was called to give the rest of life and, as we can now see, his death also. He wrote one letter from the hermitage on 13 November to a close friend:

> I hope you are well. I am here staying in Merton's hermitage out in the woods beyond Gethsemani. It is quite extraordinary how solitude brings everyone so close. I have just celebrated the most loving mass of my life in Merton's little chapel. You were all so close to me as I prayed for you and all your family.
>
> My purpose in coming here was to talk to the community about prayer, but in fact I have learnt so much myself while I have been here . . .

The full story of what John Main had learnt continues to unfold through the growth of the teaching which he was given to experience so purely in his own spirit and to pass on to future generations. He stands in the great tradition: the living tradition of Christian teachers of prayer whose authority derives from the humility and love of their discipleship to Christ.

Father John's knowledge of Christ began in his earliest years in the heart of a warm and Christian family. His love of Christ grew and matured through the richly varied years that led him to the monastic life. It was a quite unsentimental love, a disarmingly intense and honest love. It hungered for absoluteness. It was progressively inclusive and excluded nothing except what compromised the absolute.

16

He had always felt he would not live to old age. When he saw that his death was coming so soon it intensified and accelerated the inner work of integration, the pilgrimage, as he called it. He felt himself drawn ever more fully into the point of concentrated light, which dilated and absorbed him more completely at each time of prayer. He died on 30 December 1982 in the monastery he had founded as a disciple of his Master. Those he was leading on the same path were beside him.

On 6 October that year he spoke on 'Death: the inner journey' to two thousand participants at an International Palliative Care Congress in Montreal. He spoke of death as an essential part of the life-process and meditation as the way we enter the paschal mystery. Though in great pain he gave his last public teaching on 18 November; and worked on his correspondence up to the middle of December. As he approached death, he lived as fully and loved as selflessly as he had ever done. It was increasingly clear to him and to those who were caring for him that the Master he served was calling him to the even greater service of love through a faithful death. It *was* so clear because as he travelled into the light that shone so brilliantly in his heart, it made his Master visible. The light shone in his flesh. His teaching became perfected in silence. The freedom he had sought in the monastery now transcended all limitations and travelled the paths of the Spirit with Jesus who greeted him and led him past the final boundary. Those paths are more knowable to us by his life and teaching, by the tradition he revitalised with the gifts of his own spirit and the energy of his loving heart.

As John Main's influence spreads through the books and tapes containing his teaching, it is important to see how his pilgrimage and mission were fully inserted into his humanity. This is why I am so grateful to the contributors of this book who help us understand how all the pieces fit together. As a group they demonstrate that it was the authenticity of his life that in the final analysis teaches us. It is an essential element of his life and vision, that we must become the person we are called to be, fully human, fully loving. Those who loved him best in this life were those who meditated with him. Those who will come to know him in the Spirit will also be those who have found the grand poverty of the mantra.

Notes

This introduction draws on research from the biography of John Main by Neil McKenty, *In the Stillness Dancing* (1986).

1 *Christian Meditation: The Gethsemani Talks* (1977).
2 *Letters from the Heart* (1982).
3 Remark of colleague on Trinity College Law Faculty.
4 cf. *Community of Love* (1984).
5 *Christian Meditation: The Gethsemani Talks.*
6 Remark to his sister Yvonne.
7 *Christian Meditation: The Gethsemani Talks.*
8 ibid.
9 ibid.
10 *Letters from the Heart*, Introd.

1

Early Family Life and Youth

We were very happy in our home life and as well as being brothers and sisters we were all great friends. (John Main)

That summation of John Main's early family life echoes the comradeship and happy, carefree life of the Main family, punctuated by humour and underlined by a deep Catholic faith. Two of the six children, Yvonne and Kitty, confirm the fact that growing up in the family was, as Father Laurence Freeman points out in the introduction, 'colourful, entertaining and often dramatic, dominated by David's [father] strong temper and flamboyant but generous hospitality, moderated by Eileen's [mother] equally strong but steadier will and quieter spirit'. Unconsciously St Benedict's injunction to 'receive all guests as Christ' was an essential ingredient of the Main family. Contributor Molly Curran, a friend of the family, gives us a humorous account of the acceptance of one such stranger into their home. It would seem guests, waifs and strays were common visitors to the Main household.

YVONNE (MAIN) FITZGERALD

Douglas and all of his five brothers and sisters grew up in a happy family in London. We did the usual things, birthday parties, holidays to the seaside, and eventually settled in a house in Sussex. That house was a great joy for many years. One of our favourite activities as children was drama. Douglas was very good at producing plays. We had an Irish maid and once as we were practising for a play she decided to introduce us to our Irish heritage ... (IRA songs). When mother

19

discovered our newfound ability at singing Irish songs she was horrified.

A few times as young children Douglas would celebrate mass with an altar on top of a chest of drawers. I was encouraged to be an altar girl but was frequently dismissed because I either started to laugh or rang the bell at the wrong time.

Douglas always had a tremendous sense of humour. Once in the early years of the war he stood up at the top of the house and shouted to women at the bus stop, 'There is an unexploded bomb in the area, would everyone please evacuate the area at once.' All the poor ladies with their shopping baskets would trundle down the road terrified and not knowing that it was all a 'put-on'.

My older brothers Ian and Douglas were always involved in practical jokes. One day my mother and a friend were listening to the funeral of George V on the radio. The commentator was saying: 'Now the funeral has arrived at Euston station and the Royal family are following the hearse and the coffin.' A voice then cut in: 'Oh, good gracious, a terrible thing has happened, the coffin has fallen off the hearse and the king is rolling down the steps . . . ' My mother and her friend were duly horrified. They did not know that my brothers Ian and Douglas had rigged up another piece of radio equipment and managed to interrupt the radio broadcast with their horrific announcement. The rest of the children were in the hallway in hysterics.

When the war broke out (1939) Douglas was thirteen and he and I were fire watchers. We were both issued with helmets (tin hats). As soon as an air raid siren would sound the two of us would put on our hats and madly dash out of doors; Mother would say, 'Come back here immediately.' We were both convinced that with the protection of our tin hats absolutely nothing could possibly happen to us. At that time we did not realise the dangers of war. My memory of those days is sleeping under the dining-room table during air raids and the innumerable 'Let's have a cup of tea'.

KITTY (MAIN) STANLEY

I was just five when my brother Douglas was born. I do not remember much about those early days except that he had a very fair complexion, almost white hair, and was rather a solemn baby. My mother always thought he had a delicate disposition. As he got older he encouraged this to his advantage by pretending he could not do odd chores, such as weeding in the garden, when my father asked us all to help him. Douglas would wipe his brow weakly and pretend to faint. 'I told you that child is not strong,' my mother would say and take Douglas's hand. He would turn round to the rest of us with a sly smile as he was being half-carried into the house.

When he was older Douglas was fantastic with children and they all adored him. He hated noise and when the children, my two daughters and my sister's three sons, started to get excited, he would gather them all together and tell them a story. He would just make up a story on the spot, and they would all sit enchanted. He often got carried away, however, and the story could become frightening. I remember once when my sister's child, aged about five, fainted during one of his horror tales.

Douglas was really different from the usual run of boys. He was gentle and quiet, though mischievous and loved to play practical jokes. He also loved music. He hated noise and rough behaviour and was not interested in sport; in fact he loved just being at home and chatting away with all my mother's friends. Old people loved him because he was interesting, amusing and peaceful to talk to. He was about ten at that time. He had not got many friends of his own age; he was afraid of violence and fighting, probably because he wore glasses and felt vulnerable.

He was about ten or eleven when he went to the Westminster Choir School as a boarder. That school suited him because he was quite religious. He loved pomp and ceremony. He had always been available at our local church in Muswell Hill for funerals, weddings and so on, where he sometimes assisted at the altar or sang in the choir. The choir school was a small and sedate establishment with all those angelic-

21

looking, serious young boys. Little sport was practised but lots of pomp, music and liturgical ceremonies. All this suited Douglas's theatrical character. He was acting a part and he loved it. I used to call at the school on Sundays to take him out to tea. One day I called but the priest said that Douglas was still 'on duty' in the cathedral and would be out in about ten minutes. I went into the cathedral and there was Douglas and his friend David Gothard in front of the Sacred Heart Chapel for Exposition. They looked so devout and serious I was quite impressed. But later at tea Douglas turned to David and said, 'How many candles did you count?' And I realised they were just normal small boys after all. Douglas always loved playing church. Even as a very small child, he loved saying 'mass'. But *he* was always the bishop!

His sedate and peaceful life came to a sudden end with the outbreak of war in September 1939. He was just thirteen and a half years old. The choir school closed and a new school had to be found for him. He was sent with his elder brother Ian to the Jesuit College of St Ignatius, which had been evacuated to Welwyn Garden City, north of London. The priests were tough and so were the boys. It was a far cry from the peaceful and pleasant life in the choir school. I was evacuated at that time, with the Civil Service, to Blackpool, so for a year or two we only saw each other during holidays.

Douglas really came into his own when he joined the *Hornsey Journal*, our local newspaper, as a junior reporter soon after he left school. His imagination ran riot and we could hardly mention a thing at home without finding ourselves in print in the next edition. He loved journalism and I think might well have made that his career had he not been called up for military service in the army.

MOLLY CURRAN

I first knew the Main family when I was eight years old and going to school at St Martin's Convent in Muswell Hill, where Kitty, Yvonne and Diane Main were also students. Yvonne became my special friend as we lived very close to her home at 108 Muswell Hill Road. I was often at their house after school, at weekends and school holidays, for the next five years, until Kitty and Yvonne left the convent and went to one in Belgium.

I was fascinated by their home, which seemed to me at that age large and luxurious in comparison to mine; it was in fact comfortable and lived in. I think I was first drawn to the Mains as a family by the fact that their mother did not work, as mine did, and never appeared to mind the house being full of her children's friends. Eileen Main was a lovely person; gentle and soft-spoken and never seemed to lose her temper with her family – at least, not in my presence. She fed anyone who happened to be around. She was quietly firm and the children listened. She must have had quite a hectic life and I remember the father only vaguely as a handsome man who was not often there. He travelled a lot to Ireland and I had the impression that it was something to do with sweepstake tickets.

Though there were six children, I remember that they were not a particularly rowdy crowd; in fact they were rather quiet with the exception of Ian and Yvonne, who were the extroverts of the family. Douglas was one of the quieter children and the most serious of the six. Because he wore glasses I thought of him as rather an intellectual person.

I remember particularly that Mrs Main would allow us the run of the house and that it was a great place for hide and seek and she was not put out in the least to find me one day hiding in a laundry basket.

The top floor of the house was vaguely off limits but no one seemed to adhere to that. It was usually occupied by someone and I later learned that Eileen regularly took in people who were down on their luck. One particularly funny story was that the father came home unexpectedly one day to find that not only was the top floor occupied but that strangers were sleeping in his bed.

2

The Canons Regular

Is it too fanciful to suggest that, in God's providence, it was in Rome in 1950 that the cage was opened and the spirit of John Main was set free? (Paul Bowe OP)

In the autumn of 1946, following his discharge from the army, John Main joined a religious congregation, the Canons Regular of the Lateran, at their novitiate in Bodmin, Cornwall. After taking first vows in November 1947 he was transferred to St Edmund's, Ware to study philosophy. Then in the autumn of 1949 he was assigned to Rome to study theology at the Angelicum. However the following June 1950 he abruptly left Rome and the Canons and during the summer applied to Trinity College, Dublin to study law. Many people have conjectured on the reasons for his leaving the Canons. Two priest contributors who knew John Main at the time, Dominican Paul Bowe and Carmelite Brocard Sewell, attempt to shed light on this period of John Main's life.

PAUL BOWE

In his book, *In the Stillness Dancing*, Neil McKenty writes, or rather speculates, about John Main's reasons for leaving Rome and, as it turned out, the Canons Regular of the Lateran in June 1950. He begins his short account by saying that 'problems began to emerge, the nature of which is not clear'. What I have to say may only add to the mystery; but at the time it was no mystery to me, at any rate.

John arrived in Rome around the same time that I did. I had completed my philosophy studies in Dublin, as well as one year of theology in the Dominican House of Studies in Blackfriars, Oxford. My superiors decided that I should complete my theological studies with a lectorate and licentiate in theology in the Angelicum. John and I found ourselves studying under the same professors, one of whom was to end his life as Cardinal Michael Browne OP, and who was regarded, with considerable justification, as one of the great conservative theologians of Vatican II. Father Michael Browne, as we students knew him in 1949, in my humble opinion had a considerable impact on the future of John's vocation.

I knew John variously by his baptismal name Douglas and what I took to be his name in religion, Victor. But by and large he was known to me as Victor Main.

To be perfectly honest I had never heard of the Canons Regular of the Lateran at the time. God knows we had enough religious orders and congregations in Ireland, but Rome was something else! As far as I could make out Douglas/Victor/John enjoyed his studies at the Angelicum; we had become quite friendly and frequently went walking together. I learned that he had been in some branch of the army during the war. My recollection was that it had something to do with Intelligence but he rarely spoke about it. I never suspected then that John was destined to become a world-renowned master of the spiritual life! At that time he was no different, to me at any rate, from the hundreds of other clerical students I met in the course of my studies. It was through John that I met another of the Canons Regular who seemed to be particularly friendly with him: Albert Wyatt. I have never met Albert since but my impression was that they were the only two students from the English branch of the Canons living at their international college in Rome at that time.

Strangely enough I have a very distinct recollection of John's appearance. He wore spectacles, was sandy-haired, slightly thinning on top, was about my own height, around 6 ft 1 in, and had, as I have, the reputation for a marked sense of humour. He had a very winning smile. We had some good laughs together at what we considered to be the antics of some of the native-born Roman curia. A time was to come when even John's sense of humour in that regard was to desert him.

By and large I remember the various 'international' seminaries as being rather unpopular with their non-Italian students. In a way it was inevitable, as the Italians were usually in a fairly substantial majority. It was not all that long after the war and food was not the best, not to mention their strict, indeed harsh, regimes. However John seemed to take it all in his stride. He used to remind me from time to time that we, in San Clemente, were very fortunate in having our own 'Irish' regime. It went back to penal times when it was not possible to educate Irish students for the priesthood in Ireland. The Irish Dominicans got San Clemente, the Irish Franciscans St Isidore's, and the Irish Augustinians had St Patrick's. Consequently our 'regimes' were not as Italianate, if that's the right word for it, as those of the international colleges. At least that was the impression we had.

I mentioned that John seemed to take it all in his stride, but I wonder about that now. Some time towards the end of the academic year in 1950 he called to see me in San Clemente. He and Albert used to drop in occasionally for a cup of coffee in the afternoon. This time, however, he was on his own. To my great surprise he was not his usual good-humoured, sensible, balanced self. On the contrary he was very agitated and disturbed; there was no sign whatsoever of his sense of humour, or even of ordinary indignation. In fact his whole demeanour was quite out of character. He went on to tell me that he was thinking of pulling out altogether. I was greatly surprised and, indeed, shocked, for as far as I was concerned there had been no indication up to this that anything was wrong, never mind seriously wrong. It had nothing to do, he told me, with his studies in the Angelicum. It emerged in the course of his conversation – 'monologue' would be a better word – that he was desperately upset about the atmosphere of the international house of studies in which he was living. As an example he mentioned the kind of 'edifying' book that was currently being read in their refectory during mealtimes, and he was especially angry over the material that had been put before them that day.

Apparently, to use a modern term, it was extremely anti-feminist; in fact, as far as the priests were concerned, it was quite simply anti-woman. (I have no idea what the book was

26

or who was its author.) According to John, 'women' were, as far as priests were concerned, to be regarded as 'snares of the devil'. Given half a chance they would lead us, seminarians and priests, astray from our vocations. And he went on to mention other attitudes which shocked me deeply. He was so disturbed about the whole business that I felt, and still feel, that he was exaggerating, but his seriousness about dropping out was quite definite. John had his wartime experiences behind him, and the maturity that goes with them, so one can imagine the effect the kind of tommyrot he was being exposed to was having on him. The strange thing about the whole business was that he had never mentioned anything like that to me before, even though we used to meet nearly every day. I could only conclude afterwards that it must have been festering away like a boil that needed to be lanced but never was. His outward bonhomie obviously concealed a deep malaise which must have been eating away at him for months.

Anyway, when he had got it all off his chest I suggested that he should not do anything on the spur of the moment or in the heat of an obvious anger. Father Michael Browne – the future Master of the Apostolic Palace, personal theologian to Pope Pius XII, a traditional Dominican appointment, future Master-General of the Dominican Order, and to be created Cardinal by John XXIII – was still, at the time of John's crisis, a simple professor of theology in the Angelicum. He had been rector for a time. He also had, very deservedly, the reputation of being a very wise spiritual counsellor, so I suggested to John that he should go and talk to him and ask his advice.

I never did get an account from John as to the content of their conversation, but as far as I could gather Father Browne advised him to leave the Canons Regular and pursue his vocation elsewhere. I emphasise that last point although it may be a kind of hindsight going back forty years. For what it is worth my impression was that Father Browne did not advise John to give up all ideas of the priesthood. His vocation to the priesthood, John seemed to suggest, as a result of his conversation with Father Browne, lay elsewhere! The immediate effect, however, was that in June 1950 John left Rome and the Canons Regular.

The next time I saw John was in Dublin in the middle 1950s. At that time I had been appointed a junior lecturer in economics and politics. I had taken degrees in those subjects when my studies in Rome were completed in University College, Dublin. John was studying law at Trinity College and we used to meet from time to time in an organisation called *Tuarim* (Gaelic for 'opinion') of which I was one of the founders. It was a forum for young academic people who were anxious to break with what we considered to be the dead hand which the old civil war divisions was still exercising on Irish political life. How right we were! John and I never resumed the kind of friendship we had enjoyed in Rome, and our paths seldom crossed.

The next thing I heard was that he had gone to Kuala Lumpur; then I heard that he was back in Trinity, but I never met him. It is now a matter of great regret to me that we never had the chance to discuss his discovery of eastern prayer, or even to reminisce about our days in Rome together. I have an idea that he did not particularly want to rake over those particular embers.

When I heard that he had joined the Benedictines in Ealing the memories of our days in Rome came flooding back to me. Why was I not surprised? Why did I, in some way, consider it to be the resumption of an interrupted vocation?

It was some years later that I began to hear of a mysterious figure called John Main who was developing some kind of original spirituality. I had never known him in Dublin except as 'Douglas'. Eventually three, two and one came together; Douglas/Victor/John had eventually found his vocation. It was a journey not in length but in depth; it was short, but, as we all know now, it was long enough.

I am sure that there is room for a sense of humour in heaven, at least I hope there is, so Douglas/Victor/John will smile when I tell him that his spiritual way is not quite my cup of tea; it may be that I am too much of a Thomist, and who knows what would have become of Victor Main had he completed four years of rigorous theology in the Angelicum? Would there ever have been a John? Is it too fanciful to suggest that, in God's providence, it was in Rome in 1950 that the cage was opened and the spirit of John Main was set free?

One way or another it's nice to have known him.

BROCARD SEWELL

There seems to have been a good deal of misunderstanding about the religious order in which John Main was professed before he joined the Benedictines. The Canons Regular of the Lateran are the senior Congregation of the Canons Regular of St Augustine, or Austin Canons, and in fact are the senior religious order in the western Church. Theirs is a long and distinguished history.

John Main joined the order at an apparent period of post-war expansion; but the appearances were deceptive, and it was about to enter a period of decline. A principal cause was the early and unexpected death of the 'great' prior of Bodmin, Dom Richard Alphonsus McElroy, an outstanding personality and a man of marked practical ability. It was confidently expected that he would soon be created Abbot, and that he would replace the venerable Abbot Aloysius Smith as Visitor (roughly equivalent to Provincial) of the order's English Province. But it was not to be.

Dom Victor Main, as he was called in the order, made a successful novitiate at Bodmin, and then was transferred to St Augustine's Priory at Hoddesdon, just outside London. Here he was much appreciated by his fellow-students, and was of the greatest help in raising the standard of the chant, for the mass was sung on all Sundays and main festivals, and vespers also was sung on Sundays and major feasts. He was a brilliant student, and shone in the philosophy course, which was taught by able Canon Regular professors. For theology the students went every day to St Edmund's College at Ware, only a few miles away, which was the seminary of the diocese of Westminster. Here too John Main distinguished himself, and was very well liked by the hundred or more divines, as the theology students were called.

Being sent to Rome for more advanced studies, he decided while there to leave the order. The reason or reasons for this decision seem not to be known. Douglas, as he was called familiarly, had a great sense of fun and humour; one story is that a mild practical joke played on a former superior who was visiting Rome was the root of the trouble; but another tradition is to the effect that there was a serious, though entirely friendly, difference between himself and Abbot Smith over the interpretation of the vow of poverty. Who shall say?

Possibly too he felt that at that time the 'active' element in the canonical life was over-prominent as compared with the contemplative.

In later years John Main did not much like to be reminded of his canonical experience; but he did say that he owed the Canons Regular a considerable debt, because it was they who taught him how to study.

3

Ireland, Dublin and the Law

About this time he emerged in the academic body with the all-important post of chairman of the college wines committee. Douglas was responsible for laying down vintages which his colleagues were to enjoy years later after he had left. (John Boland)

In October 1950 John Main began the study of law at Trinity College, Dublin. This was a productive and happy time of his life, as recounted by his sister Yvonne; and by fellow Trinity College students and friends, John Boland and Neil Porter. Upon graduation from law he spent two years in Malaya with the British Colonial Service. Then in 1956 John Main at thirty years of age was appointed to the law faculty of Trinity College to teach Administrative, Roman and International Law. He taught at Trinity from 1956 to 1959. John Boland's hilarious recounting of a pilgrimage to Lough Derg and Yvonne's account of a racetrack snafu shed light on this period of John Main's life.

JOHN BOLAND

He first came into my life about September 1951 when I was a Law School student in second year at Trinity College, Dublin. I remember our first encounter particularly well. My mother had a near neighbour and friend who was a cousin of Douglas's. It was mentioned to my mother by this neighbour that her cousin Douglas was about to enter Trinity College, Dublin. Since I was a student at Trinity, it was thought it might be helpful to Douglas that the two of us should meet. This was certainly helpful to me in the friendship

31

which blossomed from it. This meeting took place at my home in Ranelagh in Dublin on a September evening. I remember talking at length to Douglas about a number of things, including the (then) present state of Ireland, and about his impressions of Ireland on his return from Rome. He was in many ways a man who perfectly married two totally different and almost irreconcilable backgrounds. He was, on the first encounter, English, possibly very English, and yet he understood the Irish scene remarkably well. He had a great love for the Irish county of Kerry, which I shared because my parents also came from Co. Kerry, though from the north of the county while his connections were with the south. We spoke about this, and about Ireland, as it were, after the Raj, the evolution of the new Republic. In 1950 the Republic was one and a half years old, and we spoke about our feelings of this break from the United Kingdom and aspects of the British tradition in Ireland.

Douglas's arrival in Trinity was itself of interest. He had abandoned his vocation in the Canons Regular – or maybe it had abandoned him. He had spent some time in Rome and was probably upset at the failure of this first vocation, although he never spoke about it; he had emerged with some form of diploma, a licentiate from the Gregorian University. It was alleged, I cannot quite remember whether he told me this or whether it became a part of the folklore which grew up about him, that he approached Professor Michael Tierney, then President of University College, Dublin, to say that he had spent two years in Rome and could he have a year's credit off his legal studies. Michael Tierney, who was a somewhat robust character, bluntly told Douglas in no uncertain terms, 'You may join with every other student this coming September and you will do three years like the rest of them.' In other words, no remission.

Douglas then turned his attention to the Protestant institution in College Green, the College of the Holy and Undivided Trinity of Queen Elizabeth I, near Dublin, as its motto proclaims. He approached a very precise Registrar, Captain Shaw, who listened to Douglas's submission across a large Victorian desk one morning in October 1951 and said, 'Yes Main, of course you may have your year's remission and we

32

will be delighted to have you here.' I suppose that great contrast shows how simple it was in 1949 or 1951 when we were both students, to enter a university. One simply had to take the Irish Leaving Certificate and the National University of Ireland's matriculation and without even booking a place in Trinity, one turned up about three weeks before the start of term, parted with eighteen guineas, and you were in. There was no nonsense about waiting lists or points or all the rest of it. There we were, entrants to the university.

Douglas, it must be said, was an instant success in the student body. Let me put the student body in context. University students very often are slightly immature. The scene in Dublin in the period 1949 to about 1953 was strangely different in that the immediate post-war period and the tide of ex-servicemen leaving the British armed forces had not yet spent itself. There were any number of people who had spent four years or longer in the army or in the Royal Navy or in the air force and they ended up in Dublin as mature students, people with experience of the world. They blended with us, and by 'us' I mean those who had left school in Ireland at eighteen. They had had an extraordinary extension to their post-school period and we had had none. Not only that, we had lived in the very closed society of wartime Ireland when there was censorship. We did not even have newsreels in our cinemas because Ireland was neutral. The blend between those who came from without and those of us who had come from the hothouse within was in itself an interesting confluence of two different streams. There was one further difference, that in the University of Dublin, Trinity College was viewed by the Irish Catholic hierarchy as a Protestant institution. I remember in my young life Lenten pastorals thundering over my head on the Sunday before Ash Wednesday, 'No Catholic may enter the Protestant University of Trinity College, Dublin.' Michael Tierney's institution, on the other hand, up the road, founded in 1911, which was avowedly secular in its status, was deemed by the bishops of my Church to be sufficiently safe to guard the faith and morals of young Irish Catholics. The consequence was that Trinity had a mixed student body of about 3000, with 600 Catholics including Douglas Main and myself in that number.

The extraordinary thing about that number of Catholics was that the vast majority were from outside Ireland. We were also totally ignored by the Archbishop of Dublin. No provision was made for our spiritual welfare, there was no Catholic chapel in college, there was not even a chaplain. In the middle of our Trinity stay a few of us, aided by Donald O'Sullivan who was a lecturer in International Affairs, decided that there should be a society for Catholic students. We had great difficulty with the archbishop on this account. He felt it would need to be a social society and it could not presume to orchestrate anything in the nature of giving spiritual guidance. We did arrange a mass on the first anniversary of the founding of the society but permission to arrange a special mass at the time of the second anniversary a year later was refused by the archdiocese. The society was known as the Dublin University Laurentian Society after St Laurence O'Toole, the patron saint of Dublin. We had earlier attempted to call it the Dublin University Society of St Patrick. However the Provost of the College took the view that St Patrick was 'a Protestant saint' so we could not claim monopoly of his patronage. The Laurentian Society was a body of which both Douglas and I were members. It had a nice, comfortable little room on the ground floor at number 5 Trinity College. Douglas and I used to park our bicycles conveniently outside and go in and have a coffee or sit and read the morning newspapers in comfortable armchairs beside a fire.

Douglas was also a member of the college Historical Society, the oldest student debating society in western Europe. It owes its origins to a club for students founded by Edmund Burke about 1745. Douglas did not play an active part in the debates of this body but he was to be seen at meetings of the Laurentian Society. He was also to be seen at meetings of the Dublin University Law Society. Every now and again the fact that he was some five years older than the other group of Irish students tended to assert itself and he sought to escape to the pleasures of his extended family in the Dublin area. I saw a great deal of him because we were near neighbours and it was our practice to cycle home from college to Ranelagh. We must have done this on a daily basis for the best part of three years, both on good days and bad days. We even bicycled when it was raining or when we were faced with an examination for which we had not done adequate preparation. The aspect one remembers of Douglas in these days is his magnificent and rather dry sense of humour. He also had a marvellous skill in which he would lead an unsuspecting debater to say things they had not intended, only to cut them down to size in the ensuing dialogue.

When I think of the spiritual life of the student body there were things Douglas was involved with. He was a member of a small group of Trinity students who sang in a choir at Clarendon Street, which was the nearest church to our college. The church was in the care of the Carmelite fathers who had a particular interest in plain chant. I was on the committee of the Laurentian Society and Douglas was supportive. This was a period when he had already made a number of friends in college, including Mary Lodge. Mary Lodge makes a quite memorable contribution to Neil McKenty's autobiography of John Main, where she refers to Douglas as a man apart and of a deeper spiritual sense than possibly most of us who were his contemporaries then recognised. Douglas also got to know my parents quite well. My father, like his father, was born in Co. Kerry and there were certain points of similarity; my father had worked in England for quite a long time and greatly liked Douglas. We often referred to Douglas as 'The noblest Roman of them all.'

There was one other incident of some spiritual significance. When Douglas and I were about to take our final examinations we grew a little worried as to whether we would in fact pass this ordeal. The examination was phased over four days, spanning thirteen subjects and four years work. This was four years work for me and three years work for Douglas. We felt we had not made adequate preparation and were slightly apprehensive. Now, there is in the North of Ireland a penitential island called Lough Derg which is part of the Irish religious scene. Irish Catholicism, it is fair to comment, is devotional rather than dogmatic and this often leads to a fairly aggressive regime of penance. I decided I needed to invoke a measure of spiritual aid and I remember saying to Douglas that 'I think I will' – the word was *do* – 'do Lough

35

Derg before we take our examinations.' And he said, 'I will do so too.' I had reached my decision in a point of desperation, towards the end of July 1954. I remember telephoning Douglas and saying, 'I'm going to Lough Derg tomorrow, do you want to come?' and he said, 'Oh, I don't think so.' The following morning (one had to leave for Co. Donegal quite early in the morning) the phone rang about 6.30 and Douglas said to me, 'Tell me, did you say to me yesterday you were going to Lough Derg?' I said yes and he said, 'Hang on, I'm coming with you.' So at 7 a.m. we met at a bus stop in Ranelagh without breakfast, because one had to arrive fasting. We then set off for Co. Donegal and boarded a special train: the railway still operated in that remote region at that time. The pilgrimage was under the patronage of a Dublin branch of the Society of St Vincent de Paul. There was nothing to be had in the way of breakfast on the journey apart from a cup of water. This was dispensed from a large pail with a communal mug and was presented to Douglas who took it with good grace. And then for some obscure reason someone requested his address and his name. So he piped up and said, 'Douglas Main, Trinity College, Dublin.' And, of course, the pen poised on the paper practically stopped. There was a sudden hush. The extraordinary thought that a Protestant might be engaging in this kind of penitential activity defied belief or past experience. We carried on and I, of course, picked up Douglas's cue and said, 'John Boland, Trinity College, Dublin.' They were then convinced that there was some kind of anti-popish plot. Douglas said to me with some glee as we reached the lakeside in Lough Derg, 'Well we certainly won't see anyone else from Trinity.' But he was wrong. As we rowed across the rather wide stretch of freezingly cold brown water with a gathering wind towards the island with its church, there were four fellow Trinity students, all girls, bathing their battered feet in the water at the lakeside. We had met at parties some weeks previously and greeted each other with a strange surprise and said to one another, 'What an extraordinary place to meet you.'

We then embarked on a round of endless rosaries, processions and prayers. It got colder and colder and I have a memory of Douglas going blue, without his shoes, and the rain coming down with some force abetted by a howling wind from the lake. At Lough Derg you are allowed one meal in the course of your pilgrimage; the meal is merely toast without butter and tea without milk but with the grace of sugar. I remember going in, having nine slices of toast with sugar to stave off hunger, enjoying some of the very best of company and then going off for an all night vigil in the church. The wind positively howled around the church. There was a marvellous visiting American priest who spoke about how he had been beguiled into conducting a Holy Hour on this pilgrimage at Lough Derg. I could see Douglas's face falling with lack of interest as the priest's voice droned on and on, culminating in the revelation that this was not a Holy Hour, it was a Holy Hour and a half. The night went on and on and on. It was very difficult to stay awake. The next morning at mass there was a marvellous, flowery, Elizabethan morning offering, which went as I recall it, 'Thank you, O Lord, for having preserved us from the dangers and temptations of this night'. There was a large gentleman to the right of Douglas who mumbled in his sleep, 'In the name of God, what dangers and temptations were there last night?' I then disgraced myself by going to sleep during mass and Douglas did not see fit to wake me up. He just commented a little later, 'I did think it was a little odd that you didn't at least kneel down for the consecration.' But no more was said.

We eventually got back to Dublin and we both mercifully passed the necessary examinations. Douglas referred with passing kindness and even mild affection to our experiences in Lough Derg but to my certain knowledge he never went back again. This was an experience, I suppose, of a form of spirituality which was not for him. I did, years later, embark on it again and I remember with great glee sending him a postcard. I believe I sent it to Ealing, to tell him that I had at least made my return trip and when would he come again to join me?

I remember also Douglas's enthusiasm for the elegance of the restored Trinity Ball. When we were students the Trinity Ball was held outside the college. However in the period when Douglas was on the academic staff they initiated the present practice whereby the ball is actually held in the college. We had old time waltzes in the exam hall, West Indian steel bands in the Graduate Memorial Building, ceilidh dancing on the lawn, absolutely raucous pop in one or two other locations and an elegant supper served in marquees. I remember Douglas coming to London very shortly after the first of these restored balls in college, reporting very favourably on the whole experience and how elegant it had looked and what an enjoyable occasion it proved for all who attended it.

Douglas was nostalgic, as we all were, when we came to leave Trinity. I remember him commenting about the strange force that bound a group of thirty people together in our class for three or four years as members of a student body before we were dispersed to the four corners of the world.

It was a small injection of much-needed money which made it possible for him to accept in 1956–7 a somewhat underpaid appointment on the academic staff of Trinity College, Dublin to teach private international law and to branch out into other legal topics. I think he later blossomed into contract and possibly constitutional law. He was popular with the student body. He had a good speaking voice and took care to prepare his material well. He was popular also with his fellow staff-members. About this time he emerged in the academic body with the all-important post of chairman of the college wines committee. Douglas was responsible for laying down vintages which his colleagues were to enjoy years later after he had left. I particularly remember one autumn visit to Dublin, about 1958. I met Douglas and he said, 'Come and have supper with me, we'll have a simple supper in my room.' I suppose I had embarked at that stage on a modest appreciation of some of the better wines, but Douglas was to introduce me for the first time to a vintage Chateauneuf du Pape which I have never forgotten; we also had some sausage, liverwurst, cheese and coffee.

Around this time he became interested in the social and political scene in Ireland and concerned about high emigration, and the massive number of young Irish graduates leaving the country. In consequence of this intellectual drain there were aspects of Irish life which lacked a cultural base. A number of journals promoted devotional piety of the 'drink-Catholic-tea' variety but there were few papers which analysed the contemporary religious and social scene. A group of people did get together to constitute a Dublin alternative to the *Tablet*, the English liberal weekly magazine. I think that was the intended model. I remember Douglas ultimately presenting to me the articles of the association or the company which was to produce the paper. It was going to be called 'Outlook'. I remember pointing out to him that the legal name of the company would read Outlook Limited, and I said, 'That isn't the happiest of omens, don't you think you ought to change the title?' The money had been put up in part by the Catholic archbishop. Then followed a *coup d'état* on the committee and the intended editor was felt not quite the man for the job. Douglas then emerged as the chairman of the intended publishing company, which included among others Garret FitzGerald, a future *Taoiseach* (Prime Minister). The disagreements on the governing committee reached the point where Douglas began to doubt the capability of this particular group of people to produce a paper of any worth or merit. In the end 'Outlook' never saw the light of day.

Douglas, as I mentioned earlier, was a keen observer of the Irish scene and had a marvellous understanding of the various levels of society in Ireland. In one of the long vacations when we were students Douglas made off to Co. Cork, where he acted as tutor to the children of a retired British army officer who had spent a period in the Colonial Service. I remember Douglas being astonished at the social scene in this household in Co. Cork where life really went on as if the family were still in the Sudan. I remember particularly his commenting on the fondness of the family for informal quizzes by way of entertainment. Members of the family had not the slightest difficulty in coping with questions such as who may have been Governor-General of the Anglo–Egyptian Sudan in 1894, while the same participants in the same game would find it quite impossible to report accurately who was Prime Minister at the time of the Irish Republic or who might constitute the government.

He was always a keen and active walker and from time to time, on visits to Dublin when he was on the staff at Trinity, we went out on the 44 bus to the foot of the Dublin mountains; we would walk in the countryside around Enniskerry and basically put the world to rights. He could think very clearly when walking, and I am certain he met many other friends in this way, taking exercise and enjoying fresh air and the countryside.

YVONNE (MAIN) FITZGERALD

In 1948 my husband died in America and I returned to Ireland. Father and Mother also moved from Belfast to Dublin. Douglas was absolutely marvellous with my children, he was very firm with them, he would snap his fingers and say, 'Time for bed now, boys,' and off they would go. After putting on their pyjamas they would come down for their evening story. Douglas would excel at making up incredible adventure stories.

Douglas was also very fond of the theatre. He was always organised, would already have the tickets and would come home and say, 'Everyone is invited tonight to the Abbey Theatre.' And off we would go. He loved music, especially opera. It was a pleasant life. On many evenings at home everyone would join in singing or playing the piano, our parents too, especially my father. Douglas and I would often sing an operatic duet and half-way through break into uncontrollable laughter. My father would berate the two 'laughing hyenas' and accuse us of not taking anything seriously.

Douglas would often bring home diverse friends and acquaintances, from the simply lonely visitors to Dublin to ex-Jesuits from Trinity College. I remember once remonstrating, 'Douglas, are there no normal people at Trinity? Couldn't you bring home some ordinary people for a change?' Douglas was always very kind and considerate to his friends.

In the 1950s Douglas (a student at Trinity College) and I became very interested in horse racing and went quite often to the races to view the horses on parade and place our bets. If we were winning at the half-way mark Douglas would say, 'I think it is time to treat ourselves to a brandy at the bar.' Then one day Douglas hit upon a system whereby three of us would put £10 into a kitty: the idea was that if we lost on the first race we would double our bets on the second race and so on. It was a little more intricate than this. But we did extremely well using this system and at one point we had £200 to £800 in the kitty. Then one day Douglas came home with a hound-dog look on his face and said, 'I am sorry but I've lost the lot.' So that was the end of the system and our career at the racetrack.

Douglas and I took great joy in looking at properties, checking the papers and visiting homes. We went charging off at a moment's notice. One time a cousin in America wrote that they wanted to rent a castle over the Christmas period. Douglas inserted a suitable advertisement in the *Irish Times* and we went about castle-searching. We eventually got them a wing of a castle in Co. Meath. They seemed to enjoy their stay but like most overseas visitors found it cold with no central heating. They did hold a few large parties and Douglas and I went to a Hunt Ball with them one evening.

Douglas loved company, he loved people, his family and relations. He also loved picnics and crowds of friends, and he loved dancing. Often, if we were affluent, we would go shopping on a Saturday in Grafton Street and then repair for a coffee, sometimes even an Irish coffee. Douglas once ordered red and white vermouth (sweet and dry) to be mixed on ice and this became a traditional family drink. He loved wine and good food too. But he was easy-going and if there was not much food available he would say, 'I'll go down to the shops and get some sardines and rolls.' He was adaptable to the situation at hand.

After his ordination at Ealing Abbey he would come to Dublin to visit and say, 'And where shall we go today?' We would then plan a visit to friends. On his last visit home in 1982 he said to me, 'I have two free days.' I asked him where he would like to go. He had previously visited the women's Benedictine convent at Kylemore Abbey in Galway when they were electing an abbess; so he said, 'Well, perhaps I should go and see the "girls" at Kylemore.' So off we went and had a marvellous visit. We had a lovely chat on the way up and talked about earth-shaking topics like sin and prayer. I said to him, 'What is your biggest sin?' He thought for a moment and said, 'I know my greatest sin is pride . . . it's something I'm constantly battling with.' We were greeted warmly by the sisters and had a lovely tea. This was June 1982 and it was to be his last visit to Ireland. Many of the sisters approached him asking if they could see him privately for spiritual counselling. I finally said to him, 'What could these good sisters possibly have to discuss?' Douglas replied, 'You would be surprised, Yvonne. They are human like all of us and they have human problems. You probably couldn't understand their problems and they probably couldn't understand yours.'

The tradition of a Dublin family mass once a year developed and there always seemed to be good weather for the occasion. There was a wonderful *joie de vivre* surrounding the outdoor event and stimulating conversation followed. On one occasion Douglas asked if anyone would be interested in knowing about meditation. Some of us withdrew to the drawing-room and he gave us a verbal introduction to meditation, followed by a period of meditation. He did that only once. He was never pushy with meditation, although I remember him saying to me once, 'Have you ever considered meditation?' I replied, 'I think it's a great idea, Douglas, but I don't think I have the time.' Gerald, my husband, had been more serious about taking up meditation. I felt at the time that something like this was for the élite and that I was not worthy enough or holy enough. It was only years later that I discovered how much I had missed all those years I had not meditated.

Douglas had a great respect for women – all women. He was very courteous, very gentle, very helpful and very sympathetic to widows. I personally experienced this sympathy as a widow for many years. He also thought highly of religious women. He once told me he was so impressed by the nuns of Ireland because of their clear understanding of the needs of the Church. He was above all impressed with their involvement with people – in education – in visiting the poor and the sick.

At Westminster Choir School Douglas learned to appreciate music and this interest stayed with him for the rest of his life. Many times he would bring members of his family presents of records or suggest we buy such and such a record. He loved classical music and choral music, and would never miss listening to the King's College choir from Cambridge at Christmas.

The whole family was shaken when my eleven-year-old son David died suddenly. It was a great shock to everyone and I feel this was a turning point in Douglas's life. He came to me soon after David's death and said, 'I have decided to enter a monastery.' I said, 'What do you want to do that for, you've got a wonderful law career ahead of you at Trinity College.' He said, 'It isn't that I want to, Yvonne, it's that I must.' He suddenly knew this was the path he had to take. It was very hard because he loved life, his family, friends, the work at Trinity. But he simply knew he had come to a crossroad and he never regretted taking the decision and entering the monastery. I recall saying to him, 'Where are you entering?' He replied, 'Ealing Benedictine monastery in London.' I said, 'If you must enter, why not join a monastery in Ireland where we would at least see you.' He replied, smiling, 'No, I could never enter in Ireland. I must go to England. If I entered in Ireland I might lose my religion altogether.'

NEIL PORTER

John Main has been described by Dom Bede Griffiths as 'the most important spiritual guide in the world to-day'. John Main came to this position by a varied route, part of which lay in Dublin. I was privileged to witness some of it.

In 1952–3 a small group of men and women students of University College, Dublin sang Compline on Sunday evenings in University Church, St Stephen's Green. We were helped and encouraged by the late Father Patrick O'Kane. Our motives varied from the purely religious to the musical to a simple interest in one of the girls in the choir. We enjoyed this immensely, but Compline does not make enormous demands on ability in plainsong. To our chagrin we began to hear rumours that a group of Catholic students from Trinity College were singing the much more demanding and complex vespers in the Carmelite church in Clarendon Street (the church of the discalced, or 'footless' Carmelites, as they were popularly known).

43

On enquiry this proved to be true. The students' leader was Douglas Main who at the time held a quasi-staff position in law at Trinity College. After some discussion we joined them, increasing the size of the choir considerably, though not its competence. Douglas had a splendid plainsong voice, and on his occasional absences we lost much of our accuracy. He left Trinity in the late fifties for a branch of the British Colonial Office. His account of the appointment interview was entertaining. A member of the interview board, hitherto silent, was asked by the chairman if he wished to ask Mr Main any questions.

'Yes, Chairman, if I may. Mr Main, do you consider yourself an Irishman or an Englishman?'

'Well,' replied Douglas, who had been half-expecting this question, 'I was born Irish and my parents were Irish. But of course I served in the Eighth Army and I have other British connections.' Well, to hell with you, he thought: 'I'm an Irishman.'

'Thank you, Mr Main. I'm an Irishman myself.'

The answer was the correct one, and he got the job.

4

Malaya

I was first introduced to meditation long before I became a monk. My teacher was an Indian swami who had a temple outside Kuala Lumpur. When I first met him I was deeply impressed by his peacefulness and calm wisdom. For the swami the aim of meditation was the coming to awareness of the spirit of the universe who dwells in our hearts and in silence is loving to all. (John Main)

As Laurence Freeman points out in the introduction, in the spring of 1954 John Main applied to join the British Colonial Service. This adventure would dramatically change his life. One day he was sent on an apparently routine assignment to deliver a goodwill message and a photograph to a Hindu monk, Swami Satyananda, director of the Pure Life Society ashram and orphanage school. This visit was to change his life and to set in motion a passionate search for his true vocation. His goodwill mission accomplished, John Main asked the swami to discuss the spiritual base of the many good works carried out at the orphanage and school. Within a few moments John Main knew he was in the presence of a holy man, a teacher, a man of the Spirit whose faith was alive in love and service to others.

John Main was so moved by the swami's intensity and devotion that he asked him to teach him to meditate his way. The swami agreed and invited him to come to a meditation centre once a week.

The swami pointed out that since the young western visitor was a Christian he must meditate as a Christian, and he gave him a Christian mantra. He also insisted it was necessary to meditate twice a day, morning and evening. For eighteen months John Main meditated with the swami and it was this

45

encounter that led him to the pilgrimage of meditation and eventually to discover the mantra tradition as taught by John Cassian. As Laurence Freeman comments, he was never to forget this experience of holy presence. John Main's own confident openness to the religions of Asia is directly attributable to this Hindu monk who had accepted him as a Christian disciple.

JOHN BOLAND

Douglas left us, joined the British Colonial Service and went to Malaya. He wrote to me quite frequently in this period. I suppose one of the tragedies as I now look back on this time is that I kept none of the letters – though I did keep some of them for quite a long time. The general type of letter that came from him in Malaya was to the effect that life in the Colonial Service while it might have intrinsic moments of beauty was really intensely boring. I remember one comment to the effect that if he had to go to another cocktail party and meet the same group of people again he would start screaming. The strange thing is that this was a period when he had made his first encounter with the practice of meditation. And yet as I now recall it, he did not mention meditation to me even once in any of his letters.

It was quite clear that he was not going to make a career in the Colonial Service. One of the difficulties in talking about his experiences there is that he would so magnificently pull your leg. You could never be quite certain that what was written to you did not suffer from at least a measure of mild exaggeration. He was then a member of a team entrusted with the task of preparing Malaya for self-government and there were to be some elections. Douglas, being astute, could see that these elections could only have one possible result: the emerging government would be one that would wish to terminate, in its then existing form, the British connection and this would lead to the end of his career.

JAMES SCARLETT

In January 1955 Douglas and I sailed from Southampton in
the P and O liner *Carthage*. We had spent the previous three
months learning Malay in the School of Oriental and African
Studies at the University of London under Miss Lewis, a
former Chief Education Officer in Malaya. She was a gifted
teacher, and Douglas, with a sensitive ear, could respond to
the recorded Malay conversations to which we listened, without drawing the criticism, which rightly was my lot: 'Don't
speak Mayfair Malay.'

Snow fell on the decks of the *Carthage* as we left Southampton with the prospect of a long sea voyage; it was soon
clear that the voyage would be entertaining. Douglas had a
timely sense of the ridiculous and was quick to fit nicknames
to many of the passengers, selecting imaginary and suitably
junior appointments for the most distinguished. The voyage
was a delight; we were committed to the ship for a time, but
not for too long; the ship's passenger list was long but not
too long, and there was room enough both to meet and to
avoid one's fellow-passengers; ahead lay the land in which
we were to work and discover a different life.

For some reason we disembarked at different ports,
although our destination was the same – Kuala Lumpur.
There we did different things; Douglas entered the Chinese
Language School, and I went into the Secretariat. From time
to time we met but our work was different. We met for the
last time on board one of the Blue Funnel liners at Port
Swettenham; Douglas had embarked to return to England on
a ship which carried but few passengers, and we shared a
glimpse of some of them. I never learnt what nicknames he
gave to them, but in the conversation which we had, there
was the promise of an entertaining voyage home.

5

Ealing Abbey, London

And his teaching made a deep impression on the people because he taught them with authority. (Matt. 7:29)

When he began to speak about meditation it was with authority and assurance and no pussy-footing around. His message was clear, simple and straightforward. This was the teacher I had been looking for. (Tom Abraham)

In September 1959 at thirty-three years of age John Main surprised everyone by joining Ealing Benedictine Abbey in London. In November 1962 he was chosen by Ealing to go to Rome for theological studies at the International Benedictine College of St Anselmo. He enjoyed the cultural atmosphere of Rome, his holidays, hiking trips with fellow-students and the excitement of preparations for the Second Vatican Council. On 21 December 1964 he was ordained at Ealing and then taught for three years at the Ealing boys' school. It was at Ealing in 1975 that he began to teach meditation and formed the first lay community of meditators. Two monks who knew John Main comment on the Ealing years and Tom Abraham recounts life in the lay meditation community.

TOM ABRAHAM

My initial meeting with John Main came about in a circuitous way. In 1975 my personal pilgrimage had taken me from my home in India to Ethiopia to Ghana and finally to London where I was preparing for a Ph.D degree in electrical engineering at Imperial College. In London I met a Chris Knollys and on a trip to visit Worth Benedictine Abbey he said to me, 'There's an Irish monk you should meet. He teaches meditation at Ealing Abbey.' That was enough to whet my appetite. I had been reading a few books on Zen meditation and was open to any kind of spiritual discipline. The problem was that all my reading talked *about* meditation but never gave a clear explanation *how* to go about it.

In December 1975 I finally got an opportunity to meet Father John at a regular Monday evening meditation meeting at Ealing. I had conjured up an image of this priest as young, inexperienced, and probably into meditation as a fad, as the thing 'to do' in the 1970s. On that particular evening I had just placed one foot in the meditation room when a firm, strong voice behind me said, 'We take our shoes off when we go into the meditation room.' So much for my preconceived image of Father John. Here was a mature monk who, I subsequently learnt, had been meditating for twenty years. He had an impeccable English accent and an imposing personality. When he began to speak about meditation it was with authority and assurance and no pussy-footing around. His message was clear, simple and straightforward. This was the teacher I had been looking for.

After attending a few more meetings it became clear to me that this was an authentic path of prayer and that I had to make some kind of move towards a deeper commitment. At Easter 1976 I spent five days as a guest at the monastery. Father John was open and welcoming and I was attracted to the discipline of the Benedictine rule. This visit confirmed to me that living in this environment would enable me not only to develop the practice of meditation but would also offer the right environment in which to write my Ph.D thesis.

I asked Father John if I could join the other two members of the lay meditating community at Ealing. After checking my character references he welcomed me to the community with open arms. A few days later on visiting me in my room he noticed a transistor radio and a record player. He gently reminded me that in an effort to preserve the spirit of silence radios and record players were prohibited. I was learning. In all my dealings with Father John he came across as a disciplinarian, but fair, just and invariably kind. He was practical and you always knew where you stood. He asked me how much I could contribute towards my upkeep. I had carefully budgeted fifty pounds a month. He accepted this offer but probably had to make other arrangements to make up for my shortfall. In my first visit for a meal to the monastery dining-room I wore jeans and an open shirt. After the meal Father John pointed out that I should wear a jacket and tie at subsequent meals. In my youthful exuberance I protested but Father John insisted that this was the rule and I would have to abide by it.

Living and participating in the lay community was a happy time for me. Laurence Freeman, then a novice, joined the members of the lay community and Father John in meditating each day. I did, though, have a great deal of chagrin that so few monks in the Ealing community seemed to see the value in this form of contemplative prayer.

At our evening recreation in the lay community house Father John would often join us and entertain us with hilarious stories and mimicry. He had a gift of accents and could imitate Irish, Australian, Indian and a variety of other dialects. Up to this point we had two meditations, morning and evening. Then one day I accidentally discovered Father John and Brother Laurence meditating at noon. This was another aspect of Father John's character. He never put any pressure on anyone in regard to meditation. No persuasion or armtwisting. He always hoped you would on your own accord join in. Needless to say we all freely and joyfully joined in this third daily meditation.

In August 1976 Father John gave a series of talks at the Cistercian monastery of Gethsemani in Kentucky. On his return one could detect this had been a spiritual turning-point in his life. He shared with us that 'when I was there I felt a oneness with everyone here in the community'. It would seem that Gethsemani was in fact the catalyst that opened Father John to a wider role as a teacher of meditation. At this point none of the lay community was aware of developments in Montreal.

I do though remember the date of 4 January 1977 when Father John, Pat Hawes, Nicholas Wardropper and I went off for a day of leisure and a visit to the south of England. Before leaving Father John picked up his mail. On his return to the car he opened a letter and said, 'This one is interesting. It's a letter from Bishop Leonard Crowley of Montreal asking us to start a new foundation there.' That was his way of letting us in on the news. It was quite a bombshell. Personally I felt he would never get permission from the Ealing community and so dismissed the thought from my mind. That turned out to be a wonderful day. We went to the town of Bosham to see a great-aunt of Father John's but she was not in. We had a pub lunch and a beautiful walk along a beach. He also showed us a house he lived in as a child. We drove back in time for meditation.

In April 1977 I got a job with the firm ITT at Sidcup but continued to visit the monastery at weekends. At this point Father John and Brother Laurence had received permission for Montreal. When Father John asked if I was coming I at first declined, but subsequently decided that indeed my path lay in Montreal with Father John and the meditating community.

Life in the community at Vendome Avenue was a wonderful experience. In the beginning of course only a few people came out to Father John's meditation talks. Nevertheless he talked with the same intensity and authority whether there were two or twenty in attendance. It amazed me that he never worried about numbers. Even if only one person came from outside on a given evening he would give a talk of the same duration and with the same preparation and concentration.

Nor did his humour ever diminish. One evening at recreation he had our entire community in convulsions with a story from his diplomatic service in Malaya in the 1950s. It is really worth repeating. My memory is a little hazy and I cannot vouch for its literal accuracy but, as I recall, he was chosen as an official translator of an obscure Chinese dialect to accompany a British general on a visit to a village under Communist control. The rather rotund general stood up on the jeep in front of the people and in a loud voice said to John Main, 'Tell the people that if they don't behave and if they don't get rid of the Communists in their midst, we will come and teach them a lesson and flatten their entire village.' John Main looked out at the scowling faces, all of them

51

Communist sympathisers, and decided not to translate the message literally. Instead he said, 'We have a message from the Queen who lives across the ocean in England. She sends her best regards to you.' At this point the villagers started smiling. The general then said, 'Tell them, Main, that if we find one single Commie in the entire village we will come and each one of them will be punished.' Realising the villagers were all well equipped with long knives and could easily dispatch in short order the general, the driver and himself, John Main again decided that diplomacy was the best policy. Addressing the crowd he said, 'The Queen in fact sends her special regards to all of you in the village.' At this the villagers smiled, clapped and cheered, appreciative of the Queen's great interest in their own particular village. The general turned to John Main and said, 'I told you, Main, if you give them some tough straight talk you will get a good response and they will fall in line very quickly.' Father John ended the story by saying tongue in cheek that if he had given them the general's message they would probably have had a fifty-fifty chance of getting out alive.

One thing that always struck me was Father John's equanimity. He had been trying to purchase or rent additional accommodation across the street from 3761 Vendome Avenue. An offer had been made to the owner. Father John, Laurence Freeman and I were out for a walk one night and suddenly discovered in walking past the house that it had been sold to someone else. I remember being so disappointed but Father John took it all in his stride with not so much as a hint of frustration or anger. He accepted it casually with utter detachment.

The Prior of the Benedictine Monastery had no qualms about doing humble tasks. There was an accident on Vendome with a great deal of broken glass. He asked me to get two brooms and out we went to clean it up. During the work he casually mentioned that he had quite a bit of this kind of cleaning experience because his father often put him to work 'cleaning up after the horses'. Another time Father John and I had to return a large carpet to Pascals' department store. He carried the front and I carried the back, to the amusement of staff and customers. No task was too menial or treated as drudgery. He always concentrated on the job at hand.

Another characteristic was his courtesy and deference to women. In Indian culture if a Catholic priest came into a room all the women would leave. I shall never forget a visit to the Priory when I brought my wife Ivy into a room to meet Father John and other members of the community including a bishop (all male). The men all stood up, but it was Father John who stood up first. He had this special courtesy to women.

In the final analysis, though, it was his teaching on meditation that won the hearts of so many people who listened to him including myself. He always emphasised the simplicity of meditation, the discipline required and the importance of fidelity. He knew full well it was a difficult journey, that it sometimes required courage, and so he was always giving encouragement. How often he would say, 'Don't worry if you stop saying it – just come back to it.' He felt that the teaching would be handed on organically in small groups. It was not going to be a 'boom' or 'bust' process. After fifteen years of meditating I still need to belong to a weekly group. There is both a 'giving' and a 'receiving' in a group. We need the support and encouragement of seeing others faithful to the journey but others need to see our perseverance and faithfulness. With Father John there was no need to discuss religion. He sensed that meditation brought us to the heart of religion itself and that the practice took priority over discussion.

My last visit to Father John took place in late November 1982, the Sunday on which he celebrated his last mass. I had arrived with the family a little late and was standing aside while Father John and Father Laurence, fully vested, came down the steps to enter the chapel. He noticed me, stopped and gave me a firm embrace. It is something I will never forget. His eyes lit up and there was joy on his face, and he said, 'How are you, Tom.' That was it, nothing more. After lunch I took Ivy up to his table to see him for the last time. In great pain he stood up to greet us.

How can one sum up Father John's life? All I can say is that the way of the mantra, that great leap of unconditional love, changed my life for ever. He will always be my teacher.

JOHN BOLAND

Douglas was to drop a positive bombshell in my direction when he announced that he was leaving Trinity to be a Benedictine novice and would be joining the community at Ealing. This came as an enormous surprise to me. Although I could see Douglas as a Benedictine monk, I could never quite see him fitting into what was my image of the community at Ealing. Nevertheless he left us, went into the novitiate, the door was closed and we did not see much of him for quite some time. There was an interesting episode in that while he was in Dublin he had decided he would read for membership of the English Bar. He had taken all the necessary examinations. He was in the novitiate when the moment came for him to be called to the Bar. He emerged from the monastery at Ealing in the clothing of a novice monk, came to my flat in Chelsea, changed into evening dress, borrowed my wig and went off to take his call before the benches of the Honourable Society of Gray's Inn. Some little time later he came back, changed out of the evening dress, got into his habit and disappeared back into his monastery. That, I suppose, was the end in some sense of a legal career which certainly bore a great deal of promise. I always thought he had a very good legal mind. He did not write a great deal in the way of review material for law journals but he certainly made his presence felt on the very few occasions when he attended meetings of the Law Society. He was someone who was respected and certainly his reputation long survived his departure from the Law School at Trinity.

JACK PEFFERS

Dom John Main, the new young monk, walked across the playground. He approached the playground in a different way to other adults. He did not seem to be abiding by those unwritten conventions about the relationship between monks and pupils. He did not circle the edge of the playground and seek to pass unnoticed or make extravagant sallies to inspect the shape of the ball being used in playground games. Rather, he walked slowly through the middle of the playground with his head and eyes eager to make contact and engage with the boys. He meticulously responded to every greeting. He declared himself available to the students. Some boys sensitive to this lack of cultural conformity sought to induce it by exaggerated greetings. These faded and a new method of engagement between pupils and staff was on the agenda for all.

The same approach by Dom John Main was to be found in the classroom. There was no radical pedagogy being pedalled, rather it was a question of style. Dialogue was more open, more pupils were drawn into discussion – a gap was becoming apparent; the gap between instruction and education. Such was the approach for fourteen-year-olds in Religious Education and eighteen-year-olds in Government and Politics seminars. The approach left each student feeling a valued and valuable individual and a member of a learning community.

The learning process was never cramped; it was ongoing. The start and finish of lessons were somehow organic in spite of being separate in time and space. The learning was never truncated. It was for life, not for the exam. It was not the content, although it was always stimulating, that was important; it was the process of learning that was important. Learning became something about growing, less about being fattened for the market.

The relationship with Dom John did not end with the transition from school to university to work. There were many issues about growing and living that had to be tackled. His approach remained constant: openness, approachability and non-prescriptive support. He gave of his time effortlessly.

His death, though untimely, has not interrupted the dialogue between all those who knew him and the teacher. It could not be broken. His philosophy of life is alive in us today and is being passed on to new generations. Thank you, John Main.

EDMUND FLOOD

My first strong recollection of John Main is of his insisting on carrying my cases, quite unnecessarily, down a steep hill in Rome in 1962. Always there was the charm, the kind courtesy, the zestful humour. But already, in the early 1960s, there was the practical content to it.

In 1963–4 I came back from Oxford and John from Rome. In our different ways we were absorbing the theology of the Vatican Council: John with the sweeping enthusiasm of the Irishman. In sixth form religious education teaching our pupils' most frequent question was 'What is the position about birth control?' At that time only John had worked out his position, and he was willing, if requested, to deal with it for other teachers' sixth form groups. Inevitably he became known in the school as 'our expert in birth control' – a sobriquet he accepted in good humour.

In 1967 our elderly abbot decided to retire. Although he was a long way from having (or wanting) a reputation as a 'progressive', the abbot sometimes seemed to assume that John would succeed him – a most exceptional assumption for someone only recently ordained. Those who supported John's candidacy were realistic about the odds but saw it as immensely desirable. There seemed to be some hope that we would be led by a leader who had been totally won over to the theology of the Vatican Council and would boldly, imaginatively and with great conviction help us to apply it to our urban situation, and who could light quite a beacon in London and beyond.

Another was elected; and John was made deputy head in our upper school, where I was also serving. In the sixth form (about 150) – or at least among its livelier and brighter echelons – John was, predictably, a stimulating influence. Sixth form societies rapidly proliferated, founded and enlivened by John, with a sophistication and geniality which delighted the abler student.

John found his metier chiefly among such students. Much of his contribution came from his being a worldly-wise university don, rather than a pedestrian schoolmaster. This reinforced his sense of freedom from – and sometimes irritation against – pettiness and over-institutionalisation. It was combined with his love of fun, of wit, and with the marvellous but bizarre richness of his humanity. And since religion and life were, through the Vatican Council, beginning to overcome their long divorce, all this influenced his religious practices as much as anything else. One was hardly surprised to hear that John heard senior students' confessions over a glass of sherry!

For John, and for others of us, those were impatient times. There was such an evident need for the perspectives underlying the Vatican Council to be allowed to shape our religious practice. Yet the obstacles to this in the English Roman Catholic Church seemed so blind and unyielding. The autocratic streak in John's character made it at times still more difficult for him. How far the pejorative implication of 'autocratic' is fair to John is a discussion that would take one to central areas of his personality. He *did* want power; he sincerely believed that he could rule best. Fired by his impatience at what he saw as quite a measure of greyness, he had little taste for the varying tones of a range of options. But the opportunities were, in principle, immense. And he sincerely believed that he was best placed to harness them. Had he been given the chance to do that, there is little doubt that, at that stage in his life, he would have made great mistakes (his plan for rebuilding the new monastery at Ealing was ludicrously grandiose; and he might not have listened to wiser counsel). But he would have lit a torch in London with huge effect – and might have managed to disarm a large proportion of the opposition in the area.

Instead, after a dispute about school policy, he went to Washington DC, and after a few months at St Anselm's was invited to be headmaster of the Benedictine school there. On business trips to the USA I visited him there in 1973 and 1974. Part of him found some fulfilment in being a headmaster, but not the whole of him. He loved the variety and sophistication of the Washington scene. But he clearly felt called to what he saw as more fruitful fields. We talked in Washington about what these might be. He said he would like to establish a prayer centre. It seemed to me a most promising avenue, and when I returned to Ealing I mentioned this to the abbot.

From some points of view John's prayer centre at Ealing was a great success. People from every age group and every sector of society regularly attended the centre. There was then (and of course still is) a hunger for help with prayer. John was, literally, a godsend. But hardly any Benedictine houses had then felt able to reappraise their prayer in the light of new insights. The meditation 'across the garden at the Prayer Centre' was peripheral to our community life. And how well-suited John would have been to help effect some synthesis I am not entirely sure.

In the light of this, the Archbishop of Montreal's invitation to John to found a monastic prayer centre there was evidently providential – and of course even more clearly in the light of how long he was to live. To some of us at Ealing it was a great personal loss.

Because of the pressure of my own work, my visits to John in Montreal had to be short. Hence my impressions of him then are inevitably more piecemeal. The fun, and the litigious Irish wit, were still a delight. I remember staying with him for a few days at the home of a rather conservative judge, who repeatedly greeted John's theological and political views with expostulations of 'Rubbish. Absolute rubbish'. John thrived on this tough, genial argument well into the morning.

John never seemed personally threatened by opposing views: he could almost always discuss them in a relaxed way, and with what he hoped was an open mind. But there were considerable limits to the openness he achieved.

This was no doubt linked with his autocratic streak. I noticed it in my visits to the first Montreal house, where John seemed to insist on preaching when there were others who could have done it better. It was linked more strongly, I suspect, with the role of founder to which he had been called. In the first years of a new enterprise a clear-cut shape is required: an easily recognisable identity. In his work of marking that out for the new Priory, John's gifts and his limitations both contributed marvellously to something that bears great fruit in the lives of so many today.

ANTHONY GEE

I studied with John Main in Rome from 1960–1, and we were the only two students from Ealing. Peter Flood, a monk from Ealing, was a professor there. I got to know John very well. We passed many an hour over an 'illegal' bottle of wine or pizza, discussing all the new ideas in the air as the preparatory commissions for the newly called Vatican Council got under way. We did, however, go far beyond theology, with common interests in literature and music. Looking back I realise that he was one of the most formative influences in my early life.

I was a young, inexperienced and immature student; he was some years older with considerable experience already behind him. One of my most delightful memories is of a holiday at Easter, when we rented a cottage with four other monks in an isolated village in southern Italy. We found the cottage by going to a travel agent in Rome. John, in his best Italian, proclaimed from the centre of a large shop, 'Does anyone here have a cottage to rent?' to which a customer replied, 'Yes, I have.' The days (and nights) were spent in play-reading, poetry reading and singing madrigals. Fortunately we all enjoyed singing, often to the amazement of the villagers, who admitted when they discovered at the end of a week that we were monks that they had never met monks like us. They confided, almost apologetically, that they were all Communists! I still remember John in the forceful role of Othello. He always took the major part! Like many shy people he was a born actor; he once confided that he felt he was playing a role most of the time. Stimulated by John, I devoured T. S. Eliot and tussled, rather unsuccessfully, with Rilke. I well remember the enthusiasm with which we devoured the newly published *Phenomenon of Man* by Teilhard de Chardin. We were possibly encouraged by the vehement condemnation of the book by Peter Flood, which echoed our own desire to break down the old dualisms between nature and grace, religious and secular, science and Christianity.

Back at Ealing, an amusing illustration of his liveliness as a schoolteacher was his founding of an upper fifth society called the Termites – to nibble away at the foundations of the Establishment! A popular aim for sixteen-year-olds!

We remained close over the next few years at Ealing during the 1960s, sharing the excitement and promise of the Vatican II years. But I gradually became aware that his large personality could be somewhat stifling, and I suppose I distanced myself from him a little as time went on, to assert my own independence and need for personal growth. But I retained a firm belief in his suitability as a potential abbot, and shared the disappointment when he failed to be elected.

Would he have been successful as abbot? In retrospect, I have my doubts. Certainly life would have been exciting and lively, and he would have cut a great figure in the Church. More than that, he would have been an inspiration to many. But whether he would have been a sympathetic father of a Benedictine family, with its cross-section of personalities, is more doubtful. He inspired great affection and devotion in his disciples and also in those with differing views but similar big temperaments. He enjoyed a battle of wits. But he also inspired fear and mistrust in lesser mortals with more pedestrian qualities. I largely lost touch with him, sadly, when he went to Montreal, but I have the impression that he mellowed somewhat in this respect in his later years; perhaps he would have done so earlier had he been elected abbot, but I have my doubts.

I suspect that had he been elected, he would not have developed into the significant person he eventually became. He would probably have been significant in other ways. After his disappointment (and this was very real, he wanted to be abbot), he was clearly looking around for a new role. The resignation from the school was, in my opinion, not a matter of principle but a largely engineered excuse to set out for new pastures. It was inevitable; he was already looking beyond Ealing. He had found his role. In retrospect he found his meaning in life in the mantra.

6

St Anselm's, Washington

To our youngest daughter he was quite plainly 'the funniest man she ever knew'. Our sons saw him as a headmaster, teacher, a no-nonsense disciplinarian, who very transparently had a warm and generous heart. To close friends who met him in our home his spirituality often came through like a laser beam. And there were others who just didn't know what to make of him. (Jack Davitt)

From 1969 to 1974 John Main spent five years at St Anselm's Benedictine Community in Washington DC. His first assignment was to enrol in graduate theology studies at the Catholic University of America. Dissatisfied with the curriculum at CU, he was happy to become headmaster of St Anselm's Abbey, a private Benedictine school for boys. It was to become the busiest and most productive period of his monastic life so far. He took over an American school with severe administrative and personnel problems and threw himself into the work of improving morale, ensuring a sound religious education programme, upgrading the academic standards of the school and fund-raising.

JOHN FARRELLY

When John Main first came here his plan was to take graduate studies in religious education at the Catholic University of America, and this is what he did for the first year. During that period he and the community got to know one another; he made friends among fellow students and faculty at the university, and through participating in some of the community's ministries he became acquainted with changes that were occurring in religious life in the United States at the time. He had a vivid sense of the differences between people and places that he experienced in the United States in that period after Vatican II and their counterparts in England. He was amused at times by this and amused others by the way he recounted his experiences. It seemed that he was frequently having rather outlandish experiences – as when he went for a picnic with some Christian brothers in a national forest in Virginia. As a bear approached their picnic table the picnickers retreated and left the bear consuming their food. This and other incidents lost nothing when Father John retold them to us, or by letter back to community and friends in England.

His heart was not, however, really in his studies. At the end of that school year, St Anselm's Abbey Preparatory School was in need of a new headmaster. Father Abbot Alban Boultwood, with the advice of the monastic council, asked Father John whether he would take the position; a position for which John's experience as assistant headmaster at Ealing had fitted him. The Abbot of Ealing was amenable to this proposal, and Father John accepted. This was a troubled time for many preparatory schools in the United States; a period when many parents were disturbed by the direction some Catholic schools were taking after the Vatican Council. John reassured our students' parents of the importance to the faculty at St Anselm's of the religious dimension of the school. And he conveyed a strong sense of the school's commitment to update the academic programme as needed.

In the school he got on very well with the students, teachers and other staff, and was always willing to take the most menial tasks on himself when circumstances called for this. He taught the senior religion class, considering this more as an opportunity to face problems of belief and its implications in the students' lives than as a course in which a certain amount of content had to be covered.

During all this time John was quite faithful to the community liturgy as well as to his personal prayer. In his last year at St Anselm's his interest in the form of meditation that, as he recounted many times, he had initially learned from a Hindu swami in Malaya, revived. This was occasioned by the interest shown in meditation by a young man who was staying for an extended period at the Abbey. John suggested Augustine Baker's book on prayer, *Holy Wisdom*, to this young man. Reading it with him, he was struck by similarities between the advice of this spiritual master and the advice of the swami who had introduced him to meditation before he had entered the monastery. He saw this as a turning point for himself and as a background from which he later taught meditation in prayer groups at Ealing when he returned there, and still later in the Benedictine Priory he founded in Montreal; and also for the many people to whom he taught prayer from that centre.

As a member of St Anselm's I know that I speak for many here in concluding that John Main made significant contributions to our school and was highly esteemed in our community. The esteem and affection in which he was held were manifested in many ways while he was here and in later years.

JACK DAVITT

John Main opened the door into my life with a flourish. That was the way he did things, with verve and assurance. He knew precisely where he was going and why he wanted to get there. And if he chose you to go along the way with him, you were the luckiest of men.

He chose me in the autumn of 1970 after addressing for the first time the parents of the student body of St Anselm's Abbey School, Washington. He took my elbow as we all moved from the auditorium to the refectory and enquired in his strongly British accent, and with a decidedly Irish twinkle in his eyes, whether I might be a relation of Michael Davitt (founder of the Land League in Ireland and a prisoner of Her Majesty in the 1870s for high treason against the Crown).

And so, as in our introduction, he appeared to each person who had the pleasure of accompanying him, briefly or at length, along that path in totally different ways. To our youngest daughter he was, quite plainly, and she told him so, 'the funniest man (she) ever knew.' Our sons saw him as headmaster, teacher, a no-nonsense disciplinarian, who very transparently hid a warm and generous heart. To close friends who met him in our home his spirituality often came through like a laser beam. And there were others who 'just didn't know what to make of him'!

As I said, I was the luckiest of men. The face he turned to me was his merry one. He was John the *schanachie* (Irish story-teller), who could spin the most outrageous tales in much less than a moment's notice, or relate a mundane event in a perfect dialect, if need be; but always in a way that left you convulsed with laughter. He was a leg-puller *par excellence*; yet, as he often confessed, his own leg could be pulled more easily than most.

Our home in Washington was always enlivened by unex-pected phone calls from him: a 'collect' call from 'Sydney, Australia', with John playing all the roles, the Australian and American operators (and himself, of course), as he chatted on interminably about our children, asking for each by name and probing for every bit of trivia in their lives at the moment, as the costly minutes ticked by – and not revealing, until the most expensive half hour in Ma Bell's history had expired, that he was in town and would be out presently to share the evening with us.

Over a decade relatively few serious words passed between us. We shared the Irish proclivity for gallows humour and he was a master of it. There were, I suppose, other times and places in his regimen for serious matters. But in John's ordered view of life – 'ordered' by his British background and training, though well-tempered by his Irish – our relationship was to be one that the closest of friends enjoy; no pranks need ever be weighed in the offing, no words to be 'chosen carefully'.

There were a few serious moments. We were brother lawyers and we shared from time to time our love of the law, debating judicial decisions (of which he was always *au courant*) or politics (of which his knowledge was global). When he was with us on Cape Cod he awakened to the BBC short wave and would come to breakfast with news of how things were that morning in Bangladesh. On religious matters he was direct: spirituality, above all else, a *sine qua non* if the Church was to survive and flourish. So substance (read: spirituality) could never take a back seat to form as it did in the Middle Ages, he said, when monks who violated all of their sacred vows continued none the less to observe the form by fastidiously saying their office.

He preached what he practised, and in the most meaningful and practical ways. If he was guest in your house he had already baked his unique Irish brown bread when you came down to breakfast: 'The secret is honey, that is the *only* way.'

He professed to believe that there was only one way to do most things. Orange and grapefruit juice, for example, must be taken daily, but only freshly squeezed and ingested in less than a minute after squeezing. The curative powers he attributed to the drink prepared 'the right way' were mind-boggling. Yet, his 'one way' of doing things in matters of minor importance did not reflect intolerance in things of moment. His charitable attitude towards transgressors of the law, God or man's, had no limits; he fully understood the problem of priests who sought to be laicised; or the plight of divorced couples; or students who over-imbibed; or confrères who did not return the charity he showed them.

On a temporal plane, his 'Irishness' was, to me, the great force that moved him. It accounted for his humour, his abiity to spin a tale or to deprecate himself, his love of music and literature and, most of all, of life and people. The then *Taoiseach* (Prime Minister) of Ireland, Garret FitzGerald and his wife were among his dear and close friends, and on more than one occasion I recall watching Washington's officialdom, Irish and American, bristle as John drove FitzGerald to appointments around the Capitol. Not protocol!

An Irish friend of John's, a prominent physician from Belfast, was fully convinced that if John was made Archbishop of Armagh, Primate of all Ireland, he could bring the warring factions of the south and north together. So was John.

Others will see him in a totally different light. And they would be, I think, quite right. Does anything come more quickly to mind when one thinks of John than the post-Pentecost audience of the apostles, who heard them 'each in his native tongue' (Acts 2:6)? So each of us saw him in different lights because he communicated to each of us in a singular and special way.

His delightfully wry wit, however, came through to everyone in the same way. Still, if this brief portrait of him seems to make too much of his jocular and humorous side, I must in defence say that is the part of him, I believe, that he would have wished we remember most. But this is speculation.

What is not speculation and what we can say with Tomas Critlin (*The Islandman*) when he drew the veil on the end of life on the Blasket Islands, just a stone's throw from John's beloved Skelligs off the coast of Kerry, is: 'The likes of (him) will never be seen again.'

And, Douglas John Main, the likes of us will never be the same – because of you.

SEAN MULLIN CSSR

My first meeting with Father John was on campus at the Catholic University, Washington DC. He was standing examining a map of the campus, immaculately dressed in black blazer, Roman collar and grey slacks. He turned and asked me in a very pronounced English accent, 'Do you know, Father, where nursing (pronounced nussing!) block is on the campus?' When I said, 'I'm going there,' he said, 'Are you Irish?' My accent was quite clear and so we gave our names. When I heard Main, I asked him if he happened to be a relation of Ian Main of Ballinskelligs in Kerry. Immediately he changed into a clearly Irish accent and said, 'My heavens, do you know Ian – he is my brother.'

We became good friends. I have many happy memories.

One day in the torrid heat of Washington he arrived on campus dressed in his Benedictine habit. When I asked why he replied, 'Just to show these people here what a medieval monk looks like.'

We had been listening to dangers in the Church at a lecture and were told that institutionalisation, localisation and reification were perennial dangers. Some time later John was hospitalised and underwent a series of examinations. He was not impressed with hospital practice in the USA – so very impersonal. I asked him how he was and he tersely replied, 'I feel totally reified.' He was so clever with words.

John wrote a superb poem for our first Hallowe'en party in our department.

Once when he was asked about taking over the principalship of the local Benedictine school he told me about his worries and that he went back to Ealing to consult his abbot there. He told me he was very conscious of obedience, and also was interested in his obedience to the whole Benedictine family: if his taking the Washington job was for the benefit of the whole family, then he felt that he should accept the offer. He was also offered a lectureship in Oxford (in law, I think) and the post of senior chaplain in the new Catholic University in Australia. That offer came as a result of meeting somebody over lunch when he went to Oxford about the law job. He made an impression on everyone at first meetings.

I was privileged to be his friend.

ELTIN GRIFFIN

The John Main I knew at the Catholic University of America was first of all a very civilised man, beautifully spoken; he was a very striking-looking man with silver hair, long face, long nose and a delightful smile. In addition to all this he was one of the most brilliant conversationalists I have ever encountered. He was also a superb mimic and could literally 'take off' any person or accent. His mimicry of the Co. Kerry accent was unforgettable. I'll never forget his description of 'the day in the life of a Kerry curate'.

I never really knew why John Main came to the Catholic University. I thought it rather strange why a man of his calibre and intelligence, with such a marvellous academic track record behind him, came to study at Catholic University. In retrospect it seems to have been a 'holding action' for the next step of his personal pilgrimage – and a step towards his real vocation of teaching about prayer/meditation.

I think John Main has made an enormous contribution, not only to the Catholic Church, but to all Christian churches and indeed to many people of little or no religious beliefs.

The genius of John Main's teaching on Christian meditation is that it has opened a spiritual path for people of varying degrees of faith. He has unearthed something very precious from the earliest Christian tradition of prayer; that prayer is not really a 'head-centred' practice, but a way of simplicity, silence and stillness. John Main rediscovered for us the basic truth that prayer is not based on 'thinking' or 'reason' but on seeking God in the silence and stillness beyond word and thought. Today John Main's contribution to our understanding of spirituality is being realised around the world.

Everywhere we see that in a rapidly disintegrating world people are looking for healing, harmony, integration, wholeness. There is an extraordinary interest, indeed a hunger in prayer for being with God, rather than talking to God.

This then was the genius of John Main in reintroducing us to the path of meditation – a path that fills a great contemporary need. It is an interior path that leads us into the presence of God within.

7

New Beginnings in Montreal

On 23 October 1976 the Holy Spirit breathed a fresh wind into the spiritual life of Montreal . . . I met John Main for the first time . . . It began a process that neither of us could have imagined would bear the spiritual benefits that have come to our people in Montreal and universally. (Leonard Crowley)

To understand John Main's founding of a Benedictine monastery in Montreal with its role to pass on the prayer tradition of Christian meditation, it is necessary to backtrack to Washington and a crucial turning point that took place in his life there. In *Christian Meditation: The Gethsemani Talks*, John Main recounts that one day:

> a young man came to the Washington monastery asking to be taught something about Christian mysticism. He had spent some time with a Hindu teacher but was now looking for the Christian standpoint. So, with some malice aforethought, I gave him Baker's *Holy Wisdom* as his first book of study, thinking that this would keep him quietly occupied for several weeks, unravelling its loping, Drydenesque sentences. To my amazement, however, he reacted with real and immediate enthusiasm, to such a degree that I felt I had to read it again myself. We began to read it together and very soon afterwards we also began to meditate together.
>
> Baker's frequent reminder of the emphatic insistence St Benedict lays upon Cassian's Conferences sent me to them seriously for the first time. It was with very wonderful astonishment that I read, in his Tenth Conference, of the practice of using a single short phrase to achieve the stillness necessary for prayer: 'The mind thus casts out and

represses the rich and ample matter of all thoughts and restricts itself to the poverty of a single verse.'

It was this discovery in Cassian of a Christian tradition using a prayer phrase or mantra that led John Main to found a Christian Meditation group at Ealing Abbey in London in 1974 and subsequently to founding the Montreal Monastery in 1976.

LEONARD J. CROWLEY VG

On 23 October 1976 the Holy Spirit breathed a fresh wind into the spiritual life of Montreal. How strange and wondrous are the ways of the Holy Spirit. On that Saturday morning I happened to be in my room, a rarity in itself, when the porter rang to tell me there was someone at the door to see me. When I came down to the front door, I met Dom John Main for the first time.

Everything surrounding my initial meeting and encounter with Dom Main happened in a mysterious way. Six months earlier, following the celebration of the Sunday Eucharist at the Ascension of Our Lord parish, I stayed at the back of the church to meet the parishioners. It was there I met the Kruitwagen family for the first time. Originally from Ealing in London, Hans Kruitwagen had been transferred to Montreal by the international Dutch company for which he worked. Hans and Dom Main had met each other in Ealing. They developed a close enough friendship for Dom Main to be invited as a guest to the home of the Kruitwagens in Montreal while on his way to Gethsemani. It was Hans who suggested to Dom Main that he stop in to pay me a courtesy call while he was out for a Saturday morning stroll.

The first visit of Dom John Main lasted one hour. It began a process that neither of us could have imagined would bear the spiritual benefits that have come to our people in Montreal and universally.

During that first visit Dom Main informed me that he was the Prior of Ealing Abbey and then proceeded to give me a succinct account of the principal periods of his life: namely

70

that he had been a soldier with a special assignment during the Second World War; had studied law, became a professor at Trinity College; served in the British Diplomatic Corps, and was appointed to Malaya where he met an Indian swami who taught him to meditate using a mantra. Eventually he became a Benedictine monk and founded a meditation centre at Ealing Abbey in London. For some reason he thought that I was familiar with this centre. In fact I had never been to England and knew nothing about Ealing Abbey.

While Dom Main was recounting the highlights of his life, I recalled one of the most important documents published by Rome, entitled *Mutuae Relationes*, published jointly by the Roman Congregations of Bishops and of Religious, regarding the relationships between bishops and religious in their own dioceses. I remembered that one of the recommendations was that each diocese should have a contemplative centre of prayer. I then asked Dom Main if Ealing Priory had ever sent monks on mission to establish a new foundation in other parts of the world. He answered in the negative. I asked him whether their Abbey would consider coming to Montreal where the social, cultural and religious revolution was taking place in our Province of Quebec. Many of our people felt uncomfortable and were leaving the province during the 1970s for other parts of Canada. Some of our parishes lost half their parishioners. Some of our clergy were thinking of leaving to serve their people elsewhere.

I suggested to Dom Main that one of the characteristics of the Benedictine monks was their vow of stability and that the presence of such a community in Montreal would enrich the spiritual life of our people and give them a sense of stability and hope during this crisis period. I was also inspired to tell Dom Main that the fruits of their contemplation would have an impact not only in the city of Montreal, but that their influence would be felt in the whole of North America and elsewhere.

At the end of that first encounter neither of us realised the magnitude of what our meeting would mean for the future. He went on his way. After his stop in Montreal he went to Kentucky where he preached a retreat to the Trappist monks at Gethsemani. While still there Dom Main phoned me to

71

ask if I were serious in my suggestion. I responded that I was obviously very serious because, like himself, I was convinced that contemplation should be part of the spirituality of all Christians. In fact the motto of our graduating class at the seminary in 1947 was *In actione contemplativus*. My own spirituality was based on the indwelling of the Holy Spirit.

In the light of my response, Dom Main changed his flight plan and returned to London via Montreal rather than Washington. We met again and shared on the process to be followed. I also informed him that I would guarantee him $25,000 per year for three years to begin this foundation in Montreal.

I came to the conclusion that the Holy Spirit works in strange and wondrous ways. As an auxiliary bishop, I had to submit my project to Archbishop Paul Gregoire. He endorsed my vision and signed the necessary documents, which were sent to Abbot Rossiter, asking him to establish a Benedictine foundation in Montreal and to send the necessary personnel. Some time later I received a phone call from Ealing. Dom John, in a rather disheartened tone of voice, informed me that the decision of the Abbey chapter was negative. I told him that I had an inner personal conviction and deep feeling that the foundation would happen some time in the future and that sooner or later the chapter would reverse its decision. We should both pray for this turn of events to take place.

And that is exactly what happened. Dom Main was very happy with the final and positive decision of the chapter, and that he would be one of the monks sent to begin the Montreal foundation.

In view of the political crisis in Quebec I suggested that he should come and spend three weeks in Montreal at my expense. Such a visit would help to acquaint him with the local circumstances before moving here. Dom Main did come and during this stay he lived at Ascension parish. From there he visited various groups of people, read the newspapers and listened to the news of what was happening here.

On the eve of his departure for London I invited him to speak to the diocesan clergy and tell them about his visit and final decision about coming to Montreal. Strange as it may seem, the first question he was asked by one of the priests at the gathering was: Why are you coming here at a time when we are thinking of leaving? Dom Main replied that the monks had been, in the course of history, told to leave England and yet today they are very much present in that country.

While awaiting the arrival of the Benedictines in Montreal, I had been in touch with Mr Joseph McCauley, a real estate agent, and asked him if he could find a suitable place to begin the foundation of a contemplative community of monks. During John Main's visit I showed him a property that was available. He agreed with this choice. I then bought the building, located just west of the downtown area of the city. The house needed renovations and this was done by oblates from England. The large house was very modest and unpretentious-looking. It served its purpose for the first three years, after which time it was sold to another religious community.

Approximately two years after the foundation had begun I received a call from Dom Main asking me if I knew the McConnell family. He told me that one of their sons who came to meditate said that his parents had a large home that would be of great advantage to the monks due to the increase of persons coming to the centre on Vendome Avenue to pray. The McConnell family was of Presbyterian tradition. I advised John to pursue the matter as the McConnell family had a foundation which, in the past, had been generous to various organisations in setting up establishments for needy causes.

A few months later I received a call from the executive director of the McConnell Foundation, Mr Peter McEntyre, asking to meet me. The director, a board member and Mr Jean Prieur came to seek information on the Benedictines regarding their stability and what would be expected of them in the future. The board wanted to be sure that if the building was to be donated, given its quality and the numerous artefacts it contained, the people receiving the building could put it to good use. However they also indicated that they could not consider giving the land on which the house was built. All the artefacts, if not used, were to be given to the Montreal Museum of Fine Arts. I told them that neither Dom Main nor I knew anything about the building or its artefacts.

We arranged to visit the premises, accompanied by the

executive director of the foundation. On the day of the visit we were told that any noticeable repairs to the building would be assumed by the foundation. The condition that we could not buy the land was still being maintained. Dom Main was convinced that this location, on the south side of Mount Royal just above the downtown area, and the size of the building compared to the house the monks were presently occupying, would suit their purposes.

As we ended the visit, we were surprised to be invited to afternoon tea by Mrs Laing, the daughter of the deceased McConnell owner of the property. She had raised her family in that house. Over a cup of tea we told Mrs Laing of the suitability of the premises, but that if the condition set by the board was maintained it would not be suitable to the monks, who needed the space just as much as she needed space for her family when she lived there. Mrs Laing answered that it just happened that at this time she was chairperson of the foundation board with a right of veto. In her capacity she could make a decision then and there. Mrs Laing told us that we could have both the house and the land, and that her own decision would be endorsed by the foundation. Thus the McConnell Foundation gave the monks the property for relocation of the Priory.

Concerning the means of livelihood for the monks, from the beginning I had told Dom Main that the community would not initiate financial campaigns as a means of establishing the community. I wanted the monks to devote themselves to ministry and leave the financing to my own initiative. I promised $25,000 per year for a period of three years, along with the hope that, without solicitation, persons benefiting from the services of the community would spontaneously and voluntarily make donations. During the first three years, with the encouragement of Dom Main, I approached a number of local religious communities and invited them to donate towards a capital fund that would ensure the stability of the community. I also got in touch with a foundation that donated to Catholic causes. In view of the nature of this project, my request was received affirmatively and both the religious communities and the foundation continued to help the monks financially over many years. Apart from voluntary donations, the monks depended upon their publications and books and tapes on meditation.

I had told Dom John that he would be expected to share the life of the community with the city, including persons of other Christian traditions and other world faiths. Dom Main never lost sight of a much larger project than the Benedictine Priory on Pine Avenue West. He shared with me his vision of establishing, in a quiet environment and hopefully within the Diocese of Montreal, a fully contemplative monastery with sufficient grounds to provide a sharing in their community life through a centre modelled on Taize. The city house on Pine would be serviced by monks during the day, who would then return to the monastery to rejoin their brethren. This dream was not realised and the project died with Dom Main.

Under the direction of Dom Laurence Freeman, the Benedictine community saw their mission as a universal one that consists in sharing Dom Main's spiritual message and method of silent meditation with people around the world, starting with North and Central America and extending to Europe, Australia and New Zealand, and to various countries in Asia.

From the moment of his courtesy call in 1976 until his death in 1982, my personal relationship with Dom Main was open, warm and honest. We believed in each other and we were authentic in the sharing of dreams into the future. The quality of our friendship was based on mutual support and acceptance of the other. We were both aware of our solidarity in powerlessness and depended on the one who said 'without me you can do nothing'. My conclusion is that open-heartedness and detachment are the qualities that allow God to use us as his means to attain his goals. Jesus calls us to act in his name. John Main's picture is on my desk and the deep spiritual relationship with him continues.

A few days before Dom Main died, I was anxious about the future of the Benedictine community and its stability into the future. I prayed with him on his death-bed, imploring him to oversee from heaven the work that he had begun on earth.

In October 1978, prior to leaving for the ad limina visit in Rome, I discussed with Dom John the possibility of obtaining a transfer of the community from Ealing to Mount Saviour

Abbey so that future candidates could be trained in America and better adapt to the North Anerican culture and be prepared to serve people with a better grasp of their life environment. The Abbot Primate was away from Rome at this time, but his secretary advised me to inform Dom Main to select an abbey of his own choosing. That is how the monks changed their stability from Ealing to Mount Saviour, and the reason why Dom Main was buried there.

On my way home from Rome I stopped over at Ealing for a few days to meet Dom Rossiter and thank him for allowing Dom Main and his companion, Laurence Freeman, a newly professed monk at that time, to come to Montreal. I was also curious to find out why the chapter had replied negatively to my first request to allow Ealing Abbey to set up a new community in Montreal. The only reason that I was given was that the chapter feared that John Main's personality was somewhat overbearing and that the Priory would have trouble finding candidates due to John Main's exactness, authenticity and strong personality. It was through prayer and circumstances unknown to me that the Holy Spirit allowed a change in the attitude and a change on behalf of the chapter.

JEAN R. PRIEUR

Father John Main had so many beautiful human qualities and attributes. Someone once said 'he could meet the Queen in the morning and spend the afternoon with a car dealer'. He had the great ability of being at ease with everyone no matter what their status. And he had the gift of bringing himself to the level of the person he was talking to. I think this is the sign of a great person, a person who is 'all things to all men'. He was a great listener too. With Father John you had a chance to finish all your sentences. He was not always barging in. He allowed you to say what you wanted to say.

My friendship developed one afternoon when he and Father Laurence came in to buy a car. I managed to get a good price for him and thereafter they brought the car in for service.

We used to go out together, maybe once a month, and

would go to different places and have a bite to eat. He was not a big eater; as they say, he did not live to eat, he ate to live. But he liked some fancy things and he liked to experiment with different dishes. I always remember the time I told him that one of my favourite meals was a dish of cow's brains. He had never heard of that dish and he thought it was funny. But the next time we went out, there were cow's brains on the menu and, sure enough, he joined me and we had cow's brains. And it was fun, it was an enjoyable outing. We did that several times. We would go to the country, to St Jean, Quebec, for instance, and around the Richeleau river exploring. He really seemed to enjoy the company of others. We would talk about different things including the city of Montreal. And he was always questioning, and always very interested in a variety of things. I remember we visited old cemeteries together. He had a great interest in looking at old buildings too. I remember going to the old city of Montreal several times with him and he really enjoyed walking up and down these little side streets and reading all about the history of the different places.

He met my family and came home to my house several times. I always remember his presence when my first grandchild was baptised. We had a little ceremony here at the house and a reception. He came in and with his *savoir-faire* and his personality, he knew exactly what to say, how to say it and who to say it to. I also remember how good he was to some relatives of mine. My sister-in-law, for instance, had just lost her husband and he was extremely sympathetic and helpful. And everybody who was here at that reception, probably thirty people, all thought that Father John was a special man.

On one occasion in old Montreal Father John mentioned to me that the house on Vendome was getting a little small. He thought that perhaps it was time to find a bigger home. He mentioned to me that Laurence had met some people on a plane coming back from England and this had led to the possibility of obtaining the large McConnell house on the side of the mountain (Mount Royal). The people involved in the offer were David Laing and his mother Kit Laing, who was president of the foundation administering the estate. Father

John asked if I could be of some help. Luckily enough, I knew Peter McEntyre, Mayor of Westmount and administrator of the McConnell estate. In no time at all the whole thing gelled. We made several visits to Kit Laing where Father John and she talked about the furniture that was to be left in the house.

It was unbelievable. Getting the house was almost like a miracle, what you might call a gift from heaven. Anyway I shall always remember the memorable occasion when we went one morning to sign the papers in a big office building on the corner of Sherbrook and Stanley Streets in Montreal. We were all dressed up in our Sunday best. The directors of the foundation were there and all the papers were signed and that was it. There we were, Father John and the Benedictine Order were the owners of this beautiful property on the side of the mountain. We went out and celebrated that day. We had a nice meal in a restaurant and we talked and talked about it. And that was the beginning of the Pine Avenue residence.

I shall always remember the sad day when Father John and I watched the great fire at l'Eglise Notre Dame. It was a very historical building and many old records were destroyed. It has now been rebuilt. During the fire I asked Father John, 'Why would the good Lord allow a thing like this to happen?' There was a brief moment of silence and then he turned to me seriously and said, 'Jean, there's always a reason for things to happen. It's up to us to discover or to find out what the reason is. God has a message to give us with everything that takes place.' I shall never forget the look on his face and that answer to my question which was so to the point. He spoke with an economy of words but a message that always made such good sense.

Another thing comes to mind: Father John had a sensitivity and empathy with everyone. One day we were visiting an old cemetery in Montreal where one of my ancestors was buried. My ancestor was part of the 1837 rebellion of the French against the English. When he saw the monument and epitaph he immediately complimented me on coming from such a fine family with the courage of their convictions. He had this insight and could always see the good in every situation and in every person.

I always enjoyed doing things with Father John. It was a wonderful three years of friendship. He always had nice things to say about other people and never put people down. He always enjoyed himself and life in general. His good nature sprang from faith. One time he said to me, 'You know, Jean, when you have faith you are never alone,' and I have never forgotten that remark.

He was such a great man really, and I don't have any better adjective in my vocabulary to describe him. He was just, to me, a super gentleman, a wonderful priest, a person who knew how to work hard, who knew how to relax, how to live and also how to get along with people. Of all the times that I spent with him I never heard him say anything that was bad about a person. He never, never passed remarks that were not favourable about others. To me that is a remarkable achievement when I think about it.

After Father Laurence was ordained I noticed that Father John was not feeling all that well. Despite our friendship, he never mentioned to me anything about his sickness. He told me once about an operation he underwent but he never talked about his personal health or the seriousness of any ill health. In the autumn of 1982 we saw each other occasionally and spoke on the phone but the days of going out together were over. He was sick and, to the consternation of all of us, died on 30 December 1982. It was a sad occasion. I lost a good friend, a friend I will never forget.

PATRICK MURRAY

John Main himself was the epitome of all of his teaching. He really practised what he preached. He was always faithful and one saw him coming into the Montreal meditation room day after day. I was also impressed by his powers of administration and his financial acumen and how he ran the monastery. I am sure he was always on a tight budget and there was always a sufficiency but nothing was wasted. There was no meanness, no stinginess but there was a reverence and a respect for reality in all dimensions, even the care he took of the laundry facilities.

Sometimes he would have difficulty with people when he would ask them to do some cleaning. It might simply be sweeping the floor. Often a person would complain that they had come there to make a retreat and not to work. They had come for their spiritual life. He always saw the falseness of this position. He saw that connection between prayer and work. He had insight into work. He saw that everyone wanted a job, wanted a salary but very few were prepared to work. He saw work again in the wisdom of St Benedict. It was not concentrating on the fruit of the action but it was attentiveness and concentration on the action itself. If we were concentrating on the action then the fruit was going to follow. So again it was contemplation in action, it was attentiveness in action. It overflowed into life. I always observed that John Main was attentive to whatever he was doing. He was fully alive, fully present. As we would say in Kerry, 'he was all there'.

PATRICIA GUY

Recently I came across notes made during my first summer at the Benedictine Priory in 1980. I wrote this about Father John: 'He can be as gentle and submissive as a baby, as radiant as the sunshine, as dignified as only he can be and as foolish and as clownish as any jester. He provokes a loving response from all our hearts.'

In the years that followed there was a growing experience of that greatly loving and immensely generous heart that 'provoked' such love in others. My awareness of his spiritual depths expanded beyond those peripheral, but true, observations made in 1980.

Talking about Father John with people over recent years I hear a constantly repeated phrase, 'My heart leapt when I listened to him for the first time and I knew I had found what I had been searching for.' It was also my own experience.

The summer of 1980 was the most wonderful of my life, and there have been many wonderful summers. There was a developing rhythm and harmony, and an energy I had never known before. The days at the Priory had an order as regular as a heartbeat and, as with a heartbeat, new life was generated

80

in a pulsating energy. Tremendous amounts of work were accomplished at the Priory with ease and simplicity. Dom John loved order in all things. At the hub of the work Father Laurence would be saying, 'Now, the art is – do it fast.' But there was never an atmosphere of rush or hurry.

In the first serious personal conversation I had with Father John he emphasised, 'We must take great care in all that we do. We must do everything with great care.' There was not the smallest detail which escaped his eye. It was a revealing experience to watch him take 'care' of his plants inside the house. Each drop of water was given with gentleness and concentration. The fragility of the leaves and blossoms was precious to him, and the plants responded by blooming in profusion, much to his surprise.

His sensitivity to simple needs in others was obvious. One time, recovering from surgery and feeling somewhat fragile, I took my seat in the chapel. At the very moment I became aware that it was a long stretch from the bench down to the floor Father John came quickly across the room with a cushion to place under my feet. He knew the need before I knew it myself.

Perhaps I can be forgiven for writing at the time: 'He is so absorbed in the Lord that light shines from him; from his silver hair and fresh complexion. His life is spent in caring for and loving God in the human beings around him, his novices, his friends. He has learned how to listen.'

8

The Funniest Man in the World

*True humour springs not more from the head than from the heart;
it is not contempt, its essence is love. (Thomas Carlyle)*

This chapter is all about John Main and his mischievous side,
the mimic, the comic, the leg-puller, the humorist, the joker,
and as Jack Davitt's youngest daughter put it, 'the funniest
man I ever knew'. Evidence of his humour is also found
throughout this book, and especially in the 'personal memories' in Chapter 9. John Main's humour was not a *sometimes*
thing but was ingrained in his very character. A wise man
once said 'there is something wrong with a man who is only
partly humorous, for humour ought to be a yeast, working
through the whole of a man and his bearing'. The yeast of
humour was always fermenting in John Main. It was part of
him.

JOHN BOLAND

I lived as a bachelor in London for almost twenty years after
my arrival from Dublin, in a small flat in Chelsea. Douglas,
when passing through from Dublin, very often stayed with
me. On one occasion, about 1958, he visited in a remarkably
cold February with a sort of chiselling period of really icy
weather. In the middle of this period Douglas took his aunt
to a wedding, possibly a family wedding or the wedding of
an acquaintance. This was pre-Vatican II and the mass had
to be celebrated before midday. There was no wedding breakfast but just a glass of champagne and a few titbits circulating
in the ballroom of an expensive hotel. If one has a lot of
champagne before lunch without much sustenance you begin

to feel remarkably hungry and not particularly well pleased with the world. So Douglas decided he would take his aunt to lunch at Derry and Toms, a store in Kensington which no longer survives. Douglas was in full morning dress and had covered this up with an off-fawn-grey colour cavalry coat which he was fond of wearing. He marshalled his aunt into Derry and Toms where they paused at a bookstall, bought a book and then went up to the restaurant to have lunch. Douglas shed his cavalry coat and appeared in his resplendent swallow-tail coat. At this point his aunt said, 'Oh, Douglas, I left that book I bought down on the book counter.' He said, 'Don't worry, Aunt. I'll go and get it.' So he headed off at once across the vast restaurant with his swallow-tail coat billowing out behind him. Arriving at the lift he encountered a lady up from somewhere in the suburbs with two small children holding on to either hand. Mistaking Douglas for a shopwalker and looking slightly desperate, she said, 'Excuse me, do you sell children's shoes?' Douglas quickly replied, 'Oh yes, we do, madam, but they're not very good here. If I were you I'd look somewhere else.' At that stage he disappeared into the lift.

This is one of a series of hilarious incidents which actually triggers off another memory. Douglas discovered in a cupboard in my flat a bowler hat which I had only worn on some five occasions. When I joined the Public Trustee Office I thought it was part of the uniform and that I should get one. Of course it was a mistake, no one wore them and I did not look very well in it and did not feel happy. But Douglas felt that this was just the thing to go with his cavalry coat and consequently used to borrow it on occasions. His progression down Oxford Street was a joy to behold. He would put a scarf up round the cavalry coat, look very military, put on my bowler hat and every military-looking gentleman he would see in range would solemnly doff his hat to him. Old gentlemen who had commanded vast tracks of Imperial India stopped in their tracks saying, 'Egad! I must know that fellow,' not recognising him at all.

Douglas carried this to other marvellous extremes. In the Church of Ireland, certain of the more 'spikey' (slang for High Church) clergy wear black and tend to be marginally indistinguishable from their Roman Catholic brethren. Douglas, when he went to Dublin after his ordination, wore his clerical collar but not his Benedictine habit. Instead he would wear a dark overcoat and a Trinity scarf which of course made him look very Protestant. He would take great pleasure in the magnificent confusion which arose from encounters with native Dubliners.

Douglas had great prowess as a mimic. He had a quite uncanny ability to mimic accents both Irish and British in a whole variety of accurate ways. I remember being in stitches on one occasion at his account of an auction in Ballinskelligs, with Douglas playing all the roles including auction bidders, the auctioneer, as well as people from the legal firm involved in the sale reminding the auctioneer of things about easements. And Douglas's punch line was, 'Ah, yes. The easements. Now what did I do with those old easements?'

PATRICK MURRAY

Another story I heard Father John tell was that he was giving a talk at some place in Ireland and he gave out the word 'Maranatha'. At the end of the meditation there was a question period and one of the meditators said to him, 'Glory be to God, father, I was in an awful way, I forgot the word during the meditation but thanks be to God it came back to me, "macushla, macushla".'

YVONNE (MAIN) FITZGERALD

Douglas my brother was a great leg-puller and a comedian at heart. One time he rang my mother on the phone and pretended to be a house buyer. His opening gambit was: 'Good morning, madam, I have someone in the office here who is interested in buying your house.' My mother interjected to say, 'My house is not for sale.' Douglas continued: 'How many bedrooms do you have and have you a good garden, and what about the garage?' All the time Mother would be having a fit, completely fooled by the salesman accent. Douglas finally added, 'Mrs Main, I am in fact looking for a house on your particular street,' and burst into laughter. Mother would say, 'Douglas, you really are dreadful.'

JEAN R. PRIEUR

A short time after the arrival of Father John and Father Laurence in Montreal they met Joe McAuley, a real estate businessman who was very good to the Benedictines in Montreal. Joe helped them to move to Vendome Avenue, their first residence in Montreal. I remember visiting Vendome with Father John and trying to help as much as I could to find people who could give him a hand. Being in the car business, I was able to lend them a truck so that they could pick up furniture and move things around. I remember that on one occasion I phoned Father John and I said, 'Look, I need some help. I've just purchased a piece of furniture in downtown Montreal in an apartment building and maybe you could come and give me a hand to bring it home.' So we met, and John was with Laurence. Laurence was sitting in the front seat of the truck and Father John was driving the truck and I was in my car ahead of them. When we got to the driveway, we had a funny experience. The doorman came out and said, 'Hey. Hey. You can't park here. Keep moving.' I remember Father John getting out of the truck and saying in perfect French, '*Eh. J'attends bosso.*' 'I am waiting for the boss.' It worked! We loaded the furniture in the truck. It was quite something. We got a good laugh out of that. He enjoyed a good laugh and he certainly enjoyed laughing. When it was time to work, he worked, when it was time to laugh, he laughed.

There was another funny episode with Father John. One day Father Laurence and I were taking a piece of furniture downstairs from the main floor to the basement of my house. It was a long buffet and we were struggling with it. We finally got it down without scratching it, much to the delight of my wife. Father John immediately saw the irony and humour involved in our efforts. With a very straight face he said, 'One good thing has come out of all your exertions, Jean. If you die and want to be laid out downstairs in your recreation room you know that it can be done because the buffet you just took down was about the size of your coffin.' We all had a good laugh at that over a cup of tea.

At one time Father John mentioned that he would love to have a place in the country where meditators and the Benedictine community could spend time on a farm. We talked about it and one day went to visit the Cap St Jacques area in the west end of Montreal. A congregation of sisters owned a large tract of land there including a few farmhouses. We drove up one day and there were six or seven older nuns just relaxing. Father John got out of the car and in his best French greeted them with *'Bonjour, mesdames'*. He started to talk about the Priory, about meditation and about the need for land and very quickly an entourage of sisters gathered around him. He was completely at ease in the French language and completely captured the sisters with his great sense of humour.

AGNES MURPHY

Father John was such a humorist and joker that it was hard to know sometimes whether to take him seriously or not. For Easter Sunday at the Priory I had been asked to make a pavlova for the sweet at the midday meal. I have made many such successfully but on this occasion it stuck to the paper! I was vainly endeavouring to remove the paper when Father John went through the kitchen. He stopped and asked if there was a problem. 'Oh,' he said, 'leave it on. A little paper will do no one any harm!' Undeterred, I pressed on, removing each minute scrap laboriously and getting more and more depressed and panic-stricken. Father John returned through the kitchen and stood laughing. 'Agnes, just put some hot water on it.' Heresy indeed.

In desperation I poured hot water liberally on the underside and – no – the meringue did not dissolve as I had anticipated but the paper came off in great style. The situation was resolved and I must admit that my appreciation of Father John's practical advice got a tremendous boost.

One day at Vendome I returned to find Father John cleaning the front steps. Upon my offering to take over the job he acquiesced very readily and I presumed that he went off to do more important things. Later I went round the back of the house only to find him cleaning the back steps. I was treated to a wry smile and soon began to realise that the Benedictine way of life meant prayer, study and *work*.

Another example of Father John's humour in a similar context occurred when chores were again in order. A gentleman guest wandered aimlessly into the hall where I was busy with a duster in each hand. I invited him to relieve me of one of them and join in. His reply amused me: 'I think Father John would disapprove of men wielding a duster.' I laughed and so did he but still firmly stuck to his guns. We decided to put it to the test and ask Father John. He considered for a short time and then said, 'Let's say that after deep thought not only do I approve but also give him my blessing to do the work.' Delivered in what could only be described in ponderous tones and followed by a broad grin. The job was done by us both in double quick time and amid great hilarity.

BRUCE TODD

My mother, my sister and I were in Rome and being shown around St Peter's by our cousin John Main, when he pointed to a huge marble tomb in the aisle, and said, 'That is of course of special interest to our family. It is the tomb of our ancestor, Charley Main.' As he spoke perfectly seriously, we were astonished and hurried towards the tomb. On it in huge Roman capitals was inscribed CHARLEMAGNE!

9

Personal Memories of Those Who Knew Him

Douglas was a person with many facets. To different people he was a different person. Hence the entirely different impressions he created for various people. He was truly a man for all seasons. (Gerald Fitzgerald)

This chapter is really the *heart* of this book. Those who knew John Main at various points in his life tell of their personal reminiscences and memories as well as John Main's influence in their own particular lives. Taken together as a whole they illuminate the spiritual adventure he had embarked upon and give us a deep understanding not only of John Main the man but of the teacher and the teaching. Many common characteristics come alive and are expressed vividly by the contributors. The portraits of John Main that emerge are also personal and honest. The pieces of the jigsaw fall into place as the contributors reveal as much of the private person as they can without trespassing. Their understanding of John Main as a person helps us immeasurably to understand John Main the monk and teacher.

POLLY SCHOFIELD

PAUL   Polly, tell me a little about when and how you first met John Main.

POLLY   It was early springtime in 1977. I had two children at the age of first communion and I wanted them to get the best religious education they could. My husband Mark went to Ampleforth Benedictine School, and I was always incredibly amazed by his commonsensical attitude to religion. It is a very spiritual one, more spiritual than religious perhaps, and I wanted the same for our children. It was probably the only thing I have ever prayed for in my life. One day we were at the parish church and it was announced from the pulpit that the English Benedictines had come to Montreal and I said, 'Aha, just for me!' So I telephoned and John Main answered. I explained that my husband went to a Benedictine school in England, that I had two little heathens and would he please do something about them. And he said, 'No. No. No. This is not our mandate. We're here to teach meditation.' However, I'm not one to give up easily and I kept on asking. Eventually, he gave in and said, 'All right, there is a young monk here, see what he has to say.' That young monk was Brother Laurence. He liked the idea of meeting the boys and invited all of us to the house on Vendome. That was the begining of a lifelong friendship with the Montreal Benedictines.

PAUL   What was your first impression of John Main?

POLLY   I shall never forget that first meeting. It was a lovely spring day with still a little snow on the ground. I was expecting Adrian, and Julian, aged seven, and Dom, aged six, came along with Mark and me. My first view of Father John is indelibly impressed upon my memory. He was holding on to a table trying to get it into the garage on Vendome. For some reason his eyes, clear blue eyes, looked right through me. I have never forgotten that loving look. It's one of those eternal pictures in one's mind. I have seen him transfix others with those eyes. Even when he was dying, I remember being at the foot of the bed and those incredible eyes looked right into me again and again, right through into my soul. Those eyes were one of his great gifts.

PAUL   When did you first begin to meditate?

POLLY   I started after the birth of Adrian. The other boys were already meditating by then. They also formed the nucleus of a children's meditation group under the wing of Brother Laurence. I remember once meditating and saying the office with Father John and there were only the two of us. But he was never ever concerned with numbers and was never worried by only a few people coming to meditate. He kept saying, 'Just sit down and meditate and other people will join us,' and of course he was right as usual. After beginning to meditate I saw how in the silence one transcends time and space. Having escaped from Hungary during the 1956 uprising, it has often occurred to me how meditation could save your sanity in solitary confinement. It would be the one thing that would help you escape from the four walls. I liked the way Father John always said the same thing over and over. He didn't complicate it in any way. It was always simple and straightforward – 'Just say your mantra every day.' A great sense of reality, of common sense, pervaded his judgment and he had a vision which never left him.

PAUL   Tell me a little bit about John Main, his character, his personality, his mannerisms.

POLLY   Well, he was an extremely shy and private man, in spite of his almost gregarious manner in public.

PAUL   You'd never think he was shy from listening to his talks.

POLLY   That's right. But in a sense he was an extraordinarily shy man. But not shy to the point of being diffident. On the other hand he had wonderful elegance and he loved to give parties; he would invite the oblates and other friends and of course everything was done with the greatest –

PAUL   Panache?

POLLY   Yes, it was wonderful. He would greet every person himself and he would welcome them and he was the most congenial host I have ever met. And he would entertain, and he would tell jokes and stories and he could act every part himself. This was especially true in July 1982 on holidays with the community in Nova Scotia. Everybody would be laughing and happy around him. He loved cooking barbecues there and would treat his guests royally. And then meditation time would come and he would say, 'This has been so wonderful, but now it is time to meditate.' Everything had its time for Father John. He thoroughly enjoyed the present moment, but everything was in its own time. Everything in moderation except moderation. Once he summoned me for a little chat, and he had two Waterford glasses and a bottle of port on a tray. He knew I liked it. He would pour us a 'moderate' glass-and-a-half. But of course, one could tell that meditation was the focal point of his life and what it meant to him. But he was – to me, anyway – more of a father of the family, more of a patriarch, in the old Celtic monastic sense, than anything else. He loved to have his family around him. And he was certainly not wishy-washy. He certainly spoke his mind. And he certainly ruled with authority. And everything ran smoothly in the Priory, because while he ruled with authority he also ruled with love. There was the exhilarating sense of the Absolute about the man. Nothing was out of our reach. There were no closed doors; the gift had already been given in Christ. Life was serious, but life was fun. He brought a wonderful sense of enjoyment to things both little and big. Even amidst sorrow he was never depressed. The word boredom was not in his vocabulary. 'The greatest sin,' he once quipped, 'was to be boring.' He really was the glory of God; man fully alive, and it was contagious. He said once that he always felt eighteen and was always in love. He told me that the only thing he knew how to do, the only thing of any importance at all, was, TO LOVE.

PAUL   How do you relate this shyness to everything you've been saying here, that he ruled, he was in charge, he was dominant in a social sense? In what way was he shy?

POLLY   Perhaps I should have put the emphasis on being a private person. In his personal life he would not often talk about himself. Nor would he ever infringe on another person's privacy. He would never probe. He would never push his beliefs on anyone, he would only open up opportunities for choices. A private person – yes, he was a private person rather than a shy person. He never pushed, never pushed – yet he spoke always with authority. He spoke from personal experience, with great love, great tolerance.

PAUL   Any other aspects of his personality?

POLLY   Father John was generous and not only with his life. He was always giving gifts to people and people were giving him things. But the gifts he would receive he would give away again. He had quite an assortment of hats and I inherited one of his favourites.

He would not, and he could not abide with what he called the professional religious. Even though he was an extremely spiritual man he had an absolute horror of religious complacency, or people hiding behind their habits. The monk is one who prays, he said, and the universal vocation of a monk is to love. We all have a monastic dimension in our lives, he said.

Father John found wonderful pleasure in the house the McConnell family gave the community. He appreciated the Renaissance furniture, and the beauty and craftsmanship of things. He rose early each morning, before the rest of the community. He would walk round the house, look closely at and appreciate the lovely objects around him and perhaps dust a little. He came to me one day with eyes sparkling with the joy of discovery, holding a great big book he had just found in the house. It was about the English painter Salisbury. He led me to a great painting of magnolias in the hall, and pointed in triumph to the signature on the canvas. It was by Salisbury. At another time he had tears in his eyes, he had cracked an antique vase. Once, when I suggested that the house was all much too grand, he rebuked me and reminded me of what I have since come to know, that created beauty leads as a stepping stone to the Uncreated. Beauty points directly to the Absolute.

PAUL   Did Father John ever give his views on the contemporary church?

POLLY   Well, he believed in married parish priests. Obviously he did not believe in marriage for the monastic orders. But he felt that part of the sorrows and loneliness of the ordinary parish priest would be alleviated through marriage. His views were quite explicit on married priests and he spoke to my husband Mark on this subject rather extensively. He was always sympathetic to people's needs. He once said that he believed that the only morality is the morality of love, and the only law is the law of freedom. He certainly didn't believe in restrictions and rules for rules sake. Like St Paul, he believed in the spirit rather than the letter of the law. As something of an illustration, let me tell you about Adrian's first communion. He must have been all of three years old. We always took him with us to Friday mass at the Priory. One day as the Bread was being passed round he stood on his tiptoes, and when the communicant next to him was not looking he took a piece and defiantly put it into his mouth. It seemed irreverent, but it was not, more like a triumphant innocence. Father John smiled in approval. 'Well,' he said, 'this was his first communion – an important day.'

At another time during mass – perhaps Adrian was a bit younger – Father John celebrated, facing the congregation; Julian and Dom, on either side of him, served. Adrian was on a pillow directly at the front of the altar. All of a sudden a look of absolute horror passed through the otherwise serene countenances of his brothers, the altar boys. Adrian was making horrible faces at Father John – of course no one else could see him. What some of us did notice was that Father John made a face – quite a face – at Adrian. That did it. Adrian never again made faces. Now he is the one serving mass each Friday at the Priory.

Although Father John believed in the community of saints, of love beyond time, if you will, he did not hold too much store by what some people called 'miracles' or 'signs'. To him the whole of life was a miracle and everything was a sign. 'Everything mediates the love of God,' he said. Relics, however, got short shrift. One day a lady came to him bringing a carefully wrapped relic, bones of some saint. In hushed tones she asked what she ought to do with it. 'Ugh!' Father John said, 'take it away and give it a decent burial.'

PAUL   Did he ever talk about his childhood or his early years in Ireland?

POLLY   He did talk to me about the small island of Skellig Michael (Scelig Mhichil in the Celtic language), eight miles off the coast of Co. Kerry near Ballinskelligs, where he grew up. He said it was on Skellig Michael that he first learned to pray as a young man. A group of his friends, on a dare, bet each other that they could stay overnight near the windswept pinnacle of the island where the beehive huts of a fifth-century monastic settlement are perfectly preserved. They drove down from Trinity College, Dublin, got a boat to Skellig Michael and did stay overnight. He said it was an awesome experience, and that he learned to pray there. I don't know if he learned to pray because it was such a terrifying experience or because it was a spiritual experience. It was probably both. He always thought of Skellig Michael as a very holy place. I once promised him I would go there and he said that he would be with me there in spirit.

PAUL   I can understand his emotion. I have climbed the 672 stone steps to the monks' beehive huts twice in the last few years and it is an unforgettable experience.

POLLY   Yes, my solitary pilgrimage to the Skellig in the summer of 1988 was a pivotal experience of my life. Father John was very close.

PAUL   Was John Main always on his best behaviour or did he have human failings?

POLLY   Oh, he was human all right. Once at the house on Vendome after office and meditation, he was preparing his favourite food, Welsh rarebit, a grilled cheese sandwich with onions. He proceeded to cut his fingers badly and, as I attended to the wound, I wouldn't want to repeat his sacred expletives. The first time he visited our home I offered him some Scotch and he said, 'I never touch the stuff.' But of course he did. At our holiday at Iona he thought my son Adrian had got into his shaving kit and spilled the contents over the floor. The next day he grudgingly admitted, 'It was the wind that did it.'

PAUL   Is there any one event, other than John Main's death, that stands out in your mind?

POLLY   Yes, Mark, I and the children were invited by Father John in the summer of 1982 to join the Priory community for their holiday in Iona on Cape Breton Island. The CND sisters gave Father John a house overlooking the sea. It was a beautiful setting. He said it reminded him of Ballinskelligs. Father John and Father Laurence went down first to prepare the house for the community. My husband Mark drove one car and Paul Geraghty brought the rest of the community in another car. It was a most extraordinary holiday. It was Father John's last. It was a family affair with games, long walks by the sea, salmon barbecues, and of course meditation to give a framework to our day. My most unforgettable experience with Father John took place on an evening walk as the sun was setting. Of course, by this time, he knew he was sick. We stopped by the sea. He put one of his arms around me and with his other arm leaned on his cane as he looked out to sea. He stood there silently for a long, long time and then he said, 'There are so few people we can really share things with, maybe one or two in a lifetime – if one is really lucky.' But that was it. There was just nothing more to say. And then we just walked back.

The holiday was wonderful. Father John and Father Laurence would play croquet with the children. Dominic drew a picture showing Father John and Julian (the winners) smiling very calmly while Father Laurence and Dominic (the losers)

95

smash their mallets in agonising defeat. I still have the drawing.

At one point Mark and I felt we should leave for day trips from time to time and let the monks holiday with themselves. However Father John would hear none of it and insisted we stay. He wanted us around him.

I shall never forget the scene on the last day as we left early in the morning with the mist rising. Father John had filled the car with oranges and other goodies for our journey. The community were all standing on the crest of the hill as we left. I tried to take a picture, found I had no more film and one by one they went inside. Finally there was only Father John alone, standing and waving, until we could no longer see him, a tall grey figure in the mist. It was awesome and reminded me of some of Yeats's poetry. I will never forget him waving in the receding mist. This was an archetypal, eternal experience. Of course, back in Montreal he was still not feeling well and in only a matter of weeks he was in a wheelchair.

DON MYRICK

To recount the role of John Main in my life it is necessary to go back several years. I had come through the 1960s with my faith relatively intact, despite being a little bruised and tattered around the edges. It was around this time I felt myself being drawn into some of the renewal movements that were starting to gather steam in the early seventies. One of the things I began to realise was that prayer is an important business and that I should do something about it. After some reflection, what I decided to do was to get up a little earlier in the morning and spend twenty minutes in prayer to begin my day. And so I began. I started off doing a quasi-Jesuitical style of meditation – choosing a theme, thinking about it, hashing it around in my head, this sort of thing. This got a little heavy and tedious after a while so I decided to try something a little more simple and unstructured, namely talking to God. This was great until I ran out of things to say. Then I tried listening to God, praying with scripture, and other different 'methods'. This went on for about ten years.

After our son was born – the second child in less than fifteen months – I found myself in need of rest. Working by day and up a lot at night with the babies, I felt I had to get away from it all for a couple of days. So I went to the quietest place I knew of, namely the Trappist monastery at Oka, Quebec, with one thing in mind: to catch up on my sleep. I guess almost providentially I happened to have a little chat with Father Benedict Vanier, brother of the famous Jean Vanier, founder of l'Arche community. I told him I was having a hard time getting my spiritual life together, especially in the light of my family situation. We had a good chat, and in the course of the conversation he suggested some tapes that I could buy at the monastery. The tapes of course were Father John's, and for me they hit the nail right on the head. I started to meditate in the autumn of 1979.

I had finally found what I had been searching for. The reason that Father John's tapes made such an impact on me was that a lot of the reading I had been doing around that time was on people like Thomas Merton, George Maloney and Anthony Bloom. All alluded to this type of prayer – the prayer of quiet, the prayer of silence, the prayer of the heart. These writings had made a deep impression on me. The only problem was that they wrote in generalities and made it sound as though this type of prayer was for spiritual heavyweights, which I certainly was not. I listened to Father John's tapes and the message I got was: Yes, everything you have been reading is leading you to meditation, and here is how you do it. I was overjoyed. So I started meditating, confident that within three months God would zap me and I would just sail through life on a cloud. Six months went by, and although I was faithful to meditation I felt the need for direction. But I did not have a clue where to start looking for it. There was no one I knew doing anything that even remotely resembled this type of meditation, at least not in the Christian context. Out of desperation I got hold of a Montreal telephone directory and, sure enough, 'Main, Rev. John' was listed, so I called the Priory in May 1980 and made arrangements to go down. This was at the old house on Vendome. I had a real good day at the Priory. As well as meeting Father John, I met Brother Laurence.

Things were a little more informal at Vendome in those days and after noonday office (which was then in French) and meditation I joined them for lunch. Due to the size of the community talking was allowed during meals, and Father John had a few humorously pointed remarks about the terrible bread that Brother Laurence had baked. He was also interested in my background and we talked among other things a little bit about the icebergs off the coast of Newfoundland. After lunch we set about the business I had come for – some badly needed direction on the path of meditation. We sat out in the garden and I presented my 'shopping list' of questions. Father John answered them easily and directly and without long drawn out explanations. He had the uncanny ability to get directly to the heart of the matter. One of the things I liked most about his teaching was that he would leave you with a little story or phrase which you could easily remember and therefore recall whenever the problem cropped up again. My visit to the Priory that day was not a long one – but it was important. I went home feeling much more comfortable about the whole business of meditation. All of this was due to the kindness, lightheartedness and authenticity of the community. These qualities plus his teaching authority are the gifts that I most associate with John Main.

During the next three years I visited the Priory many times both privately and with groups of meditators. Whenever I visited, Father John always found the time to have a chat with me. Our relationship, though relaxed and comfortable, was essentially that of teacher and disciple and not too much on the personal or social level.

In the autumn of 1982 I had arranged for Father Laurence to come to Ottawa to talk to the meditation groups on a Friday night. Everything was in readiness. I called Father Laurence on Thursday just to confirm. Father Laurence announced that he could not make it because Father John was ill and was changing his medication. I was polite and understanding on the phone but inside I was upset. The story that Father John had set in motion was that he had reinjured

98

an old wound in his back while doing the 'twist' on holiday in Nova Scotia that summer. It was a great cover story. Unknown to all but a few, Father John's new medication was radiation treatment for cancer of the spine.

I visited the Priory twice that autumn. In October I went down for a few days retreat and again in November with the Ottawa groups for a day. Even in October it was obvious Father John was not well. He was not able to come to the chapel. After morning meditation Father Laurence would make his breakfast and take it up to him. When I had a chat with Father John in his room he stood up to greet me even though it was obvious this caused him a great deal of pain. When I asked him how his back was he told me it required a lot of patience but left me with the impression that it was just a matter of time and rest and he would be well again.

When the Ottawa groups visited in mid-November he came down and spoke to us and even answered questions although he did not look well. This was the last time I saw him alive.

It was a shock when Doreen Romandini phoned me from the Priory in early December to ask me to pray for Father John and informed me that he was seriously ill and would likely die. Doreen called me once again on 30 December to tell me Father John had died that day. The next day I went to the Priory. It was New Year's eve. In the afternoon Andy Foley, myself and a few other people got the mailing ready for the letter that Father Laurence wrote to inform people of Father John's death. That evening at the Priory there was a beautiful memorial service in the meeting room, which was filled to capacity. The next morning there was a funeral mass at the Priory, after which the community and some close friends accompanied Father John's body to Mount Saviour Monastery for the official burial.

John Main's teaching and the spirit of his community flowed from the man himself. The three complemented each other and in a certain sense were one. To have known him personally and to have experienced the spirit of his little community was to get a glimpse of God's Spirit at work. They were the factors which, for me, authenticated his teaching on meditation.

99

PATRICK MURRAY

I remember the first time I heard John Main. It only seems like last week. Actually it was 3.30 in the afternoon of 25 June 1979. I was lying in bed for a siesta in the White Fathers House in Dar es Salaam, Africa. There was another priest there, a Father Laliberte, and he suggested I might like to listen to a tape. I was not really interested but Father Laliberte was such a kind and gentle man I said I would put it on and listen to it. I was lying in my bed and had the tape recorder along beside me. As soon as I heard John Main's voice, the very sound, the very tonality of his voice struck something deep within my very being. And as I listened to him as he explained the significance of the mantra (which I did not fully understand at the time) there was something in my inner self that said it all made sense. I sensed deep within that even if I did not understand, he was saying something significant and that I would like to meet this man.

It took me until March 1982 before I met him. But in the meantime, off and on, I had started to meditate. I got some of the tapes and wrote to him and he replied. It was at the time of his illness and he was recuperating in the Bahamas. And I remember a line of his letter, 'keep on keeping on'. Ever since then my life has been a continuous 'keeping on keeping on'.

Eventually I did get to Montreal. I got a taxi from Montreal Airport to the Monastery in Pine Avenue and when I rang the doorbell and a brother came out, I said, 'Is it possible to see Father John Main.' He asked me if I was a priest and said Father John was going to give a talk to priests that very morning. So I went in and sat down with five other priests. Eventually Father John came in and the very bearing of the man spoke to me of his dignity, his presence, his single-mindedness. We listened and meditated. He invited me to stay, so I stayed for a week. We did not have much conversation during that week. Eventually I left and went to work in a parish in Montreal for about two months. But I used to come every morning for the first meditation. I would also come in the evenings, and, if I was free, for the midday meditation. We spoke very little until May that year, just before he went to Ireland in June to give a series of talks and retreats.

I happened to know many people he knew, my mother being from Kerry. And I knew Ballinskelligs and Cahirciveen and some of his contemporaries at Trinity College and University College, Dublin. He shared many episodes of his life. He was at times so moving in his sharing. The place he liked to talk was in a room at the top of the house. He always put one leg up on the table, looked out of the window over Montreal, and would then start to reminisce. What comes to mind are his views on the Church, seminary training, prayer, the clergy and his own life story with the Benedictines. I remember one evening his saying, 'Pat, it took me about forty years to become aware of being, simply being,' and I could see in his eyes an almost living transcendence. I could see joy, and there was this joy of being in him. And yet I could see a man who had a lot of woundedness, a lot of hurt. He could be very sensitive. His sensitivity was a cross for him and he could flare up. But through his discipline, his faith and meditation he had that gift of going to the ground of his being and bearing with his weaknesses.

He often shared with me how important it was for him to meditate three to four times every day because he said there was always the danger of his slipping. By that he meant slipping into the ego, slipping into the false self. He was a man who had that deep awareness and attentiveness to the ground of his being and he saw the dangers of an over-active imagination. He saw the dangers of fantasy, and above all he saw the danger of idolatory – of making God in our own image and likeness. One thing that struck me was how he talked about prayer. He always used, of course, St Paul's unforgettable phrase 'We do not know how to pray'. He would say, 'Prayer means being absolutely still, absolutely silent before the incomprehensibility of God.' He was so aware of that and he saw the deep need of a spiritual renewal in the Church. He would often say it was fine to change structures, change veils or change habits – he was not against that – but he felt that all renewal had to begin from within. He had that deep conviction that all growth must begin from inside and from that deep inner awareness of who we are. It is not *what* we do, he used to say, it is *who* we are. He had a real insight into the meaning of presence and he stressed our own uniqueness, or, as he would say, our own originality, our own unrepeatability.

I remember vividly one day in June before he died. He said one morning rather cryptically, 'We have to give up this place shortly,' and I looked at him and said, 'This Priory here in Montreal?' At first I thought he meant Pine Avenue but I then knew that he had that impending sense that he was going to enter soon into the fullness of life. Another insight he had was about the shortness of time, how time for him was never days or weeks or months. He had that discipline of seeing time in the present moment. He had the rare gift of appreciating the present moment, something that never happened before, something that will never happen again. One of his favourite phrases was from Blake's 'Kissing the joy as it flies'. I remember the words he recited. They are imbedded in my heart: 'Simply being, is your greatest gift'; and the more I meditate the more I see the importance and meaning of those words. He had a great insight into silence: I remember him saying, 'Silence is condensed speech.' He used to say that the great things in nature, the great things in life, happen in silence – the grass grows in silence, the trees with deep roots grow in silence, and the galaxy, the earth on its axis spins in silence. He often used to say the basic condition of the human heart is silence – *silence*. He preferred the French word *silence* to the Anglo-Saxon 'silence'.

He often liked to talk about Dublin and Ireland. He found it very difficult to leave Trinity College. I remember him saying he had to give up his friends, his room there, his car, to join the Benedictines. And the struggle he had at Ealing! He often wondered whether he did the right thing – the difficulties he encountered there, the human conflicts.

He told me of the difficulties in Washington to build up the school there. He had to collect a lot of money, I think something like a million dollars, for a science lab. He used often to wonder when he spoke to the graduation class each year how well they were prepared for life. He described America sadly as one of the most success-orientated, materialistic cultures in the whole world, and it worried him.

102

He had wonderful insight into life: he would say, 'Life is a mystery, rooted in the joy of being.' Being meant so much to him and he saw the graduality of being. First of all there was being, then there was the awareness of being and then there was the joy of being. I can see it myself since I have started to meditate. If I am aware of being, I am also instantaneously full of joy, just of being myself. Not apologising for being, or being other than who I am. Just that non-judgmental state, I would say, of active passivity.

He spoke about several Dublin characters he knew well. He often spoke about Garret FitzGerald who became Prime Minister of the Irish Republic. He liked Garret. He enjoyed himself in Dublin. He told me that for a long time in his Trinity days he used to go to the racetrack every day. And I remember saying to him, 'Where did you get the time?' 'Well,' he said, 'I had one or two classes in the morning and then I had the rest of the afternoon free.' He spoke about various racing personalities. One friend of his was Vincent O'Brien, the famous Tipperrary trainer, and his favourite racecourse was Leopardstown. He often mentioned Leopardstown. It is out in south Co. Dublin – a sprawling racecourse. Whether he had a successful system for gambling I do not know. Gamblers of course will always tell you about their winnings. You never hear about their losses, but we did not go into that too much.

The few times I went out to lunch with him he always had two beers. He was abstemious in my experience as regards food and drink, although I often sensed that when he was in the university he would take a drink with the students. He liked good wine; he liked good fare. He knew how to possess the things of life without things possessing him.

In his facial expression there was a great sense of integrity and there was a transcendence in his face, the penetrating look of his eyes and his gentleness. There was a gentle movement, especially in his hands. His hands showed such character. There was dignity in his bearing – tall, alert, firm-stepped. And then his clipped, Anglified diction. These were peripheral characteristics but they were expressions of his being, of his soul. But his greatness was above all, I think, his insight into the basics of the gospel, his insight into the Beatitudes, his insight into poverty. He saw poverty as a rejection of nothing. He saw poverty as an intense reverence for everything because everything was a gift. He saw sin in the context of St Paul of 'missing the mark'. So it was a deep sense of positive awareness to seek the things that are above. Sin was not a guilt-ridden experience. It was not something to put us into a psychiatric state. In John Main you could hear St Paul's words 'Everything works together unto good for those who love God'. He saw the mantra as the deepest act of unconditional love. I remember him saying:

> The greatest thing we can do as human beings is to offer our complete consciousness to the infinity, the incomprehensibility of God. God is incomprehensible to our intellect and to our feelings, yet God can be known in love. He is essentially and above all the God of love, his essence is love.

We were once talking about God's will, and he said:

> God doesn't have a will, not in our human conceptualisation. God is immutable. If you want to use human language in the context of God's will then God's will is love. If we are living from our love, especially from the love that is in our inner self – our unconditional love – then we are saints. We are likened to God, to the essence of our Creator.

The mantra was the only way that he knew of stilling the mind, bringing all that amalgam of imagination and fantasy to rest. And the way was the way of learning to say the mantra. He always stressed that we are always learning to say the word and it was a continuous beginning. I remember him one time saying it was not only the word one had to say but each syllable and vowel. And he used to say, listen to it as a sound, Ma-ra-na-tha, to savour it and to leave all else. This was the deep act of faith. He never denied the gift of reason and the fruits of reason – philosophy, art, theology – but he was always wary of the limitation of theology. Theology, he used to say, was preceded by analogy, human analogy, human metaphor. Theology at most was a crutch and in the poverty of the mantra even theology had to be left behind.

1933, John Main at Ballinskelligs, Co. Kerry

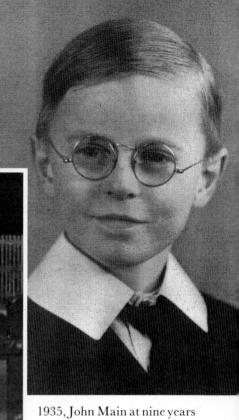

1935, John Main at nine years

1940, in London, aged fourteen

1942, at sixteen John Main began a journalistic career on the *Hornsey Journal*

1942, press pass 374 issued to John Main

CERTIFICATE OF MEMBERSHIP

Class of Membership

No. 37

VALID UNTIL

31st December 1942

Issued to

Douglas Main

Holder's Signature

Douglas Main.

(*To be signed on receipt of the Certificate*)

Issued by the Council of the Institute, under the Small Seal.

1943, Private John Main, Royal Corps of Signals

1946, John Main joined the Canons Regular, and in 1949–50 studied theology with the Canons in Rome

1952, the wedding of his sister Diane and Hugh O'Neill. John Main is on the far right

1953, with his mother Eileen Main at a wedding in London

1955, dinner
with friends,
Kuala Lumpur

1959, John, his
sister Yvonne,
Hugh O'Neill and
Diane at Trinity
College Ball,
Dublin

1970–1, Headmaster
of St Anselm's Abbey
School, Washington
DC

1976, John Main at Ealing Abbey, London, shortly before his move to Montreal

1977, with Yvonne and Diane at a wedding in London

1977, first Benedictine foundation in Montreal at 3761 Vendome Avenue

1977–82, Prior of the Benedictine Monastery, Montreal

1977–82, Prior of the Benedictine Monastery, Montreal

June 1982, last visit to Ireland: with Yvonne in Dublin

October 1982, last meeting with the Benedictine oblates at the Pine Avenue Priory, Montreal

October 1982, visiting Jack Davitt at Cape Cod

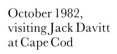

1982, in the garden of the
Benedictine Priory, Montreal

IN MEMORIAM

✠

dom JOHN MAIN o.s.b.

monk

born 21 January 1926
died 30 December 1982

teacher

*I have delivered my word to them . . .
thy word is truth.*

1982, John Main's in
memoriam card

I SAID TO MY SOUL
Be still, and wait without hope
For hope would be hope for the wrong thing;
WAIT WITHOUT LOVE
For love would be love of the wrong thing;
There is yet faith. But the faith and the
love and the hope are all in the waiting.
WAIT WITHOUT THOUGHT
For you are not ready for thought:
So the darkness shall be light,
And the stillness the dancing.

T. S. ELIOT

1982, 'I said to my soul be
still'

John Main (1926–1982):
sketch by Gerald
Fitzgerald, Dublin

1982, gravestone at Mount Saviour Benedictine Priory, Elmira, NY

1987, Benedictine oblate Connie Moore at the John Main memorial in the garden, Benedictine Priory, Montreal

I remember sharing with him one time that I had difficulties with the priesthood. The priesthood was defining my work, my value, my function, my role in life. And I remember saying to him one afternoon that I was not too happy with this priesthood. I just wanted to give it up. He said nothing, but the following evening he said, 'Pat, I was very happy you discussed the priesthood with me.' He brought the discussion of the priesthood into the context of the poverty of the single word, that everything had to be offered up. And he used the word 'holocaust' rather than 'sacrifice'. In 'holocaust' he said everything was wiped out, everything was given up. What was important was that inner death, that daily dying to the false self. He always saw the paradoxes. He came back time and time again, about losing one's life, and the need of letting go. Yet on the other side always the reminder that Jesus said, 'I have come that you may have life.'

Father John had a great love of nature. He often used to talk about the birds singing in the morning and the beauty of the trees around the monastery. He had a deep oneness with nature and there was an openness about his personality, especially with those who were less fortunate. He had that empathy and understanding with others. And yet on the other hand he would avoid seeing anyone he felt was coming to visit a guru. But whenever he got the chance of sharing the mantra and communicating the mantra he was really at his best. It was something deep within his soul. He had this notion of 'being' and 'being with' others in relationships. He saw 'being with' in the context of community life. He was so single-minded. It was so clear to him that the essence and the message of the gospel was indeed that the kingdom of God is within you. He wrote a book, *Death: the inner journey*, that is, about dying to the false self. He pointed out that we must resurrect to our true selves – the image of God within us and resurrect to the unconditionality of his love, to the fruits of the Spirit, so to speak. And the only way that he knew how to do this was the way of prayer, the way of silence, the way of stillness.

I remember him talking about the clergy and seminaries. One morning we were at the top of the house and he was talking about the powers of darkness being enthroned in

105

seminaries. I knew inside what he was thinking. He was talking about the state of the clergy. He had great compassion for the clergy. He said there was probably a bit of fornication here and a bit of adultery somewhere else, but the only real sin was a 'hardness of heart'. When priests got stuck in this harshness and hardness of heart it was a bigger obstacle than any failure in the areas of the flesh.

He had a great love of all things human and beautiful. He liked good food, good music, good wine. There was a great humanity about him in all this. He could see that God wished us to enjoy the good things of life, to use them and not to abuse them.

He had a real insight also into the meaning of work. One of his sayings was that 'true work was concentrating on the action not in the fruit of the action'. If you are polishing a mirror, he used to say, concentrate on the action of polishing. Don't worry about getting the shine, the shine will follow if one gives full attentiveness and full attention to the action of polishing. He often remarked that the art of good work had been lost, as well as the art of craftsmanship. He felt attention to detail, and attentiveness to the present moment, were important when working. Again that sprang from his deep insight into the value of time. Even in his very demeanour, his deportment, it was always unhurried, 'an unhurrying pace' in the words of Francis Thompson.

How can one sum up the life of John Main? Well, firstly his teaching on the mantra is the greatest act of unconditional love that I know of in this life. Secondly his vocation was a mysterious one. Only six years of public teaching and fifty years of preparation. Reminds one of a Galilean who spent thirty years in preparation and only three years in public teaching. Like many spiritual giants his life was full of paradox. While he was outgoing and approachable one always sensed he was on his own inner path, following an inner light. He was a man of spontaneous joy and humour and openness and yet of concealed reserve too. One sensed he was often going through a considerable struggle about some aspect of the spiritual life. He could be very abrupt but at the same time very responsive to human feelings and human suffering.

He needed silence and solitude and yet in a crowd he was very quickly at the centre.

In the final analysis it was the authenticity of his teaching on prayer that will for ever set him apart from his contemporaries. His teaching on meditation did not come out of books. It came from thirty years of 'entering into the experience itself'. He had an unusual gift of passing on this teaching and without a doubt it was a special grace from God. I am firmly convinced that his teaching on meditation will be practised as long as there are people who are interested in seeking God in the stillness beyond word and thought. And finally he persevered and was faithful to the end to that greatest act of unconditional love in this life – the mantra. He fulfilled the mission God gave him and that is his greatest accomplishment.

LUCY MCDONALD

Many people when they first hear about Christian meditation realise that it is just what they have been seeking. For them it is like 'coming into harbour'. I had not been looking for anything at all when one Sunday morning in 1978 our parish priest, Monsignor Tom Fehily, announced at mass that he wished to introduce us to a form of prayer called Christian meditation and that he would be present in the oratory next night to tell us about it. At this time I was a very enthusiastic member of the local charismatic prayer group. I loved the weekly gathering of the people, the singing, the witnessing, and nearly always had something to 'share' myself. But I decided to go to the oratory anyway partly out of courtesy but mainly out of curiosity. Only five people turned up. Monsignor Fehily outlined the method of meditation and gave us a book called *Christian Meditation* by a Father John Main. We were to read the book, practise for two weeks and then come back for individual guidance. I found the book a bit difficult to understand but being determined to advance in prayer I struggled with it and attempted to meditate for a few weeks. I did not do nearly as well at it privately as at the prayer meetings. In fact it was not to my taste at all, but I did not know what to do with this spiritual nourishment offered to us by our parish priest. One could hardly spit it out! So I guess I just swallowed it. But like a sweet that slips down one's throat too suddenly, it did not really stick. I did not go back after the second week and stopped meditating altogether.

The following March 1979 Monsignor Fehily spoke to the parish again about Christian meditation. He told us that Dom John Main OSB, author and authority on contemplative prayer, was coming to Dublin and would give a talk in the local convent school on the following Tuesday night. I decided I would definitely go! Maybe it would come across better by word of mouth than by reading. Before this happened I got a phone call at teatime on the Monday evening to say that Father John was holding a small private meeting in the Reparation Convent that night and could I go. I felt excited, but a bit unworthy, and on an impulse asked if I could bring my two sisters along with me. This was granted, and in retrospect it could be compared to Andrew bringing Peter along to meet Jesus. Whereas I was too elated and self-conscious to benefit from the encounter, for one of my sisters it turned out to be the turning point in her spiritual life and a tremendous outpouring of the Lord's love for her. The room where the meeting was held was small and the twenty people present, fifteen nuns and five lay people, sat in a circle round the speaker. My only impressions of the evening were very superficial ones; someone near me breathing noisily; how silly some of the questions were and how gently they were answered; how my view of Father John was very blurred due to the reflection of the light off his glasses and how low-key the whole event was compared with the charismatic prayer meetings I was accustomed to.

Next evening the hall at Mount Sackvill was almost full and Monsignor Fehily introduced Father Main to us from the stage. This was better. I thought Father John looked very distinctive in the long black robes of the Benedictines. The principal memory I have of that night is of someone 'blond, grand, and beyond', very handsome, and very polished. In fact most of what he said flew over my head yet again. Highly educated people always scare me and everything about him should have had the usual effect of distancing him from me.

But the candour and conviction with which he spoke to us, the gentleness and good humour with which he answered our questions, the burning intensity that seemed to urge him to share this way of prayer with everyone, drew me to a resolve to give meditation another try.

For the next eight months I tried every day to fit in twenty minutes of meditation. I meditated sometimes in the morning, but more usually it would be last thing at night when I would remember with a groan 'my meditation'. This 'going to bed' meditation caused the added complication of trying to keep awake during meditation time. But I struggled on as I really did want to become a 'contemplative', serene, beautiful and holy.

In July 1980 John Main was back in Dublin. Monsignor Fehily had an arrangement to meet him privately in a small room of one of the city hotels and a few friends had been invited to this including my sister and me. We were overjoyed and excited at the prospect of what was for me an event, for my sister an advent. We arrived early at the hotel and took our seats in the foyer, watching the door. No sign of him, in fact not a priest in sight anywhere except for one tall, elderly, bearded clergyman who was standing at the entrance. Monsignor Fehily arrived and went over to the clergyman and spoke to him, then brought him over to us. I wondered who this stranger was in the grey suit. Just as they reached us I suddenly realised it was Father John! We nearly died of shock at his changed appearance. What had happened to him? Where was his blond hair, his youthful face, his tanned complexion? This man looked so ill, so grey and with a beard, but smiling. The meeting lasted about an hour. It was an informal get together and Father John started it off by telling us about the Priory in Canada and outlining developments there. He described the Priory which sounded very beautiful and the circumstances surrounding the wonderful gift of this house. Then he told us about life there, his work and the increasing numbers who were turning out to learn the way of meditation. One could see how vital meditation was to him and how enthusiastic he was for its growth.

Then he spoke to us individually, enquiring how we were getting on at our meditation and if we had any questions.

When it came to my turn I asked him what changes would come over us as a result of our meditation? Monsignor Fehily went on to say what a difference it had made to him in a spiritual sense drawing him to a new and deeper love of prayer and reverence for the mass. Dom John kept nodding his head in assent. Then I do not know whether or not it was because of his spectacles but his eyes seemed particularly brilliant as he told us what would happen if we persevered in our meditation: 'It is like looking through a glass which at first is a bit unclear, then you polish it and it becomes a little clearer, and you keep polishing it, and gradually it becomes clearer and clearer.' Then he was still for a minute before he added, 'And sometimes there isn't any glass there at all.' I have never forgotten those words of Father John and the meaning he gave to them as he spoke. It brought to mind the scripture quotation, 'too wonderful for me this knowledge, too high, beyond my reach'.

When the meeting was over we urged him to stay and have tea with us. Though he did not seem too keen on taking tea, he kindly came with us. He barely sipped a few mouthfuls, rather carefully as though it were too hot. There was no public meeting that summer and so that was all we saw of Father John for another year.

After this meeting with Father John, I resolved to take my meditation more seriously. One morning going to daily mass I saw some joggers out running very early and I decided that if they could make this effort for mere physical fitness, how much more effort could I not make for spiritual progress. So I started then to get up earlier to make a morning meditation as well. I was determined to advance. But somehow the lovely things that Father John had told us about did not happen. Firstly I had desperate trouble with the mantra. And though I tried it and tried it from every angle it never went down into my heart. Neither did I ever achieve much harmony or stillness. Rather there was 'much wandering in my heart'. Meditation seemed to be for me a death I did not freely accept. From time to time my sister Violet used to lend me the Priory newsletter but this did not help much either. Words like 'other-centred' 'transcendent' 'rootedness' and 'person-hood' were very unfamiliar and I really did not have the time

110

to puzzle out the meaning. Nevertheless I continued with daily mass, two meditations and my weekly charismatic prayer meeting, which I still loved. I was also amassing a veritable library of spiritual reading.

In July 1981 Father John's visit to Dublin took the form of an evening mass in our tiny parish church. About two hundred people were present including my sister Violet and me. When Father John came out on the altar I was delighted to see that he looked much better than last year, though if anything taller and thinner. The vestments looked really short on him but he seemed to be beyond these externals. This phenomenon always struck me about Father John; the intensity of his presence, yet the great depth of his distance. To me he was like someone with a marvellous secret which he had an overpowering urge to share and was just waiting for the right time to do so; but he kept hoping all the time that you might guess it. A family matter had upset me during that day with the result that as soon as Father John started the homily, tears sprang to my eyes. They flowed down my face for a long time and I had to hide behind the person in front of me. I missed most of the homily. At the sharing of peace, Father John came down from the altar and shook hands with the people in the front bench. As he passed along he must have seen my sister and me in the second row because he reached through to shake hands with us. I was too ashamed to look up with my red eyes and just thrust my hand forward. I hope he understood, somehow.

After mass a few of us went into Monsignor Fehily's presbytery for a cup of tea with Father John. He seemed very happy to be among us and enquired how things were going. Nobody was keen to be the first to speak so I ventured to speak out and said that 'I'd had a horrible year'! Father John seemed immediately interested. I told him that I still found meditation very difficult, especially on winter mornings whereas I loved the charismatic prayer meetings. He answered me kindly but very firmly to the effect that 'if I enjoyed a weekly sing-song there was no harm in going to the prayer-meetings'. He did not say anything more on this subject. Someone else said that the cold mornings were now over and to 'get on with it'. I felt a bit stupid in front of the others to hear my beloved prayer-meetings described as a sing-song. It was deflating to say the least of it, but somehow I was not hurt. This was the amazing thing about Father John. No matter how often he had to teach or correct or answer silly questions he never offended anyone because of the love and the joyfulness with which he reached out to us. But from that night onwards I saw things in a different light and reduced my attendance at the charismatic meetings. Other people present then opened up about their progress or problems. Father John was attentive and concerned about them all, but firm in his replies. One lady asked, could we vary the mantra, and another 'what did he think about the method which allowed one to stop saying the mantra after a few minutes and go into stillness'. His answer to both was virtually the same, 'stay with the mantra' and keep saying it throughout the entire time of the meditation. All this time – still the same old questions! – but still the same encouraging responses. Someone else remarked that the newsletters were rather difficult to understand and most people present who had read them seemed to agree – except for my sister Violet. She said that whereas in the beginning she too had found them difficult, now, having been meditating for some time, on re-reading the newsletters she found them clear and easy to understand. This pleased Father John enormously and he was very happy that she found it so.

By June 1982 our little meditation group had expanded over the year so that now we usually had about eight people attending every week. We met on a Monday night in the sacristy of the church and meditated together for thirty minutes. Monsignor Fehily joined us whenever he could and shared with us the tapes and letters as he received them. But apart from this we really looked forward to Father John's visits. That year he planned to be with us for two days, an open meeting for the public on a Tuesday evening and then a whole day together with us on the Wednesday including meditation sessions, private visits and concluding with the Eucharist. He could have spent this extra day with his beloved family here in Ireland, but he denied himself this to be with us. All of us appreciated it. Then something wonderful happened. On Monday night the group met as usual for meditation, and just as we were starting, the door of the sacristy opened and in came Monsignor Fehily accompanied by Father John! They sat down in silence and joined us in meditation. For me it was by far the most peaceful meditation session I have ever experienced. When the thirty minutes was up he chatted to us and asked once again how we were getting on. I told him that I had kept it up 'in the Main' over the year, and this made him laugh.

He seemed to be in excellent humour. Then I told him that I found it difficult to realise that God was so present to us, that to me he was 'out there somewhere, perhaps in the Rocky mountains'. Father John joked again and asked, did I not think that God might indeed come from *Canada* occasionally! It was all very light-hearted and happy. I must say at this stage that I noticed a great difference in Father John during his 1982 visit to Ireland. There seemed to be a certain vitality about him, not only in mood but in aura. He was in excellent spirits, very available to everybody and radiating an intense dynamism of affection. On the question of my compulsion to attend certain novenas and devotions especially where one could receive Holy Communion for a second time he told me that this was a very materialistic approach to my religion (*touché*). The others had questions too and he answered them all in a gentle and sometimes humorous way.

Then Monsignor Fehily took him off for dinner in the presbytery and asked me to call back in an hour to drive Father John home to his sister's house on the other side of the city. What an evening of surprises! I sped home, cleaned out the whole car wishing it were a Rolls Royce instead of a Mini. Then I thought, how would someone so tall fit into such a tiny car. My head was spinning. I was to be back at 10 p.m. Father John never seemed to stay out late, I noticed, and they were waiting when I arrived. On the journey across town the conversation was pretty general. We discovered some mutual acquaintances here in Dublin, and then Father John talked of his family with much affection, expressing great admiration, especially for the younger members. I thought it must have been hard to leave one's family and go off to be a monk!

Next night the open meeting was held in the lovely convent

chapel in Glenmaroon. There were about 250 people in attendance. I was glad that a good crowd turned up. I tried to jot down a few notes from the talk. Father John described meditation as climbing a mountain which, as one ascends, gives one a better view, but sometimes near the top there could be cloud which would blot out everything else; then one would have to wait there. He spoke about harmony, and told us to practise saying the mantra at other moments during the day as it was important for the mantra to take root in our hearts. Now, I had read somewhere that to breathe in and out slowly was helpful to concentration, so at the question time from my seat in the middle of the chapel I asked if it would be a good idea to match the saying of the mantra to one's breathing. 'It doesn't really matter whether one does or not,' replied Father John, 'but please do keep breathing at all costs!' and the whole congregation burst out laughing, myself included. I could see the twinkle in his eye. Afterwards there was more tea and chat, but like the night before Father John departed early.

Wednesday was our big day, a happy family day, a feast day. Father John arrived at 11 a.m. and started the day with a talk on meditation for newcomers. No matter how many talks on meditation I had heard each one seemed new, and necessary! In this one Father John said that he would sum everything up into just three words: 'SAY YOUR MANTRA.' A simple, straightforward message. I wondered what I had been doing these past four years, or doing wrong. Instead of achieving the harmony he talked about I still only had extreme dissonance. Perhaps I was more concerned with 'progress' than just 'saying' the mantra. But I desperately hoped the mantra would guide me into that stillness.

We lunched at 1 p.m. and from then until 3.30 p.m. Father John remained in one of the parlours for anyone who wished to have a private word with him. A queue formed at once and although I joined it, I did not reach the top before the time was up. There was another quick cup of tea. Even here Father John was besieged by people. Though I had a very grave worry on my mind, I refrained from troubling him as it had nothing to do with meditation. But suddenly he was passing by me on his way out and, like the woman in the gospel, I seized my opportunity. Quickly I poured out my worries, and Father John, far from being amazed at such an 'uncontemplative' request, listened carefully to everything. Then, looking at me with that deep gaze of his he said, 'Do not worry, I shall offer up the mass I am about to say for this matter.' What a wonderful response, I was thrilled with joy and gratitude plus a sense of peace that all would be well now.

In retrospect I can see that about a week after this a chain of events commenced which had direct bearing on the problem, making things seem worse instead of better. By October I was overcome with worry; my prayers were not being heard and my meditation was not working either, it seemed. So I wrote a rather frenzied letter to Father John, enquiring after his health. The Reverend Mother of Glenmaroon Convent had been in Montreal and told us Father John was confined to a wheelchair. I asked for more prayers, and childishly hinted that I would like a new mantra! I did not really expect a reply and was overjoyed when one came almost by return of post. This is what he wrote:

My dear L
Thank you so much for your letter. It is good to hear from you and to know that you keep faithful to the way of meditation. It is demanding but so worthwhile if you can only keep going.

I shall certainly keep your request in my prayer. What a worry for you. But perhaps things are not as bad as they might be. It is a real grace that this development has taken place.

I am so glad you enjoyed the visit during the summer. These little visits are really terribly brief but it is very heartening for me to discover that you all keep faithful to the pilgrimage.

My back is slowly getting better. It has been a long haul. It's a slipped disc that has been very painful but the worst part of it is that it is so slow to mend. I have not been in the wheelchair for a couple of months now.

With every good wish, Dom John.

PS   Do not hesitate to write if you want to. It is always good to hear from you.

I read and re-read the letter, skimming over it lightly, attempting to make it last – 'it is good to hear from you: I shall certainly keep your problem in my prayer: do write again, it is alway good to hear from you' – marvellous words of encouragement.

And again 'keep faithful to the way of meditation' (no mention of a new mantra) . . . 'demanding but *so* worthwhile . . . it is very heartening to discover that you all keep faithful to the pilgrimage'. Still the same urgent teaching.

Then 'My back . . . slowly getting better . . . a long haul . . . very painful . . . so slow to mend'. A great sense of weariness, almost despair, seemed to linger around these words. This was not like Father John. What could we do?

Of course I wanted to write again. It would be a masterpiece. But I kept putting it off for a suitable time as I was still immersed in my problems and miseries. All through the ensuing weeks those lines from Francis Thompson's poem 'The Hound of Heaven' kept going through my head: 'must Thou char the wood ere Thou canst limn with it'. How could one write a good letter with such a sense of doom?

Then, just after Christmas Monsignor Fehily gave us the alarming news that Father John was gravely ill. We were shocked and apprehensive. I hurried home and wrote to him immediately, but it was too late. Two days later he died. 'The day that Thou gavest Lord had ended.'

In the passing years since Father John's death I have come to realise his wisdom and that to be on the path is the only thing necessary. Meditation is still a struggle, still a discipline and the distractions are still there. This is the desert I have come to learn to live in. But the slow transformation of one's life into love is what makes the struggle so worthwhile. I will be for ever indebted to Father John for his warmth, his kindness, his affection, but most of all for his teaching on prayer. It has turned my own life upside down. The mantra, it seems to me, is the most revolutionary spiritual teaching in the world today. The path of meditation prepares one to 'Make way for the Christ whose smile like lightning, sets free the song of everlasting glory that now sleeps in your paper flesh like dynamite' (Thomas Merton). Thank you, Father John!

JOHN BOLAND

By the time Douglas reached Ealing he had the same ability to come to terms with levels of English society. I recently came across a letter of mine to my parents, reporting on an occasion in February 1968 when, at Douglas's invitation, I went to Ealing to adjudicate at a debate between the boys of Ealing and a debating team from Harrow School.

Douglas was certainly very fond of and very knowledgeable about music. Frequently when he came to London, on the occasions he stayed with me, we would both go, usually without prior arrangement, to a concert at the Festival Hall. He had in his rooms in college a fairly wide collection of recordings.

Douglas never spoke to me of a variety of things: he never spoke of what had happened at Ealing as to why he found it necessary for two periods to leave the community; he said very little about his time in Washington, he said absolutely nothing ever about his time with the Canons Regular and he never really spoke to me, almost up to the last year he spent in London, about meditation. The fact that we ever spoke about meditation seemed accidental. I was under a course of treatment for high blood pressure at one point and one of my options was to adopt Yoga, which I did with some mild interest. I then wanted to practise Yoga on a Christian basis. Because I knew that Douglas was experimenting with meditation, I spoke to him on a few occasions as to how useful and helpful I found meditation and how it enabled one to cope with stress related to work and with difficulties at a time when one is busy, and how it enabled one to sleep better. He accepted all this without question and said how right I was. He never basically gave much in the way of guidance about it. I persevered for about a year and a half or maybe two years with the meditation group founded by Sister Eileen Roche at Roehampton.

117

The very last time I was to see Douglas was on one of his last visits to London when, to me, he looked his normal happy self. He spoke that evening at a meeting at Roehampton arranged by Eileen. His talk was to an enormous gathering of about 120 meditators. He was his usual tall, erect figure. We sat in this huge room in total silence for the period of meditation; even he remarked to me how still and how quiet everyone had been. At the end of it he was surrounded by the normal batch of people who wanted to talk to him. I went up to him to say what I thought would be a temporary goodbye, and I said, 'There are a lot of people here who want to speak to you, I will have other opportunities.' We said goodbye and I was never to see him again. He did write to me from the West Indies in 1980 after he had had an operation, but he never led me to understand quite how serious the operation was or what it held for the future.

At about this time Douglas told me in one of our conversations that he had been asked by the Foreign Office to comment, for the benefit of certain members of their staff, on the political situation in Ireland. In 1968 there was no political violence in the North of Ireland; this unhappy development was to come later. What struck me about this request was Douglas's comment as to the degree to which the staff at the Foreign Office failed to understand the realities of the Irish scene.

Douglas was a somewhat entertaining mixture of the two streams which made up his background: the Irish side and the British side, England being the land of his birth. I recall that when Winston Churchill died in 1965 I wondered whether or not to join the queue outside Westminster Hall to view the lying in state. The queue was of quite enormous length and wound its way back from the entrance to Westminster Hall towards Westminster Bridge. As I was debating whether to join it, out of the gloom of a February evening suddenly appeared Douglas in an immaculately cut black clerical coat with a happy smile of recognition and a quick retort, 'John, what are you doing here, gracing this event in honour of an oppressor of our country?'

He was a good friend. I miss his joyful presence, his humour, his warmth, his kindness and above all his personal friendship. I am delighted with his spiritual legacy, his teaching on prayer that seems destined not only for our generation but for succeeding generations. Douglas's life in retrospect seems to replicate Cardinal Newman's famous prayer:

> God has created me to do him some definite service. He has committed some work to me which he has not committed to another. I have my mission ... I am a link in a chain, a bond of connection between persons. He has not created me for naught. I shall do good, I shall do his work.

MARTIN BOLER

Thomas Merton, writing in an issue of *Monastic Studies*, described with considerable admiration and at some length a book by a Persian psychoanalyst, Dr Reza Arasteh, entitled *Final Integration in the Adult Personality*. Final integration is not just a cure by adaptation to society. It has to do with the final and complete maturation of the human psyche on the transcultural level. Such a person 'has embraced all of life ... has experienced qualities of every type of life ... finally giving birth to a fully comprehensive self'. Thomas Merton rightly relates this to monastic *conversatio*, which Benedictine monks not only mentally approve, but actually vow. Final integration is rare and only attained by unusually gifted persons. It involves a disintegration of the social and cultural self, the product of mere history, and the reintegration of that self in Christ, in salvation history, in the mystery of redemption, in the Pentecostal 'new creation'. Dr Arasteh mentions three such persons. I would add Father John Main as a fourth.

I am happy to be able to record these thoughts with regard to Father John and the all too brief time that I knew him. It is not merely in tribute to Father John that I write. I think of his final integration mostly in regard to others whom he will continue to meet and who will know him through the influence of his teaching on prayer.

In most of us who achieve some degree of integration, the seams are awfully evident. In comparison with final integration mentioned above, it really is not an integration at all, but some sort of compromise adjustment. I even hesitate to use the term since it gives such an inadequate impression. None the less for me the most impressive thing about Father John was one's gradual awareness that his tremendous energy and dynamism were due to his integration. His evident humanity, his monastic identity, his centredness on Christ and in God, his resourcefulness, and his past experiences and discipline, were all present in Father John: that presence of his was like a seamless garment, to quote a well-known source.

At a meeting of university people who had invited him to speak in Montreal, he introduced himself by saying, 'I am a Benedictine monk.' That was all. No name, no titles academic or religious, no anecdotes to create an impression, no stories to put the apprehensive at ease. With that introduction, coming from him as he stood before them, all was in place and they knew who he was and moreover their graciousness in receiving him was being enhanced a hundredfold. One of the surest signs of deficient integration or pseudo-integration is precisely that it fails to integrate the others you are with, but puts them off or down or makes them aware mostly of their awkwardness.

Father John came to see me about his situation in Montreal. He wanted to know how Mount Saviour had begun as a monastic community within the Benedictine confederation without being a member of any existing congregation or federation. He came simply asking for information. He was prepared to do whatever was necessary according to the requirements of the Benedictines and the Church. He was entirely open to possibilities and entirely devoid of wilfulness. It was truly thrilling to be involved with the Spirit, his spirit, and the *Fiat voluntas tua* in that visitation. I was unaware of all this until I reflected on our meeting sometime later on. That is what I mean by his integration. It did not make an impact, but it certainly had its effect.

I am sure he was not always this way. I am sure he was not like St Anthony or St Benedict who seemed to have been born into the stage of final integration or to have arrived there by the age of seven. I am sure the integration was a difficult process for Father John and an even more difficult process for those who knew him while it was going on. His final integration was an integration of their suffering and his causality which he accepted in the context of Christ's redeeming death and resurrection. That was one guarantee of its genuineness.

St Gregory says of Benedict, that if we read his Rule, we will come to know him since he could not have been other than as he wrote. It can be truly said of Father John that to come to know him, one should join him in his prayer. That was the integrating factor of his life.

It is with this in mind that I return to Thomas Merton and Dr Arasteh. They agree that a final integration was, in the past, the privilege of a few. Now it is becoming a need and aspiration of humanity as a whole. The world is in an existential crisis to which there are various reactions, some of them negative, tragic, destructive, demonic, others proffering a human hope which is not yet fully clear. Where are we to look for the true solutions? 'Precisely,' says Merton, 'from the Spirit who will speak clearly at the right time through a renewed ecclesial and monastic community.' It was this integration, this expression of God's kingdom and not merely personal psychological balance that was the goal of Father John's monastic *conversatio*. In our final integration, not his own, he will find his joy and peace.

KITTY (MAIN) STANLEY

I always thought Douglas would have made a success of any profession. He had such a personality and was so convincing that people automatically believed him. He was a bit of a rogue. We knew him so well that we would just not believe half he said and when found out he would just roar out laughing and make a joke of it all.

Strangely though, considering his character, Douglas enjoyed his time in the army. He was lucky enough to get in with a very pleasant crowd and was not injured in the war even though behind enemy lines at times. There was no formal army life and little square-bashing and saluting. He found a nice little niche for himself and I never heard him complain about any of his army duties.

At the end of the war he returned to Belfast where my parents were living then and dropped the bombshell that he had decided to become a priest. My mother was not convinced that he had a vocation and thought he would make a much better doctor or barrister or even an actor. He insisted, however, and off he went, full of enthusiasm, to join the Canons Regular of the Lateran. He had all his 'trousseau' made in Belfast by the best tailors and we had to take photographs of him in his cassock, looking very serious and holy. My mother was more convinced than ever that as usual he was just acting.

He left the Canons Regular after a few years and was rather disillusioned and really did not know what to do with his life. He stayed with me often in those days in London and then decided to return to Dublin. My father had retired and he and my mother and my two sisters had moved there. My mother was delighted to have him home again and we were all pleased when he was accepted to read law in Trinity.

Life was very pleasant then with Douglas at home. He made life go with a swing; he was the life and soul of every party with all his jokes and stories. He was also a marvellous mimic and kept us all entertained. I was living in London but on my frequent visits to Dublin Douglas was a great companion. We went to concerts and to the theatre and opera and for long walks. If theatre tickets were hard to get he always rang for them and gave himself a title to impress the staff. He did the same when booking a table at a restaurant. He felt head waiters were such snobs. His favourite title was 'The Hon. Dougal McFife'!

He graduated from Trinity College in 1955 and almost immediately joined the British Colonial Service and was sent to Malaya. He spent two years there and was then offered a lectureship in Trinity. Mother was delighted once more when he came back. He had beautiful rooms in Trinity and we thought he was estabished once and for all. He went to London frequently to 'eat his dinners' and was called to the Bar, Gray's Inn. But the Church called once more and another bombshell; he had decided to join the Benedictines. My mother was resigned this time and thought he really must have had a vocation after all. She missed him a lot but he came home on long holidays and seemed to have changed little.

I did not really think he would ever last and become ordained. I did not think he was suited to a religious order. I felt he would have had much more scope as a secular priest in a parish, as long as he was the parish priest, of course. The Benedictine rule must have been very constricting for him and for his imagination and ambitious nature. He did love the contemplative part of it though, the praying together and chanting. He liked his own way best, which he thought was right, but then, don't we all?

After our mother died he rarely came back to Ireland except to visit other priests and convents. I remember writing to him once and saying that my only hope of ever seeing him again was to ask him to give me a retreat. It was sad that I saw so little of him before he died, and not to have known even that he was ill. He was a fantastic brother and friend and I miss him greatly.

DIANE (MAIN) O'NEILL

Douglas was just a fun brother and very protective to me. He was two and a half years my senior. I regarded him as a big laugh (never knew the serious side of him).

He was always playing practical jokes on people, just for the fun of it. He would dash into a dark room (if he knew I was about to go into it) and put his hand on the light switch as I went to turn it on, just to give me an awful fright! He knew I would scream (being a rather nervous child) and of course he would die with laughter! Another time I was 'miles away' doing the washing up; I just looked up at the window and I saw this *hideous* face looking in at me; again a great laugh from Douglas. I would laugh also.

I had a cake made for him for his twenty-first birthday when he was studying to be a priest in Hoddesdon, Herts and he had me in fits imitating all the other students.

Later in life when I was first married and he was a student in Trinity, we saw a lot of him. We would go to the theatre a lot; he loved plays and the opera. He advised me on the purchase of my first record player; we shared a great interest in music. He gave me two lovely records to start my collection, Mendelssohn's Violin Concerto and the Violin Concerto of Max Bruch and two harp concertos, one by Handel and one by Mozart. He advised me to buy a certain record player; it was the best tone of any, he said. We would have great chats and cups of tea after the theatre. He was terrific with small children – he would tell our little boys stories and act all the parts, making it all come to life. We missed him terribly when he went to Ealing. He was such good company.

When he first told me about his teaching on meditation, I said, 'Douglas, I would love to do it if I had the time but I have all my planting of vegetables and picking apples and strawberries, there simply is no time.' He laughed and said, 'Well, your way of life is out in the open and on your own a lot; you are at peace.' He never pushed it on any of us.

Would you believe it – they are just playing Mozart's Harp Concerto on the radio! Doug must be watching me write this!

BRENDA BURY

John Main was a man of great personal magnetism and charm and a splendid raconteur. We chatted throughout the sittings. He told me that his role in life was exactly what he had always wanted to be. He did not remember a time when he had not wanted to be a monk. My feelings about being a painter had been similarly unswerving and we compared notes. Usually I have to and like to talk and keep my sitters interested and relaxed. With Dom John I had to make no such efforts. He in fact kept me amused and I was full of regrets when the painting was finished. I never had any doubts that I had been in the presence of a great man. It also fascinated me that he never at any time made any effort to affect or change my own personal religious convictions.

WILLIAM DONAHUE

I am not convinced that those who knew John Main are now in a better position to understand him and know him than those who have read his books, listened to his tapes – who are living the life of prayer he proposed.

Friendship is true when both persons conceive for the other that respect which is due to the particular part of creation which the other is. At one level, both are aware of shared likes and dislikes and suffer the superficial pain of differences; but always underlying appearances is the unthreatened equality of brotherhood. Following John's example, I was, I think, constant in my respect for him. But more ideally the friend perceives something of the other's direction and the lines along which his greater perfection will be realised: I lacked the discernment necessary to foresee the quality of his life and work during his last years. The lines of his development converged rapidly and he was able to reflect himself and his happiness with the charity which we all prize. I may have foreseen, to some extent, the courage and good spirits with which he bore the suffering, first of his operable then of his inoperable cancer, but I never foresaw the depth of his prayer-life in those last days and his generous, lucid sharing of it.

On several occasions when I needed help badly he went far out of his way to help me. He was always preoccupied with others, with their needs, with the perfection of their gifts, with the return of humanity to God through Christ. He kept up his own spirit and others' in this mutual enterprise. In this regard he had an ability which sometimes puzzled others: he rarely expected too much of others and rarely expected the wrong thing of them; so he was not easily discouraged by them or discouraging for them; and so too he could share his untroubled high spirits when they were most needed. It was a concerned cheerfulness all his own, adapted for the age and condition of the other, often lightened by humour, never watered down by pietistic multiplication of words.

I will follow his example and not multiply anecdotes, telling only one of his cheerful communication with children, in which he did indeed multiply words – by repeating the same ones. Once when, with John, I visited my brother and sister-in-law with their then very young family, John gave the children an elocution lesson. This was before the time he exposed his teaching on 'the little word' (which he also called 'the mantra'). He thought they would find it hard to enunciate 'rhubarb pie'; so he repeated and they repeated after him: RHU-BARB-PIE. During the course of this almost too cheerful lesson he reached into their mostly pre-verbal world and fixed his memory in the mind of children who might otherwise have been too young to remember him.

THOMAS FEHILY

It was around the year 1976 when I first met Father John. I shall never forget the occasion. The year or so preceding his arrival I had been very disturbed by my own prayer life. It seemed to be dying. Not only had the time for prayer beome unattractive but prayer itself seemed to become more and more difficult and even distasteful. That was the situation the day that Father John knocked on my door and asked if he could have permission to say mass in my church. He was staying with his sister down the road. I had already read something by him on the prayer of meditation and so I asked him if he were the Dom John Main who had written this booklet. He said he was the very same. So I told him that I needed to make a confession to him about my own prayer life and ask his advice. His advice was that perhaps the difficulties I was experiencing in prayer were the Lord's way of inviting me to turn to a different method of prayer. He asked me if I had any interest in meditation. I told him, enough to have read his book. But I said I have no teacher. He said, well, I'm here for the week and that is more than sufficient.

That was many years ago and over those years meditation has become more and more important to me, and more and more a vital part of my ministry as a priest. Indeed I can truthfully say that my priestly work has yielded more fruit since I started meditation than it did for all the prayer of previous years. And I had to work harder at prayer in those previous years. The Lord has told us that the only condition for a fruitful life is that we remain united to him. I know

126

of no better way of remaining united to him than through meditation. For now I find that the mantra has become rooted in my heart, as Father John said it would, and so every experience I have during the day is an occasion for the mantra to quietly reassert itself. When therefore I feel very happy about something or very upset; when I want to pray for somebody or some special intention; when I am tempted or inclined to worry about the future; when I am praised or when I am hurt and feel offended, then I quietly turn to the mantra. It becomes for me a prayer of praise or thanksgiving, a plea for help or submission to God's will, as the occasion demands. It brings me right into that interior castle which St Teresa liked to retire to when she needed to reunite herself with God.

The early days of course were difficult and I had the great problem of handling the temptation of all temptations against meditation, that of thinking that I was doing nothing, just wasting my time. I would be much better employed saying my rosary or reading the scriptures. How lucky I was to have Father John close at hand to whom I could readily turn.

Here is a copy of a letter which I received from Father John in reply to one of my queries to him. It may be of as much help to others as it has been to me over all these years:

My dear Tom
Thank you for your letter. Delighted you have found the tapes useful. Forgive the telegraphic style of this. I am in the middle of giving a 30 day retreat.

As to your questions: (1) I think Father Wood's summary was accurate enough. But for 100 per cent accuracy stick to the tapes – every word there was rather carefully considered. (2) Turning your mind inwards, could, I suppose, be thinking. I would rather say just 'Be'. As you sit down call to mind who you ARE, i.e. created by God, redeemed by Jesus and Temple of the Holy Spirit. Then just Be, i.e. accept everything you ARE in absolute openness and receptivity. (3) We are bringing out a modest pamphlet – the text of my conferences to the monks of Gethsemani – I will send you a dozen copies or so. They are 50c each. (4) Always write to me in Canada. I shall be in Ireland in August 1978 for retreats in Drogheda and Cork. So I hope to see you then.

We won't be leaving here until October.

Every good wish, John.

Often I like to recall the many happy meetings which we had together. For instance, the occasion when he was giving a retreat in Glenstall and the joy of walking with him up and down that long avenue. Especially do I recall the times that he visited my little meditation group in my house in Porterstown. It was the first group we established here and our beginnings were very fragile. He never failed to come and speak to us at length and encourage us and answer all our questions. Especially do I remember his last visit among us. It was a retreat for meditators given at the Glenmaroon Convent in my parish. At that time he had a lot of pain but none even suspected that. He was his usual calm, gentle, gracious self. He never criticised, never was dogmatic in his views, never in any way dictatorial. Always I found him to be so encouraging and so full of that special kind of hope that seems to inspire those chosen by God for a special mission. Many a time he asked me to come and visit him in Montreal. It was not to be. By a strange providence of God I was indeed to get there a year after he had died. The news of his death came as a great shock to us here in Ireland as we had no foreknowledge of his illness. We met to pray for him in a special mass which was attended by the Prime Minister. Each year we will meet on his anniversary to pray for him and indeed to ask him to intercede for us that we may be as loyal as he was in our service and love of the Lord.

GERALD FITZGERALD

Douglas was a big man with a large-boned physique. I first met him through my wife-to-be in the early 1960s. I was immediately attracted by his indefinable vibrancy, his enormous vitality and a barely suppressed exuberance that radiated energy. This feeling of supercharged vitality and never varying cheerfulness made one always feel the better for his company.

He once asked me, 'Gerald, what is charisma?' I remember attempting a somewhat garbled, if not hazy definition; that is, some quality that attracts people to you. What this quality was exactly I had not then nor do I now have the vaguest idea. As the word charisma became common usage I suddenly realised that whatever it was, Douglas had an abundance of it. To dismiss it simply as 'charm' in his case, I realised, was to miss the point completely.

Charm and/or charisma and unquenchable good humour were, therefore, my first impressions of Douglas, and were to increase the more I got to know him. This instant friendliness and interest in whoever happened to engage him inclined one at first to be misled into thinking of him as a bon vivant, a connoisseur, a man of *this* world rather than of the next. He could be suddenly serious but never solemn. Among his favourite words were 'civilised', 'paradox', 'balance' and 'concentration'. A lightness of touch in conversation combined imperceptibly with a rapid lightness of foot meant he was here one minute and gone the next.

Douglas was a person with many facets. To different people he was a different person. Hence the entirely different impressions he created for various people. He was truly a man for all seasons. Extremely well-read, often academic, he had a penchant for the apt but often obtuse word. At one point I teased him about this, complaining that I needed a dictionary at my elbow when reading him or listening to one of his meditation tapes. In conversation the riposte came from him quite naturally with all the expertise of the born debater.

He was a sharp critic and quite intolerant of the poor performance, especially in music. It was here we found a delightful common ground of interest. Is intolerant the correct word? Yes he could be intolerant, of slovenly work, of crude remarks, of blatant injustice. Intolerant yes, but never personally judgmental. He was disciplined and incisive in his observations but never dogmatic.

From Douglas I learnt many things, not the least of which is that laughter is the great catalyst, the defuser of so many emotional problems, of anger and resentment. In the words of Sean O'Casey he was 'a DARLIN' MAN'. He had a wonderful gift of mimicry, a trait which seems to be characteristic of many of the Main family. In addition he could imitate flawlessly an Irish Co. Kerry accent, reducing listeners to gales of laughter with his humorous stories.

Douglas, of course, was also a teacher. The unmistakable authority of his teaching comes over clearly on his many taped talks on Christian meditation. His talks combine clarity with conviction; they are well thought-out with well-modulated diction and important pauses combined with a beautiful speaking voice.

He had no time for the personality cult and discouraged any adulation or 'kneeling at the feet of the Master'. At the first sign of any 'wide-eyed' respect he would reduce the situation to absurdity by a quick-witted remark or playing the clown, which would dissolve everyone into helpless laughter.

Despite being a born conversationalist, Douglas had the gift of disappearing into the crowd at times and could listen to others intently. He once said to me, apropos of something I was trying to do, 'You know, Gerald, *concentration* is the important thing. It is difficult at times to concentrate, but it is the key.'

Douglas was always honest. In *The Hunger for Prayer* he writes: 'it would be most arrogant of me to try to set out within the confines of a single paper a sure fire methodology for contemporary campus ministry: the more so since I have never myself exercised such a ministry'. Nevertheless Douglas goes on to spell out in a trenchant way his views on how to approach young people in today's world. He points out that the current attraction of the East for young people (Zen Buddhism, Hinduism) is because the priority of the 'real experience' is put before them in all simplicity and openness. He goes on to say, 'in any religious discussion with the young it soon becomes clear that the word "experience" has a greater force and significance than the word "faith" ', and he points out that while we live in a sceptical age, it is an age in some ways more childlike because we will believe only what we have experienced. Was this the reason John Main always reiterated that it is not sufficient to listen to talks or read books on meditation but that 'one must enter into the experience itself'?

One of the major tragedies of our day is that there are so few teachers of that goodness which Jesus enjoined upon us. One such teacher was John Main who spoke of goodness out of his 'own experience'. It was a privilege and a joy to have known him.

WALTER LALLEMAND

I first met Dom John in the summer of 1977, shortly after his arrival in the Ascension parish rectory in Montreal. He and Dom Laurence had taken temporary quarters there before procuring the old Decarie farmhouse on Vendome in 1978 as the site of their first Priory. On this initial visit I was seeking a guide, a teacher of silent prayer; I had heard indirectly that this was Dom John's strong point. For I had been away from my diocese on a six-month sabbatical and had just returned to Montreal. During that time away, the Lord had taken away my – up to then – heavily discursive manner of meditation. He dried up my images and thoughts and all I could do in meditation – even in those hallowed sites in the Holy Land – was repeat the name of Jesus, over and over.

During this time, in retrospect, I felt a certain kinship to the Abbot Serapion story, related in the Conferences of John Cassian and incorporated by Father John in one of his 'Gethsemani' talks. Serapion, after many years of anthropomorphic meditations wherein he seemed to have depended too much on images and thoughts of God, was led into what Cassian calls the 'catholic' way of prayer – prayer without images that restricts itself to the repetition of a single verse, the 'prayer of poverty'. Later, we are told, rather than rejoicing with his monks he cries pitifully: 'They have taken my God from me and I have now none to lay hold of; and whom to worship and address I know not.'

Meeting John Main for the first time that August began for me a great relationship of pupil to teacher in prayer, and also provided a friend and guide. I came to understand a little more the 'God who had been taken from me' and in my

131

new prayer of poverty to 'lay hold, worship and address' the God who is, the ground of my being.

As a ministerial priest of the Lord, Dom John always afforded me a sense of joy in his priesthood, whether in a one-to-one meeting with him or with the priests' Tuesday morning group at the Priory. He loved the priesthood with a genuine depth of sense of service, understanding and wisdom.

Sometimes we spoke of the foibles of the human aspect of church life and priesthood in this post-Vatican II era. He would comment for his part, not without a touch of humour so as to take out any sting, on some innocuous quote or phrase (perhaps from the classics). We would laugh at ourselves, find grace in laughter, and once more with feeling accept our poor humanity. On more serious matters he would hold his theological ground with quiet tenacity, and if need be, criticise constructively with more than a touch of charity. He had little use for labels like 'progressive' or 'conservative'. He tried to see the 'positive' and leave the label go.

In the post-meditation discussions we occasionally had over coffee, he often emphasised so clearly the need for us priests, dispensers of the word, to be rooted in the word and in our own personal prayer life. From his own life experience and his own pilgrimage in meditation he saw the need for busy priests to have some space in their life for silence and silent prayer. He never taught priests, or others, that this was 'the only way'. He simply said it was the 'only way that I have found'. He meant the way to simplicity, reality, the heart of the matter! As a teacher of Christian meditation to priests, one was free to follow or not. But I believe the deep, quiet joy of Dom John's priesthood reflected to the listening priests a silent message: 'If you're losing joy in your priesthood, allow more time for being, not always doing; listening, not always speaking; seek out simplicity, learn to be less complex.'

Dom John Main was a multi-talented person. He had a touch of the universal man about him. He was a fine, knowledgeable theologian, lover of music and art, gifted raconteur of stories to illustrate a point, and always had an infectious sense of humour. First and foremost, however, he was every inch a monk, a son of St Benedict. I believe his lasting legacy as a Benedictine is to have brought the monastery to the marketplace without diluting the essence of monasticism. This was his great charismatic grace as monk.

Benedict said, 'A man comes to the monastery seeking God.' And Dom John Main in *The Monastic Adventure*, referring to Cassian's words on the subject, wrote: 'The monk is simply a man who seeks to be open, as the grounding experience of his life, to God's love, the basic energy of all creation.'

These two phrases, for me, form a continuum of the 'nectar' of monasticism. Hence going to the Priory to meditate, one was always, if at times confusedly, seeking God. And not only in the silence of the house which greeted one and sustained one for an hour. Silence, after all, is always present in any monastery. But in the simplicity of meditation, one was learning to be open to God's love, the basic energy of all creation. Consequently as one was immersed in silence and in prayer, one learned to be 'open to God's love' in one's centre. One came gradually to realise the monk is (or ought to be) a person primarily 'becoming' and that the monastery is more than a place for Gregorian chant or quiet learning. Living in the heartland of prayer in the Priory with its fixed times for prayer and meditation, Father John, as a teacher of prayer, was none the less always in touch with others in the world. His empathy for others – some hurting within, some searching for more discipline in prayer, others just searching, flowed freely as indirect grace from his own commitment to the pilgrimage.

His theme was so simple: God is the centre of each life and the ground of all being; seek one's roots in silence; 'be rooted in Christ', he would say, by means of discipline, by commitment to the twice-daily half hour of meditation. In his talks prior to the periods of meditation, he dispelled the false illusion that we are the centre of our life; rather, God is. God is leading and loving us into every moment of our existence, and by the gift of the Spirit at baptism we have everything we need for the pilgrimage. And this gift of life, limited, constrained and open to pain on earth, becomes an infinite gift in that eternal moment of full openness to the power and life of Jesus. Some call it death, but the Christian knows it as the more abundant life brought to full fruition. John Main's teaching was simple: 'Say your mantra, from beginning to end.' Let your heart be open to the creative silence of God. After his talks on Christian meditation to groups large or small, he always insisted on sharing in the experience of the meditation that followed. When I gave retreats on meditation later, he always emphasised the necessity of meditating after the talk. The 'experience' was infinitely more valuable, he said, than all the talks one could listen to or the books one could read about it. Though he influenced for good many lives in a variety of places throughout the world (this is evident from the many testimonials that came to the Priory after his death), Father John always eschewed any guru or personality cult. In telling him about experiences of some retreats I led in Christian meditation, he was always helpful as a teacher to advise and correct any misconceptions on my part. As a friend he cautioned that while appreciating accolades that may come after leading a group in retreat, one must always be poor in spirit; that we are all 'beginners' in prayer, no matter how long we have been on the pilgrimage. Besides, it is not our prayer, it is the prayer of Jesus in his eternal return to the Father through the love of the Spirit which goes on at all times in the depths of our hearts.

PATRICIA MCLAUGHLIN

It is very hard to put into words, written or spoken, just what John Main meant to me. My first sight of him was in our prayer room at Glenmaroon, Dublin. He was tall, erect, and my immediate impression was of a man that radiated an inner peace.

Father John was with us that first day to give a one-day workshop and to introduce people to meditation. He had a heavy day ahead but in no way showed any anxiety or worry. It was all going to take its course and it did just that. He spoke twice during the day in the church, celebrated mass, meditated, spoke to many people, and at the end of that long day he still had time to sit and relax and talk some more.

The following year Father John came and stayed in Glenmaroon for the last week of his visit in Ireland. He had three full days of retreat. And I can honestly say, morning, noon or night, Father John never lost that composure, that deep sense of peace. He always seemed to be in touch with his true self, which was God-centred.

Over the years as I listened to Father John on his visits, or listened to his taped talks and read his books, I became more and more aware of his deep love for the prayerful reading of scripture as a preparation for meditation. In discussions with him, he also took for granted that we were applying the word of God in a concrete way to our daily life. I have spoken to many people since Father John's death and each one has expressed a similar view; namely that as a teacher Father John felt that each person should listen to the word of God and find their journey in life imbued with scripture. Perhaps some meditators have missed this point. But for me, the inspiring reading of scripture at the end of each talk on meditation showed me how thoroughly grounded he was in God's word and that he lived it.

During that last week in Ireland I noticed Father John, now and again, would put his hand to his back. Once when I asked him if there was anything the matter, he replied 'oh, no, he was just tired'. And on the last Friday as I drove him to the airport, I noticed he got into the car in a gentle, easy way, and I felt there was something wrong. But again the answer 'no, he was fine'. He talked freely and easily about the week's happenings and about his family.

He felt meditation was expressed in your actions, in your kindness. And, as he has said on one of his tapes, it is not love God first, then your neighbour, then yourself, but love yourself fully, know yourself, stretch yourself to the full and then love your neighbour, but love him as he is himself, not as you would wish him to be. It is then in that full expression of love that you love God totally. That was the message from Father John that came through loud and clear to me.

We parted with that lovely smile of his and a very sincere thanks for the wonderful week that he had experienced. That thanks he expressed many times. That was the last I saw of Father John in Ireland. That was May. In September I attended a Mentally Handicapped Conference in Toronto. And having a brother living in Montreal, Father John invited me to drop in to the Priory for a visit. But when Father John appeared he was in a wheelchair. It was an awful shock. He had failed, was quite pale and thin. But his eyes were not changed, they sparkled as ever and he was so genuinely pleased to meet my brother, a sister friend and myself. We had a few wonderful hours, and once during the conversation he answered the phone. I noticed when he moved from the wheelchair he supported himself on the back of a couch. He was unable to stand erect, unsupported. As we bade farewell, Father John signed two books for me as a gift, which I have kept and treasured. And somehow I felt, 'I won't see Father John again'. But he is as much alive today as he was then. The legacy of his teaching lives on in all of us.

JUDITH MAIN

It was a year after my marriage to his brother Ian in 1980 that I first met Douglas. I had originally heard about him from his cousin John Foll. In casual conversation, I had talked about meditation and it was he who showed me the book by Father John called *Christian Meditation*. John Foll later introduced me to Father John's brother Ian. It was not until 1981 that I first met Father John himself when he celebrated a family mass in Dublin.

In the meantime I had become most intrigued to meet him as it seemed to me there were two different men in question. The first was the deeply spiritual individual of the tapes and booklets, whose teaching struck deep chords of recognition in me. This was especially true with regard to the simplicity of the message, and was a final factor in influencing me to become a Catholic. The thought that a Catholic priest of such standing could see through all the worldly aspects of the Church and then go back to the essential spirit of the teaching of our Lord made me feel that here at last was where I belonged.

The second man was the individual his family talked about with great affection, but always rather tongue-in-cheek as if one should not take him too seriously. The impression I got was of a man fond of doing extraordinary things for effect and as practical jokes. The traditionalists in the family were

136

plainly shocked by his unorthodox approach to his chosen vocation of monk. There were half-serious references to him 'going monking', his 'new religion', his grey habit, and the magnificence of the house in Montreal. At first these references shocked me too. It seemed to me quite inconceivable that the man who had made the tapes and whose whole message was about simplicity and openness should in any way be less than totally honest, totally serious. But it must be remembered that I was, to all intents and purposes, a stranger and the family would not have revealed their true feelings to me, and they also love a joke.

I finally met Father John in the bosom of his family in Dublin and for two days saw this rather austere figure (with a twinkle in his eye) thaw out more and more under the familiar family teasing and become again the much-loved rogue, the younger brother who loved a practical joke. As the newest member of the family I was, of course, fair game. And being impressed as I was to meet this remarkable man, I was somewhat 'thrown' to have remarks addressed to me with all the gravity of the great teacher, only to find that my leg was being unmercifully pulled.

The importance of the family in his life was exceptional. The Mains are unusually close, with deep ties of affection (not shown directly, but clearly understood), which are usually expressed in joking terms. All the brothers and sisters had a very close relationship one with another and kept closely in touch, however far apart they were geographically. I think that to become a monk and, to a great extent, to have to cut himself off from the family must have been a far harder deprivation than any other for him. His family ties were not confined to his brothers and sisters, of course; he was devoted to his mother in her lifetime and was the very much loved and loving uncle of his many nephews and nieces as well as taking great pleasure in visiting all his relatives whenever he could. However hard-pressed for time he was when on this side of the Atlantic, he always made time to see as many of the family as possible.

The second time I met him was in 1982 when he came to London to give a retreat, which we attended, in Neasden. It was a perfect day of peace and joy and deeply serious purpose and the first time I saw him as 'teacher'. I will never forget the deep sincerity and conviction of what he said and the look of radiant integrity on his face. No one could doubt for a second that he was totally earnest and speaking from personal experience. The atmosphere of that day, pervaded by his personality, will always remain one of the few glorious occasions in my life. Another was the day of his memorial mass, when he was most tangibly 'present' and transformed a tragic occasion into one of joy.

I think an important clue to his character is that he would (probably) not have liked me to write this. Under all their easy, teasing charm, the Mains are all deeply private people. And none more so than Douglas, who had large areas of his life about which no member of the family knew anything. I think this is the reason why some saw a dichotomy in his character; his extraordinary success in being both a man of the world in the most complete sense, and a man of God equally completely. It also accounts for his ability to communicate with people at all levels so effectively and to understand them and their needs. Perhaps it also explains how someone who was naturally drawn towards richness of thought as well as to the good things of life should have chosen the way of total poverty, especially of the spirit. He was not a man to accept the mediocre or shoddy in anything.

IAN MAIN

There are a thousand questions I could put to Douglas now. But on one particular occasion when he talked seriously about meditation he said: 'Don't try and fathom the unfathomable. No matter how much you read or study about meditation you will always come up against a brick wall. Just say your mantra with faithfulness and all will be revealed in due time.'

MARY MECHTILDE

We were privileged to have John Main with us in 1980 for what we termed 'the Centenary Retreat'. In a never-to-be-forgotten encounter with God, with Father John's dynamic presence and preaching, a new world of understanding emerged of what it means to be a Benedictine. A living PRAYER was reached; and that not by just a few. Somehow in a very strange way, a very extraordinary way, John Main's 'word' touched the young as it touched the old; it filled the sceptical as it did the enthusiastic. Why, we asked ourselves in wonder. Why should he have made such an impression? Was it the commanding presence of a great man? Was it the magic of a perfectly modulated voice? Was it the brilliance yet simplicity of his language? No, surely not, though all contributed something to the six days of peaceful reflection and surprising refreshment. No, it was the godliness of the man! For him to live was Christ. We have no doubt about it and as the days passed the conviction grew ever stronger. 'For him to live was Christ and to die was gain.'

MIRIAM O'QUIGLEY

In Dublin in 1975 my next assignment with the Medical Missionaries of Mary was announced as London's Ealing Abbey. A Father Bernard O'Dea OSB from Glenstal Abbey said to me one day, 'There's a big six-footer over there in Ealing Abbey, John Main. He has prayer groups going.' 'I'm not really interested,' I said, 'in so many prayer groups there's more talk than prayer.' Dom Bernard did not continue the topic except to say, 'You should meet him.'

In January 1976 I left for Ealing. A Sister Brenda in our community there spoke of Father John Main and asked if I would come to the Monday night's prayer hour. 'No,' I said, and gave her the same reply as I had given to Dom Bernard. 'But it's quiet prayer, very peaceful,' said Sister. I was not convinced. However as the weeks went by and Brenda and I got to know each other, and I had seen and heard John Main at mass, I was beginning to change my mind. So when Brenda said at tea one evening, 'Miriam, I think you'll like our prayer hour, there's one tonight,' I asked for details. And as she spoke of half an hour during which not a word is said, I thought, 'This is for me' and said I would come.

The prayer I had come to practise before this time was a kind of mantra though I had never heard that word before. 'I love you, I thank you' was my prayer during my usual half-hour prayer, morning and evening and at other times of the day such as walking or waiting in queues. So when I arrived at the prayer house and heard that the mantra they used was Maranatha I was reluctant to give up my accustomed way and continued during that first half hour in the group saying 'I love you, I thank you'.

We were about thirteen people. Father John read a passage from St Paul, then some quiet music was played from a cassette, after which we silently crossed the hall to the larger prayer room with chairs and cushions. A candle in the centre of the room was lighted. It was a blessed experience, the stillness, the quiet, the Presence.

Looking back I remember there was for me only one flaw. I was somehow uncomfortable. I had happened upon the wrong chair: it was too high, with my feet barely reaching the floor, and I was a bit distracted. I mentioned this to Father John on our way out. He took me back to the prayer room and pointed to a chair next to the one he always used. 'Try that one,' he said. It was perfect, and that was the one I settled for each Monday night until I left for Africa a year and a half later.

At this first encounter with Father John I felt so much at ease that I confessed, 'I didn't use Maranatha during the half hour.' He smiled and said, 'We find Maranatha has the right sound to bring us to the silence and stillness necessary for meditation.'

It did not take him long to convert me.

As I got to know Father John better I asked him if I could come and see him regarding spiritual matters. This was the beginning of a rich relationship. I told him how the letters of St Paul had come alive for me, perhaps because of the way he read passages before the prayer half hour. Passages such as these took on real meaning: 'When anyone is united to Christ there is a *new* world' or 'God's love has *flooded* our inmost heart through the Holy Spirit he has given us'. He recommended the New English Bible translation and when I brought it to him and asked him to write something on the next-to-cover page, he wrote:

1 John 5:1–5. To understand this and to know it is the whole purpose of this life. In his Love we overcome. All wisdom, all love come from him.
Aug. 13th 1977, John Main.

Faith: how often Father John was to use that word: 'Meditation, a way of faith' or 'You must take that on faith'. In *Moment of Christ* Father John says: 'Meditation takes us into the experience of faith where we become more open, more committed to the spiritual reality which is beyond ourselves and yet in which we have our being.'

Perseverance was important to Father John. He was sometimes asked, 'How long will it take to be free of distractions, to come to silence?' He would answer five, ten, maybe twenty years. 'I won't be around then,' one old sister was heard to say in one of our 'after prayer times' at Ealing. 'Keep saying your mantra,' he said.

In August 1977 a group of about fourteen of us made a month's retreat under the guidance of Father John at the Reparatrice Convent, Wimbledon. What a joy and never-to-be-forgotten experience this was to be.

Father John began by telling us we were going to spend the month with God in a very special way, on vacation with God. Vacation comes from *vacare*, to make a space for God in our hearts, he said, so let us open ourselves to receive him. He pointed out that relaxation and unwinding were necessary for prayer.

The theme of the retreat was 'Prayer and Community'. Father John pointed out that meditation is not a way of *doing* something but of becoming someone, becoming yourself, knowing who you are, created, redeemed, the temple of the Holy Spirit and of infinite lovableness. Because prayer teaches us to pay attention to the Other it teaches us to pay attention to others. Prayer is the great school of community: letting the other *be*. And the great school of prayer is community. One day the homily of the mass was based on the Christian experience of community as taught by Jesus. Said Father John:

We are a healing community: we all come to religious life wounded in one way or another. Show the people in your community, especially the novices, that we love them, so that they will know they are loved and are worthwhile, important. Let the novices make some mistakes. Don't make all the mistakes for them!

The liturgy during the whole of that month was the most prayerful and unifying I have ever experienced. After Holy Communion we had quiet prayer in which we were all closely united to one another in Christ.

This retreat was permeated with prayer, with Father John's talks, his presence, the community liturgy and homilies based on each day's readings and through our own eagerness and commitment to several hours of meditation each day.

I have written down a few extracts from his retreat talks:

- The real freedom is not to do but to be.
- The only real power is love.
- God is a sea of love; rest in that love; act out of that love. If you have a difficulty with others remember that river of love within you and begin to pour out that love on others.
- Our true self is the very self of God. Love penetrates further than one's understanding; and the impulse of love reaches straight to the heart of God.

He gave me a whole new understanding of the scriptures on this retreat, because he gave us an entirely fresh appreciation of prayer. Prayer is not talking to God, he said, but being with him. Prayer is an awareness of being loved. Prayer is the stream of love between the Spirit of the risen Jesus and his Father in which we are present. We must make our presence real, in faith, by repeating our little word, our mantra.

On one occasion during the retreat I went to Father John's room seeking some guidance. He suggested we first pray together in silence for about fifteen minutes. His presence alone geared you to prayer. When one was in Father John's presence one was filled with joy. You felt he loved you and he led you to the Father.

142

Father John had to drive each morning and evening through the London traffic. It was a stressful situation for him, not being able to stay at the Wimbledon Convent and relax when the day's work was over. He told me he could never do it again.

After this retreat we heard of the plans of Father John and Laurence Freeman to start a monastery in Montreal at the request of Bishop Leonard Crowley. In September 1977 they flew to Montreal to establish this first monastic community dedicated to the teaching of Christian meditation.

Once again I was losing a real friend, but little did I think as we said our goodbyes that I would never see him again. Only five years later he died at the monastery in Montreal. In a letter to me he wrote, 'Every parting is a kind of death. We go out into the unknown leaving familiar places and familiar faces, leaving those we love.'

But during those five years we still remained in contact.

I had written to him of my return to Africa, to Kenya this time. His return letter of 9 December 1977 says:

Your news is astounding! I must say I think it is altogether wonderful. I thought you had retired [I was then sixty] to a more quiet life in a suburban backwater; and now you are taking the gospel to the ends of the earth. It has to be right because it just hits short of the crazy and the marvellous. As you say, you will indeed take the silence of the mantra to your new surroundings. We are ready for these things, even if we do not recognise it at the time. I know you will be happy because your one aim is to do God's will in all things. The new venture represents the sort of 'leap of faith' that is required for all leaving of self behind and has just come in that moment of your life when you need to make that *total commitment* . . . We have put our prayer here at the Monastery absolutely in first place . . . three times a day for our half hour of glory.

Before leaving for Kenya, for the Pastoral Institute at Eldoret, to which I was assigned, I had written to Father John. His reply of 18 January 1978 came as a pleasant surprise, knowing how much he and Laurence were occupied with the prayer groups, guests and improvements of the building in which they lived. He says, among other things:

Have confidence in the strange will of the Lord. But it is his will that you should go back to Africa to be a good infirmarian [I was appointed Nurse, caring for the health of the staff and approximately fifty students]. Bring the one little word with you. I can't tell you how happy I am that we have a real apostle in Africa. Not everyone has understood this message but you have. And it is because you have understood it and embraced it that you will carry it with you wherever you go.

Another letter of Father John's written on 13 March 1978 gave me the incentive to start a meditation group among the students, or participants as we called them. They were from many countries of Africa, priests, catechists, sisters, black and white. They studied and participated in group work based on the scripture, theology, anthropology, counselling and Christian education lectures they received at the institute. It was wonderful how so many of them with different backgrounds and cultures got on so well together. The director of the institute, Father John Lemay, a White father from Montreal, had a real charism for leadership as well as being a wonderful person with a lovely personality. Father John Main wrote:

... you will be the apostle of the mantra in Africa. Remember, though, great patience and greater and greater fidelity. The mantra is not taught but caught. We keep you in the centre of our heart here. Do the same for us. We are hoping to bring the good news to many, but we can only do so humbly and with the recommendation of others!

After receiving this letter I put up a notice which included Father John's advice: 'The only way to teach people to pray is to pray with them.' Father John's cassettes on meditation were a great help to me and to the group. We listened to one of them before the half hour of prayer each week.

Father John's letters were infrequent though I still kept in touch with him. The newsletters were always welcome and filled in the gaps.

On 6 July 1979 he wrote in reply to a letter of mine: 'I am

so delighted that you have found fulfilment and happiness in Africa after that period of marking time at Ealing. I guess we were all marking time there, and God was marking us.'

I think it was in September 1979 that Father John had major surgery, which I knew nothing of until his letter of 8 January 1980 arrived. Here is an excerpt:

> It was a serious operation, so my correspondence has piled up into hundreds. But don't think that you have not been in my heart all this time . . . I was rather disappointed by the resolution on the Prayer House. But it will come. People are apparently threatened by it at the moment. All of us religious must soon realise that our primary apostolate is a spiritual one, and without that everything else is just sounding brass and tinkling cymbals and like those leaves no trace.

(I had spoken in my letter of the outcome of our General Assembly, and my disappointment regarding the establishing of a House of Prayer for MMM.)

Father John's letters were getting fewer, but he usually said, even when he was very ill, 'All is well'. So that when news of his death came in December 1982 it came as a real shock. I could hardly believe it and would have loved to have been with him in spirit during those last months of his life.

But to go back to a letter full of enthusiasm which came to me in September 1980. He wrote:

> Another miracle is that we have been given a beautiful house with three and a half acres of garden right in the centre of Montreal. Isn't God extraordinary? We can't keep up with him at all . . . I was so interested in all your news and the reaction of Dr B. That is the way we should really spread the Gospel, by being in God. If only we could always remember that, we would always be communicating his love. Keep us always in your heart that we may become a community of self-emptying disciples of the Lord.

Let me explain that I had been for a medical check with a Dr B in Nairobi who found that my blood pressure was unusually high. She asked me was I happy being a religious, and added, 'I always ask religious this question.' I said, 'I

145

am, and even happier as the years go by.' 'You radiate peace,' she said. And I mentioned to Father John that as I went down the avenue from the hospital my heart was singing, realising that this remark from the doctor was like a wee message from the Lord himself.

I still wonder why he did not let his friends know how seriously ill he was when he knew it. I could have prayed and been with him as he lived out those last weeks nearing his entry into the kingdom of the Father, the kingdom he so often spoke of, prepared for and prepared so many for. (See pp. 247–51.)

It was just about ten years since I had first met Father John and the richness of his love and life remain ever with me. He was a very lovable person.

BERNARD ORCHARD

Normally I should preach a homily on the gospel that we have just heard (Matt. 6:25–34). But having heard the reference to 'ye of little faith', it will be fully appropriate to comment on this gospel by telling you something about the great man of faith, Father John Main. And this of course is just a personal appreciation and not a complete summary of his life.

John Douglas Main came from an Irish family that settled in London, with deep roots in western Ireland. He was educated by the Jesuits at Stamford Hill. At the time he joined our novitiate in 1959 he had every prospect of a glittering career in the world, which however he chose to renounce. He took his first vows in 1960, made his solemn profession in 1963, and was ordained priest in this very church in December of the same year. His first assignment was teaching in St Benedict's School. In 1967 he was appointed second master; I found it a great pleasure to work with him.

In 1969 he was sent to the Catholic University of America in Washington DC to take a special course in catechetics, while residing at the English Benedictine Abbey of St Anselm's. It was during this year, as he later confided to me, that his contacts with American students at the university made him aware of the hunger for prayer that possessed so many of them and the need they felt for instruction. These contacts changed his life. From that time onwards he made up his mind to become not only a man of prayer, but to develop his own inner life of communion with God, as the most effective way of living out his own Benedictine commitment.

Nevertheless his educational and administrative skills were such that he was soon called upon to become headmaster of St Anselm's Abbey School, a position that he held with distinction for four years. In 1974 he was recalled by Abbot Rossiter for duties in the abbey here. He then became the leading spirit in setting up the house of prayer to teach Christian meditation; he was made director of the newly established lay community, was appointed novice master and then Prior.

His fame and his great achievement will in my opinion rest on his ability to speak so attractively about prayer and to communicate so effectively his own enthusiasm for union with God in prayer. He also had a special insight in being able to link up the mystical tradition of the East, which he first learnt from a swami he had met in Malaya when he was in the British Colonial Service, with the teaching of John Cassian. Cassian was the fifth-century European monk who first brought to the West the prayer tradition of the Egyptian Desert Fathers. John Main was also able to link Cassian with the teaching of our own English Benedictine Father Augustine Baker, whose method of prayer has always been standard in our English Benedictine houses.

Nevertheless John Main still hungered for the freedom to lead a monastic life that was more purely contemplative than ours. In 1977 he was granted permission to answer a call from the Archbishop of Montreal and his English-speaking assistant Bishop Crowley, to go to Montreal to establish there a Benedictine priory, a house of contemplative prayer.

His work there met with an immediate and gratifying response from both clergy and laity, and he became deeply involved in teaching Christian meditation all over North America. When it became clear that the new priory would be best established if it joined some already existing North American foundation, the monks of Mount Saviour Monastery in New York State generously agreed to take the new foundation under its protection, until such time as it was viable to become a canonically independent priory.

One of Father John's finest qualities was his continued interest in the prayer groups he left behind in this country after he went to Canada. He continued to take a personal interest in their progress and to maintain his friendships with so many individuals among them, both by personal contact and by letter. Indeed one of the most remarkable features of Father John's apostolate of prayer was the way in which he was able to gather round him a dedicated band of enthusiastic clergy and lay people, some of whom crossed the Atlantic at regular intervals not only to put themselves under his direction but also to absorb the spiritual peace and silence that pervades the Montreal Benedictine Priory. Before long he was given a magnificent mansion in the city of Montreal where his plans for expanding the work were rapidly taking shape with the aid of a few devoted disciples.

But some two years ago Father John had his first period of hospitalisation and a serious operation. He recovered well but this summer he was struck down by a spinal complaint, later diagnosed as cancer. His patience and his cheerfulness during the period of treatment were heroic, and few realised the seriousness of his illness. A fortnight ago it took a sudden and fatal turn, and he died very peacefully with the rites of the Church on 30 December, surrounded by his brethren and friends. Our Abbot Francis went over last week to represent our community at the funeral which took place at Mount Savior Monastery.

Such is the brief outline of the religious life of this very gifted and charismatic monk, now so suddenly taken from us by the Lord when not quite fifty-seven years of age (his next birthday being on 21 January).

I think it is true to say that all who met him were captivated by his cheerful, animated and sympathetic temperament; for he was a merry and witty companion; he was never boring and he stood out in any company. And he never relinquished his capacity for warm friendship, which drew people to him. Yet under the surface he was a man always seeking something better, something beyond himself, a man of vision, always searching for God. Worldly success had been within his grasp, but it did not satisfy him. When he arrived at Ealing at the age of thirty-three he possessed this great charism for friendship with young people and old, and with men and women from very varied walks of life.

He was most affable and pleasing to talk to, and full of fun. At the same time he was very practical and could turn his hand to anything about the house from gutters to drains. And he found plenty of scope for these talents in Montreal. He was indeed a builder and a doer, as well as a theologian; and he had a fluent and eloquent pen, as his spiritual writings testify. Furthermore his generous nature enabled him to appreciate the spiritual worth, the traditions of prayer and the aspirations of non-Catholic Christians, and non-Christians too. All of these he warmly welcomed to the Montreal Priory, including a retired Anglican bishop who lived there permanently in the community as a regular oblate and wearing the same habit.

His enthusiasm for the reforms set in motion by Vatican II was infectious and he was a courageous innovator and pioneer of new ways, and not afraid of trying them out. Some of his spirit and vision still survive in our community, which he greatly influenced at a critical period of its growth. Perhaps the most lasting and important memorial that he has left us is the prayer centre, which continues to flourish.

It is impossible however at this time, when he is still so near us, to assess justly all he did for us, for others, and for the Church. All I know is that he did something important for me. For when he came back in 1970 after his first year in America we had a long talk together. I was so impressed with what he told me about the American students whose need to learn to pray had changed his own life that I there and then made up my mind to follow his example and to double the time I spent in prayer, a resolution that has changed my life also. His departure in 1977 to follow his own 'star' to Canada was a loss that I and many others here have felt deeply and have deeply regretted.

So our prayers today must be for the repose of the soul of a dedicated monk who sought new ways to bring people to God and who sought to adapt our Benedictine traditions to the needs of today, and indeed of tomorrow. But we must also pray that the Lord in his mercy will not suffer all the good work he has done both in the new world and in the old to be wasted and lost; but will continue to bless it, and to aid and strengthen in a new and more powerful way those on whom his mantle has now fallen; so that the sacrifice that Dom John has made of his own life will enable him now, from his vantage point in eternity, to work more powerfully than ever for the promotion of that which was dearest to his heart, namely *the prayer life of the world, the whole world* – both Christian, and non-Christian!

THOMAS F. SCHLAFLY

Thomas Schlafly recently found the following message written by John Main on 24 August 1980 in the family's holiday-home log book:

> Two glorious days – a first experience of floating . . . delightful. On both days the dawn had the quality of the day of creation itself. The springs gave the promise of eternal life. *Quid retribuam Domine pro omnibus quae retribuit mihi*? (What can I return to the Lord for everything he has given to me?)

The following letter was sent to the family by John Main after his visit to Rainbow Springs:

> My dear Adelaide and Don
> Thank you so much for your warm hospitality while I was in St Louis. It was a great pleasure to see you both again and I was very sorry that our meeting was so brief.
> Thank you too for all the wonderful provisioning for Rainbow. Tom and I must have both put on pounds as the result of your generous hampers.
> I thought Rainbow Springs one of the most beautiful places I have ever been to. I shall never forget the mysterious power of those ever-renewed cascades of eternally fresh water.
> When Tom first mentioned the canoeing I feared I might not be up to the Schlafly enthusiasm for violent physical

endurance tests! But I enjoyed it more than I can say. It was the greatest fun and so beautiful floating between those spectacular bluffs.

Tom is of course a great companion for such a trip and we enjoyed good conversation ranging over a wide territory. By the way if you have not already read it I warmly recommend R. F. Schumacher, *A Guide for the Perplexed*, published by Perennial Library, Harper and Row. When Fritz died in London the whole of the intellectual community, agnostics and atheists included, turned up at his requiem at Westminster Cathedral. Of all our contemporaries he has had perhaps the greatest influence as a Catholic.

For your interest I enclose a brochure about our work and a copy of one of our newsletters and one of our publications.

With every good wish.

You are all in my heart at prayer, in Christ,
John Main.

MADELEINE SIMON

I first met Father John in 1963 when he came to give our community a three-day retreat. He based his talks on the Church and, though the community in general was very impressed by what he had to say, I have to confess that the talks left me cold. He asked to see me because my father, who knew some cousins of his, had been to visit him when he was studying at St Anselmo. He had been very touched that an elderly man like my father should have taken the trouble to call on him. I remember him as genial and friendly during this visit but I was not left with any particular desire to meet him again – nor did I for another twelve years.

In 1975 our Sister Sara Grant from the Christa Prema Seva ashram in Poona, was in England. We met in Southall, a strongly Indian district west of London where I was living, to discuss a possible ashram-type prayer centre there, where Sikhs, Hindus and Muslims might feel free enough to pray in silence with us. Sister Sara asked me to drive her to an

151

address in Ealing, where I intended to drop her and return home. However the tall, black-habited figure on the doorstep, none other than Father John, invited me in and I found myself, in my clumping winter boots, in a room full of silent people. Father John asked Sister Sara to speak and we then all moved to another room for meditation. I was feeling so nervous that I stomped in, boots and all. After the meditation we went back to the original room where questions were put to Sister Sara about her ashram. By the time I left I was saying to myself, 'This is for me.' Father John had scarcely spoken except to introduce his guest. From that time I was a regular participant at the meditation meetings.

One evening after the group had returned from the meditation room, Father John turned and asked me a question directly. As I answered, we both knew that we had met at a deep level. Nothing was ever said about this by either of us until the last talk I had with him in Montreal in May 1982, and he said something to this effect: 'Our love for each other, and indeed for everyone else, is one with God's love.'

His guidance, at least in my case, was non-directive; he answered my questions and he recommended books. Once I asked him what he considered to be the essential ascesis. Without hesitation he answered 'Love'. He did not expound, but my understanding of that answer has been deepening ever since. During a six week renewal period he gave me the book *Saccidananda* to ponder, and for the only other retreat I made under his guidance, he gave me Meister Eckhart. Both of these books have had a profound influence on my spiritual development. He did not ask for, neither did I give, any account of their effect on me.

Our relationship had this strange ambivalence: nothing was said, yet everything was said; I felt easy in his company and at the same time I never lost a sense of awe; we were strangers and friends; he never probed or intruded and I never asked anything personal. I only learnt of the existence of his brother when I asked him if he had a reader for mass and he indicated the man next to him, saying, 'My brother.'

This same ambivalence was experienced by many who have spoken to me. Some felt him to be aloof and uncaring, while others, accepting it, were open to his spiritual influence. His was certainly a very powerful and attractive personality. Could it have been that this seeming aloofness was, in his humility, a way of forestalling any undue attachment to himself? His personal contact through his tapes and correspondence was phenomenal. One sums up what many have experienced: 'I feel he is a personal friend though I only know him through listening to his tapes.' An elderly, very blind man wrote to me (in a practically illegible scrawl) on hearing of Father John's death: 'How I loved that man, yet I never met him.'

No memoir of Father John could be complete without some mention of his humour and gift of mimicry, which sparkled out at the most unexpected moments. Having just delivered a profound and most beautiful talk on prayer, he said he was willing to take questions. An awed silence ensued which he diffused by adding with a mischievous twinkle, 'So as General de Gaulle said at his first news conference, "Ladies and gentlemen, be so good as to provide questions for my answers."'

I do not see any value in presenting Father John as a superman without human frailties. He struck me as basically a shy person. But at the same time he could be intolerant where he sensed a lack of authenticity, and dogmatic in stating what he saw to be the truth. I remember once at Ealing, in the period after the meditation, when he had made some particularly devastating statement, and he smiled and said, 'You must forgive me. I was a public prosecutor at one period of my life and my brethren tell me I have been prosecuting ever since.'

Some people expected him to be a professional psychologist, which he was not. His subject was 'God' and few could equal him in his ability to teach people, not how to know about God and his workings, but to know him personally.

During my visit to the Montreal community in the spring of 1982 it seemed to me that Father John's spirituality had come to the simplicity of St John's 'God is love'. I remember him saying: 'God is a sea of love; rest in that love, act out of that love. If you have had a difficulty with others, remember that river of love within you and begin to pour out love on them again.'

At the Holy Saturday vigil there was a blazing fire in the hall, which lit us all up in its glow. Father John, as celebrant, was standing apart near the fire and, looking into it, he said that God is like a blazing fire of love, and that we need to throw ourselves into it, to be one with it, and then to take that fire which is the love of God out into our lives that others may burn with it too.

It was at this time, too, that I discussed with him the possibility of my opening a co-ordinating centre for his work in England. I suggested 'Christian Meditation Centre' as a name for it. He thought for some time and then said: 'Yes – that says just what it should be, and I hope that, in due course, there will be Christian Meditation Centres all over the world.'

CARLA SIMMONS

I first met John in 1977 when our congregation, the Medical Missionaries of Mary, had a thirty-day retreat in Wimbledon, which John Main led. I was going through a very difficult time and had really gone on the retreat with the intention of asking for a leave of absence at the end of it. That never happened. Through the course of the retreat John helped me to clarify my thoughts and to redirect my life. I just know that in looking at things with him they appeared different. Those talks and the introduction to the mantra changed my life.

One of the things that I remember most about John was his ability to adapt himself to his audience. He wanted to pass on the fruits of the mantra and he used all his talents to do it. He had every regional Irish accent down pat and he charmed the Irish sisters with his stories. This was even more apparent to me when we met again later. In 1980 I spent a month in Montreal on retreat. John and Laurence were in the original house and I did the cooking for them and the oblates and joined in prayers and liturgy. Two very warm memories stick in my mind. A French-speaking Cistercian was in the house for a week on retreat and one evening after dinner as we conversed over coffee John was telling stories.

The brother was rather left out until John told him a lengthy story in French. I do not speak French but just watching the animation and listening to the inflection was a delight and the Frenchman must have found it just as delightful for he laughed heartily at the end.

Another day we were entertaining a family from Toronto, a mother, father and young child. Mum and Dad were busy doing something and the child, who was about five or six, had become quite restless waiting for them. John took the child apart and told him the most imaginative story about an Indian chief who had a motor car. I couldn't help eavesdropping. Each of the characters in the story had a different voice and the motor car made a collection of entertaining noises. The child was mesmerised and John seemed to be thoroughly enjoying himself as well. John could truly be all things to all, man, woman or child, and he used his gift to spread his message.

That time in Montreal was a very special time for me. I often recall it and am so grateful that I was there in the beginning when things were small and simple.

JOHN SMITH

I first heard of John Main during retreat in Dublin in August 1981 while home from Guyana, where I worked for thirteen years. I listened to his first tapes on Christian meditation and found the breakthrough I was searching for in prayer. His simplicity and utter conviction convinced me. I have never looked back since!

I met John in Montreal in Holy Week 1982. I was on sabbatical in Toronto then and made my retreat with the community in Montreal. I planned a directed retreat but John simply invited me to meditate with the group. It was a powerful experience and further affirmed to me that I was on the right track; that I had found what I was looking for: to let go, say nothing and trust, just 'do nothing'. I was looking for the inner journey after spending years in faithful mental prayer but getting nowhere. I found the answer in John Main. When I was leaving I said to him that it was very easy to be faithful to meditation in the silence of the monastery. But I was returning to a busy missionary life in Guyana and wondered how I would cope. John simply said: 'What alternative have you?' That hit me like a ton of bricks! I knew too well from past experience that without a deep prayer life I could not exist in Guyana with all the tension and problems.

I returned to Guyana totally committed to twice-daily meditation. Since then I am proud to say I can count on one hand the number of times I have missed those two vital parts of my day. I have meditated, still do, in all sorts of places: at airports, on planes, in small and large boats on the rivers of Guyana, on buses and trains, in the jam-packed 'taxis' in Guyana with two people sitting on me, and at different times in the night. At that time the parish had six communities spread over fifty-six miles, with two islands thrown in. In addition I was a jack of all trades! I found the quality of my work was better because of the time spent in active listening.

Due to health problems I returned to Scotland recently. It is so much easier now to continue the inner pilgrimage. I feel rooted in meditation and cannot do without it. I used to get very tired in Guyana and did not have the energy to say the breviary. But I could sit and be quiet and say the mantra. John Main brought light, depth and direction into my life.

CEDRIC M. SPEYER

My first meeting with Father John Main is a remarkable story of synchronicity. I was working one day as a medical orderly on the top floor of the Montreal General Hospital, adjacent to the Benedictine Priory. On an unofficial break I was reading the *Weekend* newspaper. The details are quite clear in my mind. I was seated at a desk in the lobby between the east and west wings. The article I was reading was about a monastery where anyone could go to learn about Christian meditation. I had meditated within different eastern traditions and this article about a Christian meditation version really intrigued me.

While focused on a colour photo of the founder of the monastery, my attention was distracted by the elevator doors opening. A tall, distinguished-looking man emerged. He came up to my desk to ask directions and noticed the open page of the newspaper. He asked if he could borrow it to show the patient he was visiting. Slightly irritated at the interruption, I agreed, saying, 'Be sure and bring it right back.' Only after he had left did it dawn on me that he was the same man in the photo I had been concentrating on. I could hardly wait for his return to confirm this unlikely coincidence. Father John dealt with my subsequent surge of interest in him by being (what I thought was) excessively polite and reserved. He obviously did not relish any adulation. He also remained steadfastly neutral about my assurance that we would meet again some day.

That settles it, I thought, after he had left. I am going to find out what the priory and its founder are all about. This man seems to think my interest is a passing curiosity. Well, I'll show him it is not.

That was about eight years ago. For the past six years I have been meditating regularly and became an oblate of the Priory along the way. Father John taught me to let go of images and trust direct personal experience. I now realise that his entire teaching was contained in the first moment we met.

JOHN TODD

When I first met John Main he was a Benedictine monk of Ealing Abbey, much engaged in giving retreats. He had come to the Ammerdown Centre in Somerset. The tall, good-looking, pink-faced monk looked every inch of him a member of the English Benedictine congregation, with his well-laundered habit and his fresh face. But there was something a little unusual about him, which it was difficult to put one's finger on. There was an element of 'larger than life' about him. His preaching and his talks seemed to be in the normal mould of traditional doctrine and spirituality, full of practical common sense, with a gospel urgency and application such as is found in the Rule of St Benedict. With it all, however, there came across a special charism. It was certainly a matter both of his personality and of his personal commitment. His words themselves seemed not to differ greatly from what one might expect to hear from an English monk, but the urgency and attraction were unusually compelling. They came with a commanding smile.

I did not, I think, hear Father John talking about meditation at that time. However, the impact had been sufficient for me, as a publisher, to recognise in John Main a potential author. Then shortly afterwards I read an article of his in the *Tablet*, in which he spoke of his experience of learning to meditate from a swami in Malaysia, and the practice of using a mantra. This immediately took my interest. It linked in my mind with the Eastern Orthodox practice of the Jesus Prayer with its word-repetition. It seemed also to offer a Christian alternative to and improvement on 'TM', transcendental meditation, as recommended by Maharishi Mahesh Yogi, which had become widely popular, and was based on the use of a mantra.

I would often write from my office at Darton, Longman and Todd to someone who had impressed me, enquiring whether he or she planned to write a book. On 28 February 1977 I wrote such a letter to Father John. My letter was enthusiastic and suggested that Father John had the ability to write something that 'might reach beyond the normal religious constituency'. He replied enthusiastically, saying that he was thinking of writing something about prayer for modern man and that my letter had made him crystallise his thoughts.

And so began the process which led to Father John and his young confrère Laurence Freeman, not yet ordained at that time, coming several times to the publishing offices in London. This led eventually to our publication of Father John's and Father Laurence's books. The first book was *Word into Silence*. It was based on the text of a tape of Father John's which The Grail had published a few years earlier. He had the ability to speak to groups about meditation with a remarkable combination of clarity and inspiration. To a quite exceptional degree the texts needed little editing for publication in book form. They retained the liveliness and verve which results from communicating well with a particular group. This helped a prime purpose of Father John's: 'to place the spiritual teaching in a real context of community living', to quote from a letter to me of 20 March 1980.

For Father John meditation was always done within the community of the church, and when it could sometimes be integrated with the liturgy as thanksgiving after communion, so much the better. He liked to be in personal touch with each member of a group if possible.

For me personally, publishing Father John Main's work was a kind of fulfilment. Soon after I had been received into the Church in 1944 I had met Dom Ralph Russell and been invited to stay at Downside Abbey. In 1946 I went to live near the abbey while recovering from serious illness. I began to practice what was then called 'mental prayer', in the tradition which the late Abbot Chapman of Downside, among others, had recommended. I had the opportunity to read widely. Thanks to the Abbot, Christopher Butler, I attended choir daily as a confrater, for solemn high mass in the morning and sung vespers in the evening. I followed this regime for six years while recovering and beginning to work as an editor, publisher and author.

A recurring thought was that the Church in Europe would need help from outside the European tradition. There were many movements in it, theological, liturgical, social, and they bore fruit in the Second Vatican Council. But for me Europe sometimes had about it an air of spiritual bankruptcy. In the Church I sensed an intellectualism and an individualism beyond which, when combined with a heavily authoritarian structure, it would be unable to grow without enrichment from the eastern traditions. I thought too that maybe the 'primitive' vitality and sense of community of Africa might be a necessary further help. In any case I became especially interested in the initiatives of Father Bede Griffiths in India (DLT published his *Christian Ashram* in 1966), and realised increasingly that the Indian, and indeed the Chinese traditions, might enable the contemplative traditions of the western Church to be strengthened.

These convictions remained and led me some time later to investigate transcendental meditation. It seemed to be a genuine attempt to provide an introduction, for Europeans and the western world generally, to the oriental traditions of meditation. It was a severely cut-down, yet very carefully packaged, and so far as it went, a viable version of the techniques. Twenty minutes, twice, or even only once a day, might be possible for western men and women. They might reasonably be asked to find some place, some time where they could be silent, learn to relax and be attentive, and learn at least the preliminaries to what the eastern tradition calls meditation and the western Christian tradition had usually called contemplation.

I decided to ask to be formally initiated into transcendental meditation. I read some of the writings of the Maharishi and his disciples, attended the obligatory 'learning classes' and was then passed to the person who would instruct me. I found it admirable that even for the West, the process of personal transmission was considered crucial. I discovered two things. First, as I had expected, the techniques worked. At a purely physical level it was possible to reduce the level of breathing and heartbeat. It is a very simple matter and plain common sense. If you remain still, you get quiet. Along with the quiet, you practice holding the attention on one word. If you are tired you are liable to send yourself to sleep while sitting upright.

The experience of actually doing just that was in a way a reassurance for me. Abbot Chapman had said that the preliminaries to mental prayer were just the same as those of going to sleep – one removes one's attention from discursive thought and images. But then instead of a drift into the unconsciousness of sleep, meditation took one on into a concentration of one's own awareness. Brain scans of meditators had shown the simultaneous presence of the evidence for both deep relaxation and sharp awareness. Now came a second discovery.

The founder and sponsors of TM spoke in a general way of the transcendental goal of meditation, presenting it as a path to 'God realisation'. They made use of a number of terms from Hinduism and Buddhism. This was liable to create a difficulty. The terms came from assumptions which are part and parcel of the background of most Indians. But for westerners they could have the effect of seeming to provide keys to an otherwise closed esoteric world – an arcane or gnostic world attractive perhaps to some people but impossibly daunting to others. Meditation itself is extremely simple and was properly presented as such, but along with it seemed to come a world of specialised thought and culture. And yet, without it, TM could, I thought, seem empty. The techniques certainly worked, but for what purpose? The answers given by the founder and sponsors included improvement of one's physical and psychological health, a general raising of standards in one's life, and finally if one needed to know more, the kind of 'God realisation' which the literature talked about.

Although I found this philosophical presentation of TM unnecessarily forbidding, yet in itself I found it acceptable, as far as it went. But it was at an intellectual level only. There was no symbolical expression of it (apart from the brief moment of one's being given one's own mantra), nor any specific moral reference. 'TM is not a religion' was an important and appropriate statement. There was no communal activity apart from occasional meditation in common and possible discussion of the concepts of 'God realisation' and of the propagation of the TM movement. However for me TM had been a positive thing. It had enabled me to re-possess the habit of 'mental prayer'. I had found a new validation of such prayer and with the sharpened technique a fresh encouragement for attempting to continue with a practice far from easy to follow in our European culture. It even prompted a renewed consideration of Christian prayer. For the Christian, I thought TM must have at its heart a divine presence. For the ordinary English agnostic it tended, I thought, to have an emptiness at its heart. It was simply a kind of relaxation, enablement to be oneself. What one understood by 'oneself' then became crucial.

The 'teacher' who initiated me into TM and gave me my mantra asked me several times whether I would be willing to help spread TM, to write and speak about it. I said I would as long as she and the authorities in the movement had no objection to my always saying that for me it was at heart closely related to the mental prayer which I had learnt earlier from Benedictine monks. This was not acceptable and eventually the idea was dropped. There was a settled policy of keeping all religious affiliation and practice at arm's length.

It will be seen that it was with considerable intellectual and spiritual excitement that, soon after my experience with TM, I began to read the teaching of Father John Main. Here was the full Christian contemplative tradition, in the wholly appropriate Benedictine setting, newly reinvigorated by the simple, deep and rich experience of the oriental religious tradition. It was almost too good to be true. The very thing I, doubtless in common with many others, had hoped might be possible had happened. The detail was of course quite unpredictable, but a creative moment had occurred. Two people had met providentially, a swami and a mightily gifted British civil servant. The seed of eastern meditation had been dropped into rich Anglo–Irish soil and had begun to grow and flower.

An especially attractive feature of Father John's teaching in my view was that he saw it as drawing on the writing of Cassian, and harking back to the earliest monastic practice. And Father John always presented it within the dynamic of the New Testament, quotations from which come regularly and easily into his texts, as though written specially for them. Then again the teaching seemed to mesh effortlessly with the revival of interest in the English mystics. Finally it was entirely contemporary and brought a fresh coherence to the widely-spread movement for spiritual renewal and interest in meditation, bringing it fully into the marketplace. About, for instance, Abishiktananda, Bede Griffiths and Thomas Merton, there was always something of the exotic. Merton's reaching out to the Buddhists was a moment of special importance. But it could not be for everyone, any more than the oriental philosophies of TM could reach many people. But with Father John Main we seemed to return to a universal and gospel simplicity, while being led on a path which was profoundly demanding, just like the New Testament virtues.

After Father John's death the Montreal Priory inaugurated an annual John Main Seminar. In 1987 Father Laurence Freeman invited me to give it and I had the pleasure of living with the brothers and sisters for nine days, some of them in the small rural foundation in Vermont, USA, and the rest in

Montreal where I conducted the seminar for four days on 'The Inclusive Church'. It is a topic which I also sometimes call 'The Wider Church' or 'The Open Church'. It was a high point for me. Three times a day to share in the singing of the office in the chapel, sometimes also taking part in the Eucharist, and then to take part in thirty minutes of meditation, was a great inspiration and revelation. I was able subsequently to visit and speak more briefly to, and meditate with three groups in Canada and USA, linked to the Priory. And since then I visit the London Christian Meditation Centre regularly.

The last time I saw Father John Main was in the publishing offices of Darton, Longman and Todd, when we discussed the publication of future books of his. He had come from a visit to the Prime Minister of Eire, Garret FitzGerald, who was an old friend from his past. Transformed now in his appearance into the bearded spiritual master that he clearly was, what struck one was the man himself. The commanding smile came a little less often, but one was aware of a man concerned with everyday reality, with all its sometimes awfulness and triviality, someone for whom the serious could also be comic. He was happy to stand beside the person who wished to relax and be 'more oneself'.

GERARD P. WEBER

I met John when I was living in Washington DC, and he was at St Anselm's. An old friend of mine had two boys attending the school and she raved about the wonderful Benedictine who taught there. Somehow or other she managed to bring us together and from then on we often met for supper. During these meals he never talked about meditation or the spiritual life. They were, though, very pleasant get-togethers. I learned that he had been on his way to Australia when he was sidetracked to become headmaster at St Anselm's. My impression of John Main was that he was a rare person, the perfect gentleman.

The first time I came to know about his Christian meditation groups was when he started the meditation group in

England. I was in London, called him up, and he invited me to Ealing Abbey. He was excited about the house he was renovating. He said that he had hoped to have a good number of people praying there after one year, but he already had many people coming each week before the house was six months old. As I look back the strongest impression I have is that he never pushed his ideas nor his prayer tradition on anyone. Each person could choose or reject meditation.

When he moved to Canada I visited him in the first house on Vendome Avenue. Again he told us in general about his plan for a house of prayer, but not much more. I also visited him at the present house on Pine Avenue in Montreal. He told me about how that house was given to the community after he had turned it down because the owners were not going to give him all the land. They finally did give the land and even offered to do necessary repairs. He also told about the butler or one of the retainers who stayed on and contributed to fixing up the house when money was short. I had the impression that John really never worried much about money. Either he was confident in his ability to raise it or trusted in God completely.

I lived at a California retreat house in 1981 and asked the sisters to get him to give a retreat. After the retreat he and I took a few days of vacation driving in southern California. At this time I discovered what a fascinating past he had. He told me about his intelligence work during the Second World War. One day we went into a restaurant and were given a table in a spot where he could not see the door. After a few minutes if he asked if I would mind if we left. I said that I would not mind at all, but I asked him why. He told me that during the war in France or Belgium a car in which he was riding had been buried by a bomb and that it had taken some time to dig him out. Since then he had claustrophobia in certain circumstances.

It was on this trip that he first talked to me about meditation, but even then he did not say much. He said that I would be more at peace and not so harassed if I spent thirty minutes in the morning and thirty minutes at night meditating. He explained how simple it was and let it go at that. I told him that the kind of meditation that he recommended was not my cup of tea; he accepted that, merely suggesting that I try it sometime. However, when we stopped at motels I would find that he had risen long before I had, said his office and meditated.

On this trip he also talked about his plans for publishing and distributing cassette tapes. Since I worked with a small publishing and distributing company I had all kinds of ideas and plans that I thought would be beneficial to him. He listened carefully but did not commit himself. Nothing, as far as I know, came of the advice I gave, but I had the impression that he listened carefully even when he did not agree with what I was offering.

John was a man I wished I could have seen more often. I felt free when we travelled to talk to him about what was going on in my life. He listened, said little and at most recommended prayer. He did live a simple life and I think of him frequently as I continue to dash madly around.

AGNES MURPHY

When asked to make a contribution to this book my first thought was that such an effort on my part would be so anecdotal as to appear trivial. However, the last eleven years of my life have been a jigsaw made up of apparently trivial events slotted into place, and maybe even the smallest pieces help to provide a complete picture.

As a small child I was obsessed with the idea of God being everywhere. I was really unhappy that nobody could tell me whether God was in the table-top. It did not seem sufficient that he was above it and below it and it was a great frustration that everyone I asked seemed perfectly happy about the situation and did not question it.

Eventually as an adult I saw a review of a translation of *The Phenomenon of Man* by the Jesuit priest Teilhard de Chardin. This was in one of the Sunday newspapers and was headed 'Consciousness in Stones'. Here was an answer to all my childhood and adolescent queries; God in matter. A great light indeed and a great sense of joy and contentment which lasted for many years.

Time went by and again a need for another dimension which seemed to be missing; again a period of searching and querying for what I knew instinctively was a vital piece of the jigsaw. Somewhere there must be an almost 'cosmic element' which united and made one of all that is, but in which everything in time and space could play an obvious, individual part.

Where would I find it? Time was passing quickly and life was short.

I retired, my husband died and the last of my family married. I decided to turn my back on the queries and questions and become a 'free spirit'; swimming, painting, travelling and generally enjoying a carefree existence.

And then I happened upon John Main's tapes; the early ones made at Ealing. Father Paul Geraghty lent them to me. I was impressed and wanted to know more. Soon I had an irresistible urge to go to Montreal and see this Father John for myself. I had intended travelling anyway and the USA had been on my itinerary. Such a deviation would be no more than a hiccup and would not interfere with my plans. Paul was spending six months in Montreal so I arranged a visit to join him for a few days at the first house in Vendome. This was in July 1978, six months after Father John and Father Laurence had first gone to Canada.

I arrived in a heat-wave, hot, weary and wondering why I had bothered; but as I walked into the house I knew that this was It. A feeling of wonder and oneness, a complete answer to a lifetime of queries. Meeting Father John is another whole story in itself; suffice it to say that it engendered a great feeling of acceptance and homecoming.

I have made three trips to Montreal: in 1978 during the first summer in Vendome; after the move to the new house; and after Father John's death. The first, as I have said, was the last stage for me in a questioning and querying life. The second, as Father John explained in reply to my asking about various changes, was that stage when the infancy of Vendome became the adulthood of the Priory.

On the third and last visit I expected to find a great absence but was once again overwhelmed by a wonderful feeling, not of loss but of fulfilment, wholeness and oneness.

And now to the next few years interspersed with serious discussions and even differences of opinion which I enjoyed during my visits and now value so much. The trivial anecdotal happenings also stay clearly in my mind.

I suppose the one that springs to mind immediately was going through the car wash with Father John. This was a new experience, much longer than the British counterpart; noisier and full of enormous, vibrant brushes scrubbing and polishing. We laughed together about my naïvety and then out of the blue I asked him if he had ever been afraid. He seemed so completely fearless following such a vision. I had asked this on a previous occasion and had felt unsatisfied with his answer. He turned and looked at me and smiled. At that moment in his life I knew he had no fear, he had completely Let Go. Such maturity of spirit I had not come across before.

It was interesting to read on page 183 of his biography, *In the Stillness Dancing*, that he had earlier in his life admitted to two fears: 'He was terrified of many things – like dying and flying.' I relived this too, when I heard Father Laurence say that just before his death, when asked how he felt, Father John had replied, 'Abandoned', meaning to God and not by God. The answer to that question too was in his eyes. He had reached a spiritual maturity and wholeness in which words were irrelevant.

Upon our return to Liverpool in 1979 after my first visit and Paul's completion of his six months stay, we started meditating together on a regular weekly basis in the hope that others might join us. After a period of almost three years we were still just two. Paul then decided to become a Benedictine monk and joined the order in Montreal. In the following year I paid my second visit to Montreal. After talking to Father John it was decided that I would sell the house in Liverpool and take part in the setting up of a group in Oxford. This appeared logical since, after Paul's departure, as far as I knew I was the lone meditator in Liverpool. No one else seemed to be interested.

So much for logicality. The house went on the market in July 1981 but by the September it was taken off again. In that time ten people had come to meditate and a meditation group was started.

Before the following Christmas we contacted John Cotling's group in Manchester and they joined us in Liverpool for a wonderful evening. We knew that Father John was giving a talk in London and also in Dublin in June 1982. I had the temerity to write and ask him if he would break his journey and come and talk with our group of ten. Characteristically he wrote back immediately saying that he would be delighted to do so. This talk occurred just six months before his death.

The opportunity seemed too valuable to confine to the ten of us. We decided to acquire the use of a room at Christ's College, Liverpool which would hold fifty people. This was on the basis that with our Manchester friends we numbered twenty. If we each brought a friend and spread ourselves a bit we could fill that size room sufficiently to present a reasonable gathering. Unbeknown to me John Cotling had also written to Father John with the same request.

The night before the proposed talk the college informed us that with much regret they were unable to let us have the room for fifty but we would be very welcome to their large lecture theatre seating two hundred and fifty. Horror and panic; but impossible to make alternative arrangements.

Father John arrived and we, all twenty of us, had a wonderful meal with him. Towards the end of the meal he refused to be hurried, and at his request the hour's rest which had been scheduled for him became fifteen minutes.

Then came the evening. We entered the college by the 'Main Gate', a fact which he did not miss; nor did Laurence at a later date, the words being actually carved above the gate itself. Then, wonder of wonders – the doors were opened and people came – and came – and came. The lecture theatre was packed to capacity, two hundred and fifty people seated and standing room only. It was a superb evening. Looking back I am amazed at his courage. The condition which eventually brought on his death was well advanced by this time although none of us knew that. He must have been so tired. He had travelled and talked the previous evening in Manchester. On this day he had talked all afternoon to individuals in the group, and with hardly any rest carried a meeting, talking and answering questions in this overcrowded hall.

Yet enthusiasm and life just radiated from Father John, his humour and patience inexhaustible. No one could have foreseen the events of the following December.

We had intended having the evening on video but had not done so, saying to each other, 'We certainly will do so next time.' But there was not to be a next time. This was a wonderful, once in a lifetime, privileged event. Father John wrote to me afterwards terming it 'a night of great blessing'.

As a consequence our group grew and divided and others were started and are ongoing in Merseyside. For a few years we had the use of a centre in Kirkby near Liverpool, called Maryvale. Here for a period we had some wonderful weekends. Some were days of quiet and others provided an interchange of ideas and planning between the groups from Manchester, Preston and Merseyside. We were able to provide guest speakers. Father Laurence came on a few occasions, as did Father Benedict from Ealing. All of this was the outcome of Father John's original and only visit to Liverpool, and who knows where the ripples from these visits extended.

So to finalise – how have Father John and his teaching influenced my life?

The answer must be, in every possible way. I now have a clearer vision of the oneness which I have always sought and a new, full and real life so different to that which I had planned.

How privileged we all were who knew and talked to him. For me he produced the largest and most important piece of the jigsaw of my life, for which I will always be grateful.

CONNIE MOORE

For, behold, I create new heavens and a new earth . . .
The wolf and the lamb shall feed together . . . in all my
holy mountain. (Isaiah 65:17, 25)

As I leave midday office and meditation at the Benedictine

Priory on the last day of the year, I am surging with joy. Meditation, in this body, has done its work once more. In this community grounded in otherness, the wolf and the lamb in me, the wolf and the lamb in our members, are at peace. We know love, inside and out. We also know there are thousands around this wonderful world experiencing a similar joy in following this path of meditation. We have, indeed, reason for our rejoicing! And reason for rejoicing in John Main.

However I never 'knew' Father John in the real sense of that term. I attended meditation at the monastery prior to 1982, and frequently I would think of trying to have an appreciative word with our teacher after I had been struck yet again by his telling of the Truth. There were always many wishing to speak to him, however, and I always felt my thought of speaking to him was not really necessary. After the memorial service for him in 1983, someone on hearing this said, 'But don't you now regret that you never met him?' I replied, 'No, it didn't seem necessary to actually meet him; I felt so connected to him without this, and I still feel this.'

I mentioned this last summer to a meditator in Oxford who said she knew exactly what I meant. I think, therefore, that there are many like me who feel they 'knew' Father John at a rare, deep level that did not require an exchange of words.

He gave us this great grace, this 'skilful means', as the Buddhists would say, for co-creation of 'new heavens' in a 'new earth'. We are inheritors, co-creating 'the holy mountain'. We need not have met Father John to feel we 'knew' him.

PAUL LAFONTAINE

My first real memory of Father John Main, which left a great impression on me, took place on a sunny, clear afternoon in the summer of 1978. A few nights prior to this meeting, on 1 July, I had attended my first session on the Monday night groups in meditation instruction. However on this afternoon I had telephoned Father John from my office at the Sun Life Insurance Company to ask if I could drop by after work to talk at greater length about his teaching on meditation as well as to enquire about any reading material that might be available. He greeted me at the door and we brought out chairs to sit at the end of the long porch attached to the front of that very unique residence (the old Decarie farmhouse, located on Vendome Avenue, just north of Cote-St-Antoine in Montreal). The community had been living in this house since December 1977. After a few moments I noticed a young man come out of the front door. Father John introduced him to me as Brother Laurence Freeman. He was off for a swim at the local pool.

The occasion of being received as a guest in the Benedictine tradition of graciousness left a vivid and inerasable impression on me. It was as if Father John had nothing more important to do that day than to receive me as an honoured guest, in a relaxed manner but with fullest attention. After about an hour I rose to leave. I had a rehearsal for an opera (Menotti's *The Medium*) which I was involved in in the town of Mount Royal. Despite the fact that I was a lifelong Montrealer, I recall Father John's detailed, clear and direct instructions on how to get to my destination on the city buses.

Father John always spoke with great mastery; direct, simple and effective. The three words which I feel best describe the nature of his talks are: power, conviction and authority. But in his homilies at the masses he celebrated I was impressed with all of these above qualities as well as humility: a humility so natural yet so remarkable that I did not recognise it, at first, for what it was. I often felt that in his homilies he was talking only for my own personal benefit and speaking directly to me. He often spoke with great affection of his parents during the talks. One could tell that he had come from a very loving and very strong family background.

Father John would not mince words on the subject of vocations to the priesthood. Perhaps because of his own work as a counsellor for priests he felt that the purest motives could only suffice for the priestly vocation. One did not wonder if one had a religious vocation. One knew, as he himself had known in his own personal life, that a person simply had to become a monk in spite of all obstacles. And that was all there was to it. The existence of any uncertainty in the mind of the person considering the religious life meant, for him, that without a doubt that person had no vocation. They were better off getting on with their life in another manner.

No matter how small or how big a job I did for the community, Father John always had a way of getting around to thanking me, making me feel special for having done something good.

He had a rare sense of humour. One morning after meditation we took a walk together through the grounds of the Villa Maria Convent. Exiting on the boulevard he pointed out a rather luxurious and large apartment building. He then proceeded to tell me with dead seriousness that it was one of the best kept secrets in Montreal that that particular building, in spite of its prestigious appearance, had large dwellings available for an incredibly low rent; I believe he said less than $100 a month. Throughout this scene he kept not only the tone of his voice serious but the whole context of the conversation serious as well. But if you looked in his eyes you might see the faint glimmer of a smile or a glint. I think he was always curious to see how gullible people were.

Father John also had a wonderful gift for mimicking in speech. He would often indulge in his passion for mimicry during the recreation period after supper. On many an occasion his interpretations were so hilarious that I would laugh till my stomach hurt. As a performer, he was a 'natural'.

From my first meeting with Father John, when I told him of my interest in music, we shared a love and knowledge of music. Father John had a great knowledge and appreciation of music. He was a very musical man; and I use the term 'musical' as a musician would use it, to mean one who has a deep feeling for music in their heart, evident in their approach to execution or listening. He had a good ear, and an even, pleasing tone in singing. Hearing him sing the long and demanding 'Exultet', which he did entirely in Latin at the Easter vigil service in 1979, was for me a musical event of the first importance. He had sung in choral societies in England and once told me that he had participated in the first performance of the Vaughan Williams Mass in G minor. When I pointed out to him that the event had taken place in 1925, a year before his birth, he conceded that it may not have been the World Première.

On another occasion Father John told me that when he entered the monastery (early 1960s) he felt supremely glad to give up everything material around him, with one sole exception: his stereo system and his record collection. He then found out to his great surprise that the monastery had an even better stereo system and larger record collection than the one he had left behind.

He disliked Vivaldi's *Four Seasons* and Beethoven's Sixth Symphony (*Pastoral*) because they were over-exposed. He loved opera: not the more dense, intellectual ones of the German school like Wagner and Richard Strauss, but the bel canto operas of Bellini, Donizetti and Rossini. When it came to Verdi, he had a preference for his early works. He loved operatic tenors, especially Bjoerling, Crooks, Tagliavini, Di Stefano, Wunderlich, Pavarotti and, of course, McCormack.

Except for Vivaldi's *Four Seasons*, he loved baroque music above the music of other epochs. He told me that as he got older he found romantic music to be more and more irritating and distracting. He would point out how there existed in baroque music a relationship between the musical pulsings and the duration of a breath in a human when relaxing. Thus the music corresponded to a rhythmic harmony in humans, making it suitable for relaxation, attentive appreciation and even digestion. He felt that the Haydn symphonies and the Mozart concertos were ideal vehicles for music at meal-times, given their structures and length, about twenty-five minutes.

In the spring of 1979 I invited Father John and Father Laurence Freeman to a matinee performance of a French opera, Gounod's *Romeo et Juliette*, being put on by a Belgian troup. When the curtain rose on Act 5, the tomb scene, I turned and to my surprise saw the faithful monks heading towards the exit. They would be back at Vendome for vespers.

Father John had an artist's appreciation of the meaning of human events in life, particularly those very ordinary and close at hand. He also had a poet's command of language to draw together the threads of the ordinary life with the more elusive threads of the spiritual path. He once described to me a journey of a day's duration that he had just previously undertaken. It had involved a car trip, leaving in the morning, arriving at a northern residence in the mountains at noon, and returning to the city as the sun set. But as he described the day to me he imbued it with a wonderful spiritual shading, which gave it a rare and beautiful meaning. He was very passionate about the meaning of life, and taught me the importance of making the connection between the events of my own life together with their deeper spiritual meaning.

I have always felt very privileged to have been able to share some of those early experiences connected with the establishment of the Benedictine foundation in Montreal. Meeting Father John and becoming his friend and disciple was a great gift to me. I have often had the strong feeling since, that God called me through him specially to the work of meditation; to go beyond my helplessness into the infinite expansion of spirit. Although he was a man of humour, grand gestures and refined tastes, by far my most pervading memory of Father John Main is of a man who was very gentle, a man who saw deep into my heart.

TERESA MORTON

Douglas, like all the Main men, stood well over six feet and was well-built. He had a pleasant, cherubic face, with calm blue, highly intelligent eyes, which contemplated you seriously through glasses. Since the Main family derived their early education in England, they all spoke with an educated English accent. This made the transition to a thick Kerry brogue, during one of their frequent relapses into a family joke, quite a culture shock.

Douglas was a man of intellect and wide interests which were reflected in his conversation, always punctuated with humour and keen observation of others. He was never pompous, never without humour. It has to be appreciated that the whole family had, and has, a delightful sense of the ridiculous. The Main family were mimics, highly talented, and very keen observers of their fellow-men. Douglas had all these characteristics. They were sensitive people, capable of serious thought and discussion, but whose conversation was invariably punctuated with humour, very often quite crazy and explosively funny. Pessimism did not enter into their lives and one was always struck by the family solidarity and the effervescent sense of gaiety which was so therapeutic.

During his student days at Trinity College, Dublin, my impressions of Douglas were that of a serious student. Sometimes his seriousness seemed almost aloofness, never getting over-involved with people, though always charming, polite, urbane, yet at the same time aloof. He was an extremely private person, never verbose, and became even less so over the years. His attitude to life seemed to be one of quiet, intense single-mindedness, giving a completely confident impression to friends and acquaintances. The family gatherings in later years, when John Main was in Ealing, Washington and Montreal, were more infrequent. During John Main's visits back to Ireland as a monk, he conveyed a feeling of quiet calm and the simple Christian message of love.

10

The Teacher and the Teaching

The wonderful beauty of prayer is that the opening of our heart is as natural as the opening of a flower. To let a flower open and bloom it is only necessary to let it be; so if we simply are, if we become and remain still and silent, our heart cannot but be open, the spirit cannot but pour through into our whole being. It is for this that we have been created. (John Main)

The contributors to this chapter closely examine John Main the teacher and just as importantly his teaching on Christian meditation. They acknowledge the importance of John Main in synthesising the teaching on prayer of John Cassian and the Desert Fathers, the Cloud of Unknowing, together with his own Malaysian meditation experience, and leaving a formal teaching on the prayer of silence and stillness for those of us in the twentieth century.

John Main's teaching on how to pray was as simple as this: sit down, sit still with the back held straight, lightly close your eyes and say your mantra. The mantra is simply a sacred word or phrase which is repeated continually, faithfully, for the full half hour of meditation each morning and each evening. He urged people in every walk of life to set aside two separate periods of twenty to thirty minutes each day; he suggested finding a comfortable sitting position. 'In meditation,' he said:

You should choose a word that has been hallowed over the centuries by our Christian tradition. One of these is the word 'maranatha' . . . which means, 'Come Lord, Come Lord Jesus'. It is the word that St Paul uses to end his first letter to the Corinthians. This prayer word is recited silently, interiorly in four equally stressed syllables

176

MA-RA-NA-THA. The speed is fairly slow, fairly rhythmical. Some people say the word in conjunction with their calm and regular breathing.

John Main pointed out that the person meditating should repeat the mantra for the entire meditation period:

> We begin by saying the mantra in the mind . . . then the mantra begins to sound not so much in our head but rather in our heart . . . then it seems to become rooted in the very depths of our being. In this way a person moves from thinking about God to simply being with God . . . What's more, meditation becomes a process of self-discovery, integrating one's body, mind and spirit . . .
>
> If we are patient and faithful meditation will bring us into deeper and deeper realms of silence. It is in this silence that we are led into the mystery of the eternal silence of God. That is the invitation of Christian prayer; to lose ourselves and to be absorbed in God. Each of us is summoned to the heights of Christian prayer, to the fullness of life. What we need, however, is the humility to tread the way very faithfully over a period of years so that the prayer of Christ may indeed be the grounding experience of our life.

The contributors cast light on John Main's crowning achievement – the handing on of a twentieth-century understanding of the contemplative tradition of prayer in which God is sought in the silence and stillness of one's own heart. Most of them concentrate on an analysis of John Main's teaching on meditation rather than personal reflections on John Main himself.

BEDE GRIFFITHS

I have said that in my experience John Main is the best spiritual guide in the Church today. What is my justification for saying this? It must be understood in the context of the world in which we are now living, where for a great many people the Christian faith has lost its meaning. John Main was acutely aware that there was 'something missing' in the life of the ordinary Christian and that the Church was not answering the need of the majority of people, especially the young of our time. John Main saw the root of the problem to be that people had lost touch with reality, with the reality of themselves and of the world around them. The problem was how to recover this lost dimension, how to recover the sense of an ultimate meaning in life, how to escape from the illusion created both by religion and by the world and to realise the truth of the self and the world.

Put in these terms one is immediately led to reflect on the oriental view of this world as an illusion and to see why it is that so many people today are turning to the East to find the answer to the problems of their life. I think that it is of profound significance that John Main was led to his discovery of the deeper meaning of life by his contact with a Hindu swami, years before he became a Benedictine monk. It was in Malaya that as a young man he met Swami Satyananda and learnt from him the way of the 'mantra', which became for him the means of access to the reality behind the illusion of this world. It seems that contemporary Christianity has to learn this lesson from the religions of the East. A recovery of the depths of the Christian faith can only come when we encounter the profound experience of the inner self, which is India's great gift to the world.

John Main learned through his use of the mantra, taught him by the Hindu swami, to discover the deeper dimension of his being. But the decisive moment came when he discovered in Cassian, the Christian monk of the fifth century, the same method of the mantra and realised that it was part of the authentic Christian tradition. This tradition derived from the Fathers of the Desert and had been continued through the Middle Ages, especially in the tradition of the Jesus Prayer in the eastern Church, but also in the beautiful medieval English treatise known as the Cloud of Unknowing. It was this tradition, which had been lost in subsequent ages, which John Main saw as his vocation to renew in the Church. But he saw this as by no means confined to the monastic order to which he belonged. It was his genius to discern that it was a way of prayer which was available to every Christian, and to people of no particular religious faith as well.

John Main came therefore with a definite method, the way of the mantra, the repetition of a 'sacred word', which he found to be the ideal method for awakening this deeper sense of reality. People today need a method of prayer. So far the western Church has virtually had only one method, that of the Exercises of St Ignatius and similar forms of discursive meditation. This method is good, as far as it goes, but it does not take you beyond discursive thought and the exercise of the will. It can, of course, lead to a profound conversion and to a deep renewal of Christian life, but this depends on the exercise of the discursive reason. For an oriental, on the other hand, meditation begins with the cessation of all discursive thought. As the yoga sutras of Patanjali say, 'Yoga is the cessation of the movements of the mind.' It is the function of the mantra precisely to bring about this cessation of the movements of the mind and to awaken the awareness of the inner self beyond word and thought. It is to silence the mind so that one is brought into direct awareness of the inner self.

What exactly does it mean, to be aware of one's inner self, the self beyond the rational mind? It means to go beyond the ego. The ego, or in Indian terms the ahamkara – the I-maker – is the basis of the 'personality', the external self, which works through the senses and the reason. As long as one remains on the level of sense and reason, one remains under the control of the ego. It is only when we go beyond sense and reason that we become aware of our deeper self, that we contact the reality, the real person in us, and at the same time begin to make contact with the reality of the world. As long as we live on the surface of life we see only the surface of the world around us. Only when we enter into our own centre do we find the centre of the world around us. To go beyond the ego is therefore to find ourselves not in isolation but in communion. It is to realise our intimate relationship with everyone and everything.

John Main had discovered that through the practice of the mantra one can go beyond the ego, the limited human self, and open oneself to others not on the surface but in depth. One begins to discover what he called the 'communion of

179

love'. It is one of the most striking aspects of his method of meditation that it leads to communion, it builds up community, it takes one out of oneself and relates one to the real world. He became acutely aware that people in the Church as well as outside it were living on the surface of life and therefore were becoming isolated and alienated from themselves and from the world. He found in his method of meditation the answer to this human need. I emphasise this matter of method, because I find that most people today need a method. There is a search for God, for truth, for reality going on all over the world, but people need a concrete method to bring them into contact with this reality. In that lies the attraction of Hinduism and Buddhism to multitudes of people in our time, because they teach definite and well-tried methods of meditation. John Main found a method of Christian meditation, which would lead to the same experience of the inner self, the centre of truth and reality.

But it was his special genius to discover how this method of meditation could lead to the experience of the deepest reality of Christian faith. In the Foreword to *Moment of Christ*, which was the last book he wrote, he described it in this way: to enter into the deep centre of one's being is to enter the consciousness of Christ, or as he puts it, the prayer of Christ. 'I can describe it only,' he says, 'as the stream of love which flows constantly between Jesus and the Father. This stream of love is the Holy Spirit.' This takes us to the very heart of John Main's understanding of meditation. It is a participation in the inner life of the Holy Trinity. To enter into the depth of one's own spirit is to encounter the 'love of God, which is poured into our hearts through the Holy Spirit which is given us'. In every human being there is a point of the spirit which is open to the Holy Spirit, and when we enter into deep meditation we experience this outpouring of the Holy Spirit in our hearts, which, as John Main says, is the 'stream of love that flows between Jesus and the Father', or the 'cosmic river of love'. It is this love – the inner life of the Trinity – which sustains the whole creation and flows into every human heart. To meditate is to become aware of this river of love, the spring of water, of which Jesus speaks in St John's gospel, welling up to eternal life.

180

There are other methods of meditation than that of the mantra, and there are other ways of experiencing the love of God than that of meditation, but I do not know of any better method of meditation leading to the experience of the love of God in Christ than that of John Main. He has recovered for Christians a way of prayer which links us with the earliest tradition of the Church and at the same time relates us to the most authentic tradition of prayer and meditation in other religions.

HENRY HILL

I would like to consider John Main's prayer of the mantra and its relationship to the further realisation of our unity in Christ. I want to suggest that the theology of our unity points to an ever richer interiority and communion. It is only out of this that we can speak in the power of the Spirit, who also provides the courage to follow where we are led. After one of his conversations with Dom Jean Leclercq, Dom John Main was led to write:

> We can be blinded to the immediacy of the situation by the impressive institutional structures that still remain around us. But structures without a living Spirit issuing from committed and open hearts too easily become pre-occupied with self-survival rather than with transcendence of self. We must learn from our experience in prayer that our call is to follow Christ in death to self and in resurrection to new, unlimited life in him, with him, and through him . . . We talked together daily of the other great challenge facing the Church in the West, that of her own unity as a concerted witness to the one Lord that the different Christian communions serve. The many theological and ecumenical conferences have brought us a long way towards this essential unity, but they can only serve a limited need. What, by their nature, they cannot do is lead us beyond the multiplicity of concepts into the simplicity of God and the unity of his transcendent love found in and through Jesus.

Again, it seemed to us as we spoke that the challenge facing the larger community is the same facing each of us. Indeed, we belong to a community because we are each a microcosm of it. And our challenge as we return daily to meditate is to lay down everything we are, our very selves, before the infinite mystery of God. The ideas and experience that bring us to this moment of prayer [the sacrifice of mind and heart] are renounced together with all psychological self-reflection and theological speculation. The great achievements in ecumenical theological understanding over the past twenty years are only fulfilled by leading us beyond the fascination of differences to the prayer room, from words to the Word spoken to all people in silence. Christian unity is already upon us, demanding that we recognise and respond to the moments of grace that are opportunities for real prayer in real communion.[1]

In one of my earliest meetings with Father John Main I asked whether he would become my spiritual father. After a period of thought, he replied, 'No, but I shall encourage you to say your mantra.' This he did indeed! To sit beside him in the prayer room, first at the Priory at Avenue Vendome and later at Pine Avenue, was one of his greatest contributions to a pilgrim Anglican bishop who first came to visit the small Benedictine community in the summer of 1979. Father John's most intimate counsel, as far as I was concerned, was that deep within every one of us is a meeting place, the cave of the heart, the palace of God's kingdom within us, which belongs only to God and to our real selves. The prayer of the mantra, prayed continually for at least two half-hour periods, each morning and evening, will focus attention upon the kingdom within, leading ultimately to limitless expansion of mind and heart. I refer to this simplest of teachings at the very beginning, because that same living Presence is to be sought and found in every one of God's children. It will sooner or later lead those who meditate to the realisation that they are united in the one Spirit and that all are invited 'to enter into the communion within God himself. This communion we enter through the Spirit who breathes freely in the open spaces of our hearts.'[2]

The experience reveals that there is tremendous power in the prayer of the heart, which of course is the teaching of the Fathers of the Egyptian desert, among whom was John Cassian, the teacher in prayer of the early sons and daughters of St Benedict. It reveals as well that this prayer is indescribably enriching, because 'it takes us right out of ourselves, beyond ourselves into union with all, with the All, with God. Unity, union, communion is the threefold growth of a Christian.'[3]

As our approach to this takes us beyond the ideas and imagery given in our various religious traditions, we often find that we can pray – I am speaking here of meditation – with men and women of other religious outlooks. Many of us may have had the experience of this sort. Dom John Main summed it up beautifully in one of his conversations with Dom Bede Griffiths, when he wrote:

> What our encounter with India and the East is teaching us is something we should never have forgotten – that the essential Christian experience is beyond the capacity of any cultural or intellectual form to express. This is the 'glorious liberty of the children of God': no restriction. It became so clear to us talking with Father Bede that this experience has to be restored to the heart of the Church if she is to face creatively the challenges before her: the challenge of finding unity in the Spirit with all Christian communions, the challenge of embracing the non-Christian religions with the universal love of Christ present in the hearts of all people and which she has a special duty to release and identify. To meet these challenges each one of us must be personally rooted in the experience of God that Jesus personally knows and shares with us all through his Spirit.[4]

Characteristically he added that 'our fidelity to meditation is our preparation, our patient and ever-deepening openness to the mystery that fills and contains us. We have to be still. We have to be silent. We have to stand reverently in the cave of our hearts, the palace of God's kingdom within us.'

Again many of us have observed people of no religious background at all who have come to the Benedictine Priory, who, when encouraged to pray the mantra ('maranatha'), have in the course of time, especially when fed by the word of scripture, the office and the Eucharist, grown into the deepest of love and commitment to the Lord Christ. The power of the prayer is especially compelling, because it means 'Come, Lord Jesus' (see Rev. 22:21; 1 Cor. 16:23).

Dom John Main saw very clearly that a Christ-centred spirituality built upon the apostolic teaching and the spirituality of the undivided Church are necessary in an age in which a powerful surge of the human spirit is seeking blindly to regain contact with the divine, and diffusing a mood of dissatisfaction with things as they are. He would have agreed with Christopher Bryant who wrote that one of the signs of the gathering revolution is the ennui, the boredom, present in the world today, which Teilhard de Chardin called public enemy number one.[5] What is needed, Dom John has said, are men and women who speak with the authority which comes from first-hand experience, because the New Testament was written not for cloistered contemplatives but for the butchers, bakers and tradespeople of the Roman Empire.

We are daunted perhaps by the very idea of continual prayer, or union with God through this form of prayer; but as John Main so often pointed out, we have but to begin and at every stage we are met by God who takes us further. 'The Spirit too comes to help us in our weakness' (Rom. 8:26). The pilgrimage on which we are called is the realisation of our Theosis, our glorification, as we 'come to share in the very being of God' (2 Peter 1:3, 4). When St Paul warns Christians to keep away from fornication, he adds: 'Your body, you know, is the temple of the Holy Spirit, who is in you since you received him from God. You are not your own property. You have been bought and paid for. That is why you should use your body for the glory of God' (1 Cor. 6:19, 20).

Our prayer, as Dom John used to say, is nothing other than our entry into the prayer-consciousness of Jesus, into that stream of love which flows eternally between the Father and the Son, which we call the Holy Spirit.

Notes

1 Main, John, *Letters from the Heart: Christian monasticism and the renewal of community* (1982).
2 ibid.
3 Main, John, *Moment of Christ: the path of meditation* (1984).
4 *Letters from the Heart.*
5 Bryant, Christopher, *Jung and the Christian Way* (London, DLT, 1983).

FRANÇOIS C. GÉRARD

As long as our faith is seen as comprising a movement from man to God, we can only remain self-centred, earthbound. But in apprehending it as the movement from God to man we discover ourselves caught up in that movement, in its own depths, self-transcending and returning to the Father through the Son. Another name for this movement is love. (John Main)[1]

If one were to characterise the spiritual pilgrimage and teaching of Dom John Main in one sentence or phrase, one could suggest that he rediscovered and lived the simplicity of the gospel.

Simplicity immersed him into the depths of the divine Presence, the mystery of the relationship of the Father and the Son in the love of the Holy Spirit; and silence gave Father John the consciousness of being drawn into that reciprocated love of God through identification in his inner self with the risen Lord, the eternal Christ. Jesus prayed for his disciples, 'Father, I have made you known to them and will continue to make you known in order that the love you have for me may be in them and that I myself may be in them' (John 17:26). To be in God as Christ is in God and to be in Christ as God is in Christ through the indwelling Spirit is both the mystery of our being and the grace of our calling. To experience that union is to be 'caught up' in that returning movement. Father John constantly talks about being caught up in the mystery which is 'wholly beyond us and yet contains us'. Meditation must lead us to complete silence, to the necessary

185

void of the desert precisely because the mystery, the 'paradox', can never be fathomed: meditation is the silent consciousness of the mystery of God within us. Reflecting on the Eucharist, the mystery of Koinonia, Father John writes:

> Religious experience leads us to encounter and to enter the basic paradox, that the mystery is both within us and beyond us. And so it is that our response to mystery is always one of awe – an awe that leads us into silence, a stillness and a sensitivity that is always deepening. It is ever-deepening precisely because the paradox itself deepens and can never be fathomed or resolved. It can only be known and accepted as the *tremendum et fascinosum* that it is; infinitely great and creating in our hearts an infinite longing that only its greatness can fulfil.[2]

Father John therefore embarks on his spiritual journey towards the mystery of God in its reality. Not by the futile effort of analysing and measuring what eternally eludes the grasp of our understanding, but by allowing himself to be totally immersed in the life of the Holy Trinity lived at the centre of his constantly expanding self. It is in this sense that John Main was a Trinitarian Christian; in other words he was free of a created self that he had fully integrated and joyfully renounced to allow the self of God, the love relationship of the Holy Trinity, to rise at the centre of his consciousness. There he perfectly knew who he was. He was attentively present to himself because he was totally surrendered to the other, 'in whom', as St Paul says, 'we live, move and have our being' (Acts 17:28).

Paul's teaching here sounds an imperative note. We must find our true self in a relationship of creature to Creator. We are by nature dependent. To be, the Christian must lose his finite self into the infinite self of God. Meditation gives us the freedom to accept our reality, to discover our liberated self. In meditation, says Father John:

> You just sit still and it is in that stillness that you gain the wisdom to see that you can only be yourself, you can only become yourself who is the person you are created to be, if you are willing to lose yourself. The truth that you can

discover from your own experience is this – that any one of us can only find ourselves in the other. No amount of self-analysis or self-examination will ever reveal to you who you are. But if you can take the focus of attention off yourself and project it forward then you will discover the other and in discovering the other, you will discover yourself. The other is the Ground of All Being, the other we call God, Supreme Wisdom, Supreme Being, Supreme Love. The name is not important. Indeed, in meditation and in the silence of it, the complete silence of it, we go beyond all words, to the Reality.[3]

A theologian, yielding to the temptation of systematising Father John's thought and risking a betrayal of it, would say that the Benedictine monk reformulated an old Christian ontology of the Augustinian tradition and an understanding of the human self, rooted in the mystical experience of the Holy Trinity. He would further suggest that the twentieth-century mystic was able to pursue his own spiritual journey while faithfully maintaining an orthodox course. It is interesting, however, to notice that the subtitle of Dom John's *Moment of Christ*, published posthumously, reads 'The path of meditation'. This simple phrase reminds us that the sole intention of the teacher is not to articulate for our sake a brilliant exposé on spiritual theology, but to walk with us in our search for absolute simplicity.

Father John was a teacher and a leader in the tradition of St Benedict, whom he characterised as a heroic leader. As one would expect, Benedict's inspiration was a determining influence in the shaping of his monastic profile:

Now St Benedict, I think, is in the heroic mould because his vision of the Christian life which he is writing about in his Rule is a vision of life that is constantly expanding. The horizons are always opening and for him the reason for this is that the Christian life is an openness to the wonder and mystery of God. The mystery and wonder that is itself infinite.[4]

Father John was not a father in the negative, paternalistic connotation of the word; he does not assume the responsibility of our pilgrimage for us. He knew by spiritual instinct and experience that one has the inescapable responsibility of walking alone in the power of God's Spirit, because each one of us is absolutely unique in that 'I-thou' relationship. This is, perhaps, another reason why he never felt obliged to give a formal, rigid theological framework to his spiritual teaching and leadership.

And yet the theology is there, very solid, profound, biblical and orthodox. The time has come, it seems, to delineate that theology without casting it in a mould whatever the difficulty of the exercise. We must keep in mind that progressing spirituality is not the result of an intellectual inquiry but the fruit of a long experience.

The works of John Main, published or recorded on cassettes, already constitute a substantial collection of teachings given to groups of meditators, religious and lay people, and represent a period of more than seven years of teaching. One book, however, occupies a central place, if not chronologically, certainly in importance. I am referring to *Word into Silence*, published in 1980. A reader of John Main feels compelled, as it were, to return again and again to the central message of *Word into Silence*, for there we find the essence of his profound teaching. Like the leitmotiv of a great symphony, the theme occurs repeatedly in the orchestration of many books, pamphlets and articles; but once one has carefully studied *Word into Silence* it is always clearly identifiable. It is primarily from that source of information that I should like to examine the main focus of what we could rightly call the spiritual theology of John Main, or his understanding of deep prayer.

As I said earlier, Father John invites us to explore the nature of our human self as a precondition to wholeness, serenity and harmony. He is convinced that unless we have a healthy relationship with our own self we cannot expect our religious pilgrimage to lead us anywhere. To be relevant and effective, an authentic relationship with God must be rooted in self-discovery, self-reconciliation and true self-love. The knowledge of our self, or better, the searching for our true self, is already a sign of divine grace and the right place to begin. As we move from the periphery to the centre, from

188

complexity to simplicity, from immersion to solitude, from word into silence, from action to agape, from death to life, we leave behind an ego which has been conditioned by a world of illusions and fed on stimuli. We have the 'cloud of forgetting' behind us and in a leap of faith we enter the 'cloud of unknowing' where our true self is the very self of God, the ground of all being, the source of all love, the consummation of our human destiny. In other words, the spiritual pilgrimage starts for Father John at this level of consciousness where conversion, metanoia, calls us beyond illusion into reality. It is truly the beginning of the gospel. Referring once to the great Christian personalities of our day, Father John remarked that all of them testify to that crucial experience of conversion to the kingdom 'that is at hand':

> They testify to the central tenet of Christian conviction and experience: That once the inner commitment – or, in the old language, conversion – has taken place we are *en route* for the fulfilment, not the eradication, of our personhood: That once we have lost our life, we do, indeed, find it. They remind us, too, of Jesus' assurance that he came to bring us 'life and life in all its fullness'. It is this that our contemporaries are longing to believe and to experience for themselves.[5]

For Father John, it is through conversion or the integration of our self into the self of God that we discover reality and experience what he calls self-transcendence rather than self-fulfilment; the latter is a cultivation of the ego, the former an openness to the absolute of an unconditional love. The search for self and the need of love are one and the same pursuit: 'The first step in personhood then is to allow ourselves to be loved. It was to facilitate this that the Holy Spirit was sent into the human heart, to touch it, to awaken it, to draw man's mind into its redemptive light.'[6]

More often than not man's failure to engage or progress on a spiritual journey is symptomatic of his failure to find himself. John Main looks at the spiritual exercise, the spiritual search, and the discipline of meditation, primarily as a simple process by which man prepares himself to be at peace with his inner reality, with his inner self. Only then can he appreciate and experience that deeper peace which is the peace of God within himself. It is true, however, that the end of our journey is to find God; such a goal will never be reached unless our daily work is sustained by a clear understanding of who and what we are as human beings and as creatures in our relationship to the Creator.

The first step on our spiritual journey, therefore, is to decide that we want to be loved and be at peace with ourselves. This occurs through the transformation of our consciousness as we gradually discover the beauty of our being. The discipline of meditation allows us to do precisely that: to become aware of our self and to see ultimately that the reality of our life does not exist apart from the reality of God. It is God alone who gives existence, meaning and purpose to what we are meant to be and truly are already in God's now. Father John, therefore, is challenging us to pay attention to our self and, at the centre of our self, to the mystery of the divine Presence. We must concentrate on our self, attend to the self, with the expectation that at the highest level of our consciousness the reality of our life will be fully merged into the reality of the absolute self, the reality of the life of God.

John Main refers to that moment in our spiritual growth as the experience of 'smashing the mirror'. When we are united to God 'as our supreme power source', we break through the screen of the 'hyper-self-consciousness of egoism'. For him the original sin is self-consciousness or divided consciousness; the result of sin is a mirror, as it were, between God and our self, reflecting only our image and not the image of God, which is meant in creation to be our true identity. The mirror, says Father John, must be smashed and meditation is the tool of restoration:

> The purpose of meditation is to smash that mirror so that we no longer look at reflections of things and consequently see everything backwards, including yourself. The essence of meditation is taking the kingdom of heaven by storm. The mirror must be smashed. And Jesus is talking about overcoming self-consciousness, the mirroring self, when he says no one can be a follower of his unless he leaves self behind.[7]

190

Reflecting upon the plight of modern man generally, and of the many Christians who find most theological discussions irrelevant but who do not know how to experience the power of the gospel of Christ personally, John Main invites them to draw on the unknown forces at work in their inner self:

People today are looking for the perennial fruits of the Spirit: peace, liberty, joy, the freedom and power to love. Above all, they are seeking the courage and strength to be. Modern man knows with a peculiar insight that for this discovery he must come to terms with himself at his simplest, his most elemental. This is the preliminary work we must all undertake. As St Augustine put it, 'Man must first be restored to himself, make of himself a stepping-stone and rise from self to God.[8]

As we embark on our spiritual pilgrimage the basic discipline is to pay attention, to become alert, to awaken to the splendour of our createdness. Created by God, we have a divine origin which is the source of our being, the energy of our doing, the restoration of our self, the object of our joy. But we cannot become aware of the beauty of creation around us and within us, without sharing the very glory of our Creator, a glory we discover at the centre of our consciousness as we begin to live our life out of the power of the divine Master. This, of course, is the secret and fruit of deep prayer, the prayer of silent union:

The experience of prayer is the experience of coming into full union with the energy that created the universe. What Christianity has to proclaim to the world is that that energy is love and it is the wellspring out of which all creation flows. It is the wellspring that gives each one of us the creative power to be the person we are called to be – a person rooted and founded in love.[9]

According to John Main our spiritual experience should not be limited to our intellectual assent to a series of theological propositions. Spiritual reality has an existential dimension which gives it authority; thus the importance of experiencing our own creation. In order to do so we must try not to *think* of God as Creator, but be with him and know him as the ground of our being. The experience is utterly simple. To be with God does not demand words, thoughts or discourse, but the silent consciousness of a Presence. John Main assumes the role of prophet to our generation, reminding us that our spiritual pilgrimage has no future unless we have the courage to become more and more silent. Our inner journey will not even start unless we are willing to accept the discipline of silence. Silence will teach us that we cannot apprehend God by thinking about him, because God is a mystery infinitely beyond us and yet intimately within us. Silence frees us from the limitations of language and thought which would tend to reduce God to the anthropomorphic understanding we have of him. Silence allows us to be in communion with God as he is, not with a man-made intellectual image of the divine. Silence creates space, as it were; it opens us to the encompassing mystery of the Divine instead of restricting us to the concrete materiality of an idol.

Father John, distinguishing two kinds of silence – the 'silence of oblivion' and the 'silence of full consciousness' – attributes to the latter the power of revelation. Silence reveals the Word free of human intellectualisation:

> What brings us out of the dead silence to the living, conscious silence which leads us into the knowledge of our union with God is the Word, made living and active by the power of the Spirit praying in our heart. The personal experience of this power is the goal of the Christian pilgrimage of prayer. As we follow the pilgrimage we grow into an even deeper simplicity, an even sharper and more immediate encounter. We come less and less to seek to 'experience the experience' but rather to allow the experience to be, to emerge, to expand and to transform us.[10]

Whether we are aware or not of the mystical phenomenon we are permeated by the Light of the Holy Spirit. Speaking on 'Learning to be Silent' in the first chapter of *Word into Silence*, John Main remarks:

> In meditation our stillness (silence) is not a state of mere passivity but a state of full openness, full wakefulness to the wonder of our own being, full openness to the wonder

of God, the author and the sustainer of our being, and a full awareness that we are at one with God.[11]

Meditation is a revelation process and its teaching is that we are called to that fullness of life for which Paul prayed on behalf of the Ephesians:

And I pray that you being rooted and established in love may have power together with all the saints to grasp how wide and long and high and deep is the love of Christ, and to know this love that surpasses knowledge that you may be filled to the measure of all the fullness of God. (Eph. 3:18–19)

John Main invites us to enter into meditation precisely to seek that fullness of life of the risen Christ which the Holy Spirit, whose temples we are, presents as a sacrifice of praise to the glory of the Father. This is how he speaks of our human condition seen from a faith perspective:

We have been allowed to enter the sphere of God's grace where we now stand. Jesus has blazed the trail for us and through his own experience has incorporated us in his present state which is his glorious communion with the Father in his risen life, a life that now pervades the whole of creation. We stand in the sphere of God's grace because we are where he is and he is where we are. We are in him and his spirit is in us.[12]

Father John therefore does not hesitate to say that we are infinitely holy, and indeed called to be truly divinised. Sharing in a theme dear to eastern Orthodox mysticism he knew that 'our vocation is to look upon and contemplate the Godhead and thus to be ourselves divinised'.[13]

In meditation we realise the depth of our intimate union with God our Father through Christ and the Holy Spirit. There at the centre of our self we are purified in mind and heart, totally open to the transforming work of the love of God for us. We quietly and peacefully reflect in all our human relationships the light and warmth of that love. To be perfectly at one with God in the tranquillity of one's heart is the fruit of meditation offered by Father John not only to his Benedictine brothers and sisters but to all Christians:

> The tradition that we follow as Benedictine monks calls us both to understand and to experience our prayer as silent communion within our own heart. Union brings us to communion, that is to a oneness with God and to a oneness with all. It is a communion that is indescribably enriching, because it takes us right out of ourselves into union with all, with the All, with God. Unity, union, communion is the threefold growth of a Christian.[14]

Father John remarks that at that stage of our spiritual growth we have found our way back to our created centre where wholeness and harmony are achieved. We are fully conscious of our self and truly alive to others and to God. The continuing discipline of meditation helps us to remain within our self and thus in the presence of God our Creator. There we no longer think about the past or the future but are totally immersed into the absolute simplicity of the eternal now of God. Freedom is the fruit and sign of our new grasp on reality. Living in the now of God demands that we leave behind all false images of our self, all empty dreams of what we might have been, all illusion created by the stimuli of our peripheral ego.

We are conscious of going through a new birth. First we are unmade by experiencing the dying of Christ within our self. We become aware of being remade and then of being constantly created, and of springing from the creative love of the Father, returning to his eternal embrace. Father John can speak of a *radical* change:

> We are literally made anew in the fact of entering into the ever deeper centres of being, and of knowing ever more fully the harmony of all our qualities and energies in that ultimate centre of our being which is the centre and source of all being, the centre of the Trinitarian love.[15]

We are transformed at the centre by the contemplation of God, the absolute self in whose reality we *are*. Hence we should no longer speak of self-centredness, which is still 'earthbound', and in bondage to our ego, but of other-centredness. Mary is the greatest example of other-centredness in the spirituality of John Main, because she is fundamentally an example of poverty:

It [poverty] is the inevitable corollary of turning the search-light of consciousness off ourselves and on to the Other – the Lord dwelling within us. This is the essential Christian insight which Mary exemplifies in Luke's Gospel: a poverty of spirit that is itself a purity of heart because it is unsullied by the intrusion of the egotistic will seeking for experience, desiring holiness, objectifying the Spirit or creating God in its own image. Mary reveals the basic simplicity of the Christian response in a poverty of spirit that consists in turning wholly to God, wholly away from self.[16]

'Turning wholly to God' for Mary and all Christians is to share in the very life of the risen Christ, whose Spirit fills our inmost being. 'Other-centredness' is indeed 'Christ-centredness'. We call Father John a Trinitarian mystic precisely because of that Christo-centric relationship. The risen Christ, whose human consciousness – that is, the human consciousness of Jesus of Nazareth – we share at the level of our common createdness, is our way, the *only* way for Father John, to a higher level of consciousness where we are transformed, divinised. The Christ indwelling our human reality is the risen Lord who has returned to the Father and has re-entered the historical scene at Pentecost in the unity of the Trinity. The promise has been fulfilled; Christ continues to be with us, within us in his communion with the Father in the light, love and power of the Spirit. The Spirit within us constantly prays 'Abba, Father'. Christ is known at a deep level of immanence, of intimacy in our inner being as the God within and it is the mystery of this divine Presence which we call the kingdom.

Living that reality, that Presence, that mystery, is for Father John the vocation of all Christians. In baptism it is sacramentally signified as we die with Jesus to the egocentric dimension of our existence, and are born anew in the Spirit to the transcendent dimension of his resurrection and his eternal communion of love with the Father. Because it is a mystery – so totally unfathomable to our human understanding that we cannot even desire to possess it – it has to be received as a gift in an attitude of absolute poverty, in the experience of the void. With complete single-mindedness the void demands complete self-denial with courage, commitment and openness.

Once again Father John is squarely in line with the great theological traditions of the East and the West. God, in whose being we are, in whose love we find meaning for our lives and the hope of our ultimate destiny, is absolutely unknowable, unfathomable. The complete trust of faith is to experience in love what we cannot possibly understand with our intellect alone, nor embrace solely with our will. And we need courage to renounce our anthropomorphic language, our discursive knowledge, our need to conceptualise and rationalise in order to take a leap of faith. At the time we accept the discipline of meditation we realise that we have worshipped a God made in our own image, reflecting our thoughts, ideas, aspirations and emotions, providing the spiritual security necessary to carry us on our own pilgrimage. We are called now to experience naked faith, to feed on the creative silence of the desert with no assurance that enlightenment and the vitalisation we are seeking will ever unfold before us. The experience of the void, however, is so important that we should immerse ourselves into it, and to that end accept the 'grand poverty of the mantra', what John Cassian called the 'Catholic way of prayer': the quiet, faithful, loving repetition of a single verse or single word, seeking in complete stillness and concentration the awareness of the Spirit who dwells in our hearts.

At the beginning at least, meditating with the one word, without images, concepts and the curiosity of the analytical mind is a form of protest implying a firm choice. We turn away from what Father John, paraphrasing Cassian, calls the great danger of all Christian prayer when: 'We cut God down to our own size in order to talk to him, making a convenient shoulder for us to cry on and a convenient idol enabling us to avoid the abyss of his otherness.'[17]

Our choice is precisely the desire to be open to that 'abyss of his otherness'. Words, thoughts and imagination which attempt to define reality and impose limitations on the scope of our inner vision do just the opposite. By restricting our mind to the poverty of the mantra, the repetition of a single word, we increase our capacity for wonder, ever deepening our awareness of the harmony of God's creation and our receptivity to the work of the love of God in the depth of our being. This is why the mantra is rooted primarily in the heart, not in the mind, even though it is repeated mentally at first. Ultimately the mantra has the power in its simplicity to integrate mind and heart. Father John describes it thus:

> The mantra provides this integrating power. It is like a harmonic that we sound in the depths of our spirit, bringing us to an ever deepening sense of our own wholeness and central harmony. It leads us to the source of this harmony, to our centre, rather as a radar bleep leads an aircraft home through thick fog. It also rearranges us, in the sense that it brings all our powers and faculties in line with each other just as a magnet drawn over iron filings pulls them into their proper force fields.[18]

We must, however, leave everything in order to rest in the infinity of God himself, offering our very self to him as a living sacrifice in the hope of our transfiguration, into the simplicity of a child in the power of the Spirit:

> Meditation simplifies us, simplifies us to the point where we can receive the fullness of truth and the fullness of love. It prepares us and enables us to listen with childlike attention to the Spirit of Jesus within us. As we persevere in meditation, we enter more deeply into relationship with this Spirit, with God who is love dwelling in our heart, enlightening us and vitalising us.[19]

At that time the mantra becomes the 'murmur of the prayer of Jesus'[20] arising in our hearts and prayer itself achieves its purpose – consciousness of our intimate union with God our Father, through Christ, in the Spirit. We dwell in ourselves as we dwell in God; we are truly found. The role of the mantra is to open the door to the secret chamber of our heart where we live in the light, constantly listening to the eternal Word, ever ready to follow his guidance and taste the fruit of his love. Should we stop saying the mantra in that blessed moment? No, because by the constant repetition of the mantra we keep our mind and heart attentive to God beyond the intuitive glimpse of the divine Presence. It is important that the mantra be rooted in our self but the time may come, says Father John, when at a deeper level of freedom from the peripheral self we begin to listen to the mantra rather than saying it. At the deepest level we enter the 'cloud of unknowing' in which there is absolute silence, and where we can no longer hear the mantra. The following excerpt is of a great beauty:

> Meditation is in essence the art of concentration precisely because, the higher we toil up the mountainside, the fainter becomes the mantra sounding in the valley below us, and so the more attentively and seriously we have to listen to it. There then comes the day when we enter that 'cloud of unknowing' in which there is silence, absolute silence, and we can no longer hear the mantra.[21]

Of course we cannot force the pace of our meditation nor should we be self-conscious about its quality. The essential attitude we must cultivate is utter simplicity as we continue to say our mantra. We should not be concerned about anything else; certainly not about the lack of a feeling of enlightenment. In fact most of the time we experience nothing at all. But that is not important, the light is already within us. We are baptised sons and daughters of the day; we are children of light and those who are light can walk in the dark.

But remaining faithful to our mantra takes courage. It also takes commitment. The images used by Father John are all taken from the gospel and he speaks of purity of heart as the undivided consecration of the whole being to the seeking of the kingdom. He does not hesitate to point out the necessity of being single-minded, thoroughly pure, purity having here an ontological connotation, not a moral sense.

Such purity, however, demands openness to the other, to Jesus, whose presence we discover on the faces of our brothers and sisters, our spouse, our children, our neighbours. Our relationship to God deepens as we exercise greater sensitivity to each of his children. Indeed prayer and charity are so interrelated that they feed spiritually on each other, as it were. Father John was himself nurtured in a rich Benedictine tradition; he has this to say about it:

> St Benedict then sees these two realities in our life – prayer and community – as essentially one. Concentration upon our neighbour in love and on God in our prayer is for St Benedict the same sharing in the perpetual prayer of Christ which is his loving relationship with his Father. The monastery itself is based on and rooted in precisely this loving relationship.[22]

In several talks to new oblates Father John often addressed the theme of gentleness. One reads him as one reads the Rule of St Benedict. Both paraphrase the beatitudes. Both teach the gospel. The perfection we are called to is love, the way is self-denial, the strength is the support of the community and the gift of forgiveness constantly offered and renewed; the signs are peace and joy. In everything there is harmony, balance, moderation – the wisdom of Benedict.

One could not close one's reflection on the inner journey without thinking of its last step on earth. John Main invites us to see death as a long process from birth into life as we continue to die to the egoism of our peripheral self. From conversion to transfiguration, from metanoia to communion, we are challenged to live in the now. This is an impossible goal unless we accept that the death Jesus speaks about – 'If a man wishes to find his life he must first lose it' (John 12:25) – folds up our past and future into the eternal now of God:

> That means that we must learn to die to the ego and the state of egoism that is for ever slipping out of the reality of the present by regretting its past or day-dreaming about the future. To meditate is to learn to be present, to be still. *Be still and know that I am God.*[23]

As we fall away from our ego we discover and experience the love of God whose being is the very source of the person we are becoming eternally; we also discover that death is an essential phase of that process: 'It is the final and most demanding of the lessons that life teaches. It is the meaning of the absolute finality of the cross, the single-pointedness of the cross that yet opens up into the infinite universe of the resurrection.'[24]

The call to Eternal Life demands the radical conversion of death, the readiness to lose one's self to live in the other, the generosity of love. Death, in the experience of Father John, is an event in life, an event of love; and our physical death is a passage of consecration and fulfilment. Death is a vision of life:

> Within this vision we see life as preparation for death and we see death as preparation for life. If we are to meet our own death with hope it must be a hope built not on theory or on belief alone but on experience. We must know from experience that *death is an event in life*, an essential part of any life which is a perpetually expanding and self-transcending mystery. It seems to me that only the experience of the continuous death of the ego can lead us into this hope, lead us into an ever-deepening contact with the power of life itself. Only our own death to self-centredness can really persuade us of Death as the connecting link in the chain of perpetual expansion, the way to fullness of life.[25]

Father John invites us to look both at humanity and at ourselves individually with great compassion. There are questions we must ask but cannot answer; questions about self, life, meaning, transcendence, destiny. They confront us with the divine mystery that Jesus, the eternal Christ, incarnate, is the way, the truth, and life. In him we contemplate the mystery in which we find our origin and destiny.

Father John is a 'Christian pilgrim' who is determined to travel light. Often we spend a lifetime carrying unnecessary spiritual luggage. He calls us to the grand poverty of the mantra. He knows that a satisfactory answer to our questions will never be found in well-articulated dogmatic formulas – however necessary they may be – but in the reality of an encounter. A Christian pilgrim, Father John is also an evangelical in the true sense of the word. In the Spirit he lives the very life of the risen Lord. His business is conversion, which is the calling of the monk, the teacher, the physician, the nurse, the mother, and so on. He is willing to trust God, to be guided by the Spirit to the edge, to the limit of his inquiry and beyond in a complete abandonment to love with the single-minded dedication, the radical commitment of an Irish monk of the Celtic tradition.

He is not a theologian – but he is theologically consistent. A teacher concerned with the existential reality of our pilgrimage, Father John keeps himself within a true historical perspective, in a catholic tradition; he knows his roots. More than 1500 years of Benedictine monasticism are for him a rich heritage and yet he must charter his course. Perhaps he has learned from his Hindu master that, although our impression is that the same river always flows within its banks, it is always a new stream of water. Life for him was an adventure.

The teaching of Father John indeed, like the gospel which is its source of inspiration, is at the same time very old and very new; this is the reason why we take it so seriously.

Notes

1 Main, John, *Word into Silence* (1980).
2 Main, John, *The Christian Mysteries: prayer and sacrament* (1979).
3 Main, John, *Moment of Christ* (1984).
4 Main, John, *Community of Love* (1984).
5 Main, John, *The Hunger for Prayer* (1983).
6 *Word into Silence*.
7 *Moment of Christ*.
8 *The Hunger for Prayer*.
9 *Moment of Christ*.
10 Main, John, *The Other-Centredness of Mary* (1983).
11 *Word into Silence*.
12 ibid.
13 ibid.
14 *Moment of Christ*.
15 ibid.
16 *The Other-Centredness of Mary*.
17 Main, John, *Christian Meditation: The Gethsemani Talks* (1977).
18 *Word into Silence*.
19 ibid.
20 *Christian Meditation*.
21 *Word into Silence*.
22 Main, John, *The Monastic Adventure* (1983).

23 Main, John, *Death: the inner journey* (1983).
24 ibid.
25 ibid.

ROBERT KIELY

In E. M. Forster's *A Passage to India* a group of travellers are taken on an expedition to some sacred caves. While the visitors are deep inside one of them the torches go out, there is a moment of panic, and the articulated sounds of human voices are lost in meaningless echoes. Later, while reflecting on the event, one of the characters finds her religious faith as well as her nerves badly shaken. Suddenly the lovely cadences of the Authorised Version seemed to lose their power. In the face of darkness and emptiness and an inhuman echo, the familiar comforts vanished as swiftly as the light. What had once been her mainstay seemed only 'poor little talkative Christianity'.

To refer to the religion of the Word in such a way seems not simply a dismissal of litanies and long sermons, but a trivialisation of the great words of covenant, wisdom, prophecy and the good news. Yet more is involved than travel fatigue and a temper tantrum. Forster seems to be suggesting, through his character's reaction, that Christianity in some of its manifestations has leaned too heavily on the forms and surfaces of language. When confronted by the challenge of emptiness and darkness it is found to be inadequate. Forster remained a sceptic unfriendly to Christianity throughout his life. But the question he raises should not really be alarming to Christians, and indeed might be taken, though Forster would be surprised to hear it, as a necessary preamble to a life of meditation.

In *Moment of Christ: the path of meditation* Father John Main returns again and again to the necessity of putting words and images, even the most beautiful ones, aside. He speaks of 'descending into silence', as though it too is a cave of emptiness and darkness. But, unlike Forster and his anguished character, Father John enters in hope and does not rush blindly back, out into the dazzle. He gives himself to the moment in the faith that what he cannot fill with his own words and thoughts will be full none the less. And so one of his abiding lessons is about patience and a somewhat unexpected companion, courage. Though we tend to associate courage with action, with striking out in new directions, it is one of Father John's insights to associate it with another kind of test. Perhaps it has always, in some sense, been a trial to 'wait on the Lord', but surely it is hardest of all (and at first even frightening) for those of us brought up to associate our worth with sound and motion. The louder and faster the better!

Though conscious of the paradox involved in using language to recommend silence, Father John never doubted the power of the word. His briefest and simplest commentaries are models of clarity and of the capacity of language to convey conviction and authenticity of feeling as well as ideas. Even his sense of the limitations of the verbal is expressed emphatically and naturally: 'so, do not complicate your meditation. In my humble opinion, the less you read about meditation the better. The less you talk about meditation, the better. The real thing is to meditate.'

As is the case in most good writing, the reader hears a voice in these sentences, an experience and a person, not a mind adrift. Even if we were not reminded in the preface that the short chapters in *Moment of Christ* were originally talks given to groups learning about meditation, it would be almost impossible to read them without being conscious of a person speaking. Though Father John's life and work pointed beyond words, he was not an enemy of language. Very much to the contrary – and this is an essential motif in his teaching – the moments of silence that he believed to be so essential in every life create in one a reverence for all the most familiar aspects of existence, including language. To go beyond language in meditation is not to leave it for ever, but to return to it renewed.

Much of what we say and do in our lives is repeated hundreds or thousands of times over. In a world that appears to place a premium on originality, this is likely to be a depressing thought. Yet to the thirsty, water is never a bore. To a lover, the hundredth glimpse of the beloved's face is not ninety-nine times too many. The problem is not repetition but what we bring to the sentences and actions that recur over and over again in our lives. When Father John confronts this subject, he is not being excessively modest about his own powers of imagination, but, as usual, utterly unpretentious about what he is trying to do: 'In these talks we are always starting again. It is not that in each talk anything new is said, but our aim in each talk is to come, surely and gradually, nearer the centre of the mystery.'

The idea of 'always starting again' and, at the same time, repeating something very familiar, even ancient, is central to Father John's thinking, as it is to the gospels. The renewal of Christian meditation, and especially his tendency to see it in relation to practices within the great Asian traditions, runs the risk of being misunderstood, as it was by many who witnessed the rise and fall of various cults in North America and Europe in the sixties. The trouble with most of these groups was not that they were foreign, but that they were not spiritual; not that they were eastern, but that they were inauthentic.

'We need Christian people who realise that we have nothing whatever to fear from the Buddhist tradition or the Hindu tradition that is truly spiritual. We have only to learn to see one another in the light of Christ.' Father John's view is not one that stretches the Christian ideal beyond recognition, but rather one that returns us again and again to its heart. The descent into silence and the way of meditation, despite impressions to the contrary, are not characteristics peculiar to eastern religions. It is true that the sixties were a particularly talky time for Christianity in Europe and North America. Amidst all the discussions of Church reform and participatory liturgy, necessary as they were, the value of silent prayer often seemed to get lost in the verbal shuffle. By reminding us of Cassian and Benedict, Father John does more than recall isolated gems of wisdom; he reminds us of our own ancient and unbroken traditions of meditation.

Father John's writings are profoundly Christian. They are rooted in the word and spirit of Christ, the witness of the apostle Paul, and the experience of centuries of Christian life. There is not a single chapter in *Moment of Christ* that does not build around a quotation from scripture. The passages he selects are well known and yet there is a freshness about them in the contexts he gives them. They are not epigraphs for homilies, italicised lines that somehow stand apart from the commentary, but phrases woven into the fabric.

A characteristic and apparently favourite scriptural passage is John 8:31–32: 'If you dwell within the revelation I have brought, you are indeed my disciples; you shall know the truth, and the truth will set you free.' It is the invitation to 'dwell within' that Father John seemed peculiarly called to remind us of. His short talks on meditation all may be seen as variations on the effort to rephrase in terms comprehensible to people in the twentieth century the good news as a total environment. One of his favourite words is 'rooted', a good, simple, organic metaphor suggesting depth, connection, life and, perhaps most important of all, the capacity for growth.

With the inspiration of scripture and the clarity of his own intent, Father John wrote in *Moment of Christ* these short introductory talks about meditation. Because they form his last published work, indeed many were composed and delivered in the months and weeks preceding his death, they come to us as a unique legacy, a kind of distillation of his life's work. He often refers to meditation as 'work', acknowledging that it takes effort, time, and self-discipline, and that, at first, one does not always feel like doing it. He reveals his grounding in the Benedictine tradition by refusing to separate within himself the roles of Martha and Mary. To him, work and prayer are different manifestations of the same love. The Christian life requires both.

If silence returns us to words and the Word with renewed attention and regard, stillness returns us to the world of work and action with new energy and direction. Obviously Father John's own life, built around the rhythms of silence, stillness and the recitation of the office, was also a life filled with activity and accomplishment. His Christ was the Christ of the desert and the Christ of the multitudes, a man of quiet and a powerful voice.

A major problem, certainly not unique in our time, is how to follow Christ, an example so attractive but awesome. Various 'ways' and models of 'imitation' have been suggested

205

and tried, many with extraordinary success. The danger with imitation, however, as with a certain kind of reliance on verbal formulations, is that one can remain on the surface without meaning to. The attempt to go beyond is too difficult, too lonely a pursuit, and often too abstract and analytical.

Father John's emphasis on 'indwelling', 'rootedness', and 'entering in', suggests not so much a conscious imitation, although obviously that is not excluded, but a yielding in faith to the work of God in us. He does not advocate passivity or pious sloth, but a silent alertness that blocks out the distractions of ego and the random intrusions of the world. The titles of his talks call attention again and again to the same basic purposes: 'Leaving Distractions Behind', 'Infinite Expansion of Love', 'Silent Communion', 'Beyond Illusion', 'Rooted in the Centre', 'Beyond Technique', and 'The Life Source'.

As for words, we cannot rid ourselves of them, nor would we wish to. But there is a sacramental and mystical history of our faith that has always taught us that they cannot do everything. The gospel of John begins with the Word, but Revelation ends with 'Come, Lord Jesus' and silence. Those two poles of the Christian experience are present in a remarkable way in *Moment of Christ*. Unlike the distraught character in Forster's novel, John Main's religion is neither 'poor' nor 'little' nor 'talkative'. As a writer he was 'poor in spirit', modest; his pieces are short and his language simple. But his conviction seemed without bounds. He could say the most extraordinary things in a direct, almost matter-of-fact way. One final example might serve as a fitting summary of this book and of his life: 'Meditation invites us to enter the resonant harmony of God.'

Though there may yet be unpublished letters and other papers, the appearance in print of *The Heart of Creation*, short talks given in the late 1970s by John Main, brings home the realisation that the 'complete works' of this inspired teacher are not inexhaustible. Even if we look forward to the day when all will be available, it now looks as though the total page count will be modest: open letters and brief talks and homilies; a few hundred pages at most.

A first reaction – and a natural one – is sadness that this

teacher is gone and that he did not have time to tell us more. But a second and more powerful reaction is amazement at the fact that he was able to leave behind so much, given the relatively short span of his 'public' life and the pressures on his time and health. It is perfectly consistent with Main's teaching that the life which is rooted in the reality of God's grace is a life powerfully enabled to share that grace in whatever words and actions it adopts.

On even further reflection, it seems likely that if John Main had lived to a ripe old age he would have avoided the temptation to write a religious epic or volumes of theological tracts. The brief commentary, the short talk or letter, seem to have been his natural pedagogical vehicles. They appear now like parenthetical interruptions in the longer chapters of silent meditation, communal prayer, and active service that made up his life. Indeed it might well be said that these modest articulations gather their force and authority from the years of preparation and the daily hours of prayer and labour which produced them.

The economy of these short pieces is not only a matter of their form and length, but of their argument and theme. If readers already familiar with the work of John Main turn to these volumes with expectations of finding what advertisements call 'stunning new revelations', they will be disappointed. Of course, readers who are truly familiar with Main's work will already know that the revelations he writes about with modest simplicity and repetitious insistence are those of the gospels and epistles. What is always refreshing, engaging, and effective in John Main's writing is the clarity and directness with which he points to the central teachings of the Christian scriptures with regard to spirituality. It is one of his convictions – one that he demonstrates again and again – that these teachings, however accustomed we may be to them, *always* carry with them something new for anyone who really tries to hear them. He seemed to see his own task not in terms of embellishment or embroidery, but as a defamiliarisation of the familiar texts achieved by reflecting on them without rhetorical gimmickry or euphemistic apologetics.

All who knew John Main refer frequently to his wit and good humour and especially to his way with a story. It is all the more striking, then, and a sign of what must have been a deliberate choice, that these short talks call virtually no attention to the speaker and are almost totally without anecdote. In a particularly fine piece entitled 'Cosmic Poverty', he tells a story about not beginning his talks with funny stories, as people sometimes expected him to do. He recalls being given some friendly advice: 'Well, if you aren't going to tell any funny stories, at least warn them before you give the talk.' That is exactly what John Main proceeds to do: 'So this is really what this preamble is about.'

At the heart of the talk on 'Cosmic Poverty', as in all of the talks, is a bold invitation to let go of egotism and possessive desire, and to enter into the powerlessness of Christ in order to recover or discover with him a new kind of power whose signs are gentleness and compassion. 'The wonder of meditation is that this cosmic power which has driven back our own egotistical darkness, this power of triumphant love, is to be found in our own hearts.' It was John Main's peculiar talent and calling to focus attention unremittingly on the presence of God in the human person. Furthermore he was less interested in talking about this 'presence' than in convincing people of the necessity (and joy) of attending to it.

Since many religious exercises dwell more on the preparation for an encounter with God or its reflective aftermath, Main's emphasis can seem by contrast both deceptively simple and disturbingly difficult. The absence of apparatus marks his descriptions of meditation as the absence of digressive anecdote marks his talks. Throughout Main's writing and preaching there are numerous very brief instructions about the basics of meditation – reminders about the straight back, the closed eyes, the repetition of the mantra, the turning away from distraction. These short descriptions never vary and never become enmeshed in considerations of alternate postures, breathing rhythms, or special techniques of any kind. Once again, this can be disappointing to some people. Yet Main's refusal to become preoccupied with technique seems as deliberate and consistent as every other element in his spiritual economy. It was impossible for him, as for any Catholic who lived through the 1960s and 1970s, to be untouched by the extraordinary preoccupation with externals that marked the aftermath of the Second Vatican Council. Even if one applauded and welcomed liturgical reform, in its earliest stages it often had the effect of making people more rather than less conscious of the surface conditions of worship.

It is one of John Main's insights that no matter how intent on reform, human beings have a way of letting themselves be side-tracked (or even of creating side tracks) and thus deferring the only real point of worship, indeed of life, which is the encounter with God. No elaborate preparation or technique is needed in order to engage in that encounter. In a talk entitled 'The Process of Reduction', Main says of meditation:

> We give up thinking, we give up discursive, wandering thought. We renounce imagination, we even turn from our better insights. All this is a process of reduction. It is a process of limiting everything in our minds, for that supreme moment of concentration when we are available for one experience alone . . . the experience of Jesus.

If Main resists indulging in colourful preambles and the subtleties of technique, he also refuses to dwell at any length on the practical consequences of meditation. It is not uncommon for people to wonder about the physiological effects of meditation – the slower pulse rate, the lowered blood pressure, the strengthened immune system. Though these and other effects may be experienced by meditators, John Main never seems to have used them as a reason to meditate or even as a result to be looked for. Such concerns not only detract from the central point of Christian meditation, but they reopen a mind–body separation that meditation seeks to overcome.

But more important even than the physiological consequences of meditation in the minds of some are the behavioural and ethical effects. It seems logical to wonder whether meditation will make one 'a better person', a more charitable servant of the poor, a more patient member of a family or community, a more generous friend, a more concerned neighbour. In one sense John Main does willingly address these questions through his continual stress on love, forgiveness, compassion and gentleness. But even in regard to these, he draws back from dwelling on specifics. Perhaps, here again, his experience in the 1960s made him reluctant to identify virtue with any narrowly-defined formula for action. Whatever the reason, it seems to me that his purpose was to give the Spirit full reign and not presume to predict where precisely it will lead *and* to keep his own sights fixed on the mystery of meditation, the silent dwelling in Christ, rather than on preambles and aftermaths.

The pleasure in reading the talks is not in the surprises they provide. There are no surprises. For those already familiar with the teachings of John Main these pieces will be reminders of the steadiness of purpose, the fidelity to the gospels, the clarity of mind, and the simplicity of spirit of this man. For those not yet acquainted with Main's work, this collection will provide as good an introduction as any other. At first, as he himself says, meditation may look to outsiders like 'a process for making yourself into a cabbage'. Certainly his own life was testimony to the falseness of that fear. His words – unadorned, simple, and serious as they are – brim over with vitality and joy:

> In meditation, by learning to say your mantra, you learn to trust, you learn to be. Indeed the joy of meditation is that it is a celebration of being, a celebration of the sheer joy in receiving your life as gift, and doing what Blake called kissing 'the joy as it flies'.

This is the lyrical John Main, the choir monk in full chant. But as these short pieces each demonstrate, that singing voice is one and the same with the voice of the undemonstrative teacher who only wants to remind us, in as many ways as he can, to say the mantra.

MARIAN SCENA

John Main was a person who was important to me at a vital stage of my spiritual life. What drew me to him when I met him was that he understood the way God was leading me in prayer at that time and he affirmed me in that quiet form of prayer called Christian meditation. Another priest whom I respected had told me at a previous retreat that I was being misled by meditation and that I was not praying at all. This had upset me and kept me questioning myself. When I told John this, described my prayer and asked his opinion, he was pained that I had been so counselled previously and he encouraged me to continue on as I was doing. Needless to say I felt very grateful to him for his understanding of me and my prayer life. I could tell immediately that he understood where I was at and I appreciated that he cared enough to take time to explain it to me and also to encourage me. That helped me so much at that time. John Main was a spiritual guide, a spiritual leader, but he had the wisdom not to force his views on others. Instead he led by example with a fierce dedication and commitment to the 'path' as he saw it. I am grateful for his friendship and his counsel.

PATRICK MURRAY

Like the parable in the gospel it seemed John Main's role was to plant the seeds of prayer and the increase would come after his death. It seems he had to die in order for the teaching to come to life in the mysterious designs of providence. That mystery he used often to say was the deepest reality – meaning going beyond the senses. And transcendence to him was also that act of integration – the integrity of owning all of one's self and weaving it into a pattern of wholeness. Wholeness was his deepest insight. That wholeness meant a deep desire for truthfulness and entering into one's truthfulness in our daily lives.

He would often say if you wanted to look for any fruits of meditation not to look for them during the time of meditation, not to see how many bumps we had from hitting the ceiling or anything like that. If we had to look for results we had to look for changes in our lives. A person once complained that he had been meditating for six months with nothing happening and no changes in his life. The only positive thing he could see was that he was not screaming any more at motorists in front of him on the motorway going to work. Father John smiled because he realised that change was a greater experience than any mystical experience the man might have in a

lifetime. Father John's faith was so practical, beyond rationalisation, so peaceful and calm, rooted in his own being.

In listening to his talks on Monday and Tuesday evenings,
he was really saying the same thing the whole time, yet he
said it differently each time. He had this deep insight into
the mystery of Christ within us, Christ who is the truth, the
way and the life. He always stressed this awareness of our
inner selves, as St Paul put it, 'releasing the hidden splendour'. He urged us to release the hidden splendour within
ourselves and rejoice in the otherness of the other. He wanted
us to see and to believe in the splendour of others and to see
the splendour of creation. And the great word he used was
'harmony', or being at one, in harmony with anybody and
everything. He felt it was not so much what happened to us
in life, but how we lived life, our attitudes, to be, those be-
attitudes, those attitudes of being. He had a deep insight
into the paradoxes of the gospel, and he often quoted those
paradoxes of Jesus, 'If anyone wishes to be a follower of mine
he must leave self behind'. Discipleship for him never meant
any form of rigidity. It was that gentle attentiveness and
gentle attention to ourselves and others. He urged attentiveness, an awareness coming from our soul, from our inner
being. What had to be awakened was our attentiveness to the
mantra, that gentle attentiveness to saying the word and
leaving all else behind.

He never despised other forms of prayer. He always said
meditation was the only way that he knew and that he found
it in the living stream of tradition, of John Cassian's Tenth
Conference on Prayer. He also respected Meister Eckhart's
insights into prayer and the spiritual life. I personally feel
that John Main is one of the outstanding spiritual leaders of
this century, and that his contribution to Christianity and
spirituality will be more acclaimed over the years. One listens
to his tapes and reads his writings and we hear his message
deep within our souls.

He always saw the value of suffering. I remember something extraordinary he said to me once: 'We are often led to
meditation when our back is up against a wall.' I remember
going down the road afterwards reflecting on what he had
said, 'when our back is up against a wall'. In other words

suffering in one form or another can be the door that opens us up to meditation. That first beatitude was so deeply written in his soul. John Main heard it. He knew its meaning. 'How happy are those who are poor' and the way of poverty for him, and for all those who hear him, is the way of the mantra.

I would like to say something about my first experience of hearing Father John and his teaching, about prayer and the way of the mantra. What struck me even as I heard the tapes and before I met him was that sense of inner conviction in the tonality of his voice. Then when I met him and listened to him Monday and Tuesday evenings on Pine Avenue I could see clearly the gift that had been given to him and the insightfulness of the message of the gospel. He saw the paradoxes of Jesus' teaching and he saw the only way of leaving 'self' behind was through the way of the mantra. I often marvelled when he used to say how something so simple could be so absolute.

As he saw it poverty is the pearl of great price of the gospel. Father John did not see poverty as a rejection of anything but saw it more in the context of a reverence and a respect for everything because everything was a gift. And to cleanse the mind, to cleanse that false self, to bring it to poverty of spirit, he had discovered in the Christian tradition the use of a single word or a single prayer phrase. This demanded great faith.

Faith I would say is the second characteristic of his teaching on Christian meditation. In St Paul's famous expression, 'It is a journey that begins in faith and ends in faith.' John Main's teaching was so rooted in scripture, in depth and insightfulness, especially when he quoted from St Paul. He saw quite clearly that those epistles were written for the ordinary folk of Corinth, Ephesus, and, as he said, addressed to the ordinary Roman butchers and bakers and candlestick-makers at the time. This faith in God – faith that was trans-conceptual – was based again on the secret of Christ within us. Jesus said, 'The kingdom of God is within you.' So he taught that it was faith in the kingdom within, not faith in a concept or faith in an idea or faith in an image.

Father John always stressed the simplicity of the teaching: he never deviated from that teaching. He never watered down the simplicity of simply saying the word from the beginning to the end of the meditation and to say it gently. In his view the mantra is not a weapon. It is not like smashing a hammer on an anvil. It is simply a gentle returning to it. He saw that even distractions are a gift because the distractions provide us with a choice. When we become aware that we have departed from the mantra, we either gently return to the mantra or we allow ourselves to follow our thoughts, our imagination. He also used to say there was neither a good meditation or a bad meditation. It was basically a deepening of our poverty, the mantra being said in the present moment. He had great insight into time, the present moment, the unending now, while at the same time listening to the syllables of the mantra, sounding them, savouring them in the now and letting go.

He always used to say that meditation is a discipline and he distinguished between discipline and rigidity. He also always distinguished between discipline and technique. He used to say that a technique was always success-orientated. There was some kind of pay-off with a teaching, we were going to get something from it. Whereas a discipline is something we did irrespective of how we felt or irrespective of our moods. There again there was that great act of leaving all. He used to say the greatest thing we can leave is our consciousness and we offer our total consciousness before the infinity, the mystery, the ultimate incomprehensibility of God. That was the teaching and those of us who heard it and hear it are privileged to return to it day after day. We see the depth of spirituality, the depth of dying to the old self that is involved in his teaching.

For me, following John Main's teaching and saying the mantra day after day, getting in those half hours, is the greatest act of unconditional love that I know of, that I am capable of as a human being. We keep nothing back. I literally offer everything before that mystery – the supreme mystery of love, that God is love. There are no words really to describe what the whole thing means. The fastest way to learn is through the practice, the daily setting aside, the act of sitting down and sitting still. That in itself is the greatest act of faith and abandonment. Also important is closing one's eyes gently.

The ramifications of John Main's teaching seem to be endless. My wish is that whatever time I have left on this side of Jordan, as one would say, I will be faithful to the daily recitation of the mantra. I suppose I have not yet sat down to begin or got up from meditation but that there was a sense of joy. Of course joy does not preclude suffering. There is a deep joy which is much more lasting than transient pleasure. Father John always stressed meditation was not to experience an experience, it was more of entering into the experience itself. Whether I feel good or bad, hot or cold, in the seventh heaven or the depths of hell, that has nothing to do with the quality of my meditation. All that has to be left. It is extraordinary that we have to hear that teaching hundreds and hundreds of times before we really listen to it. So what is important is the continuous daily practice in good times and bad. It is more or less the attitude of Job. We need the faith of Job that says, 'Even if God kills me I will still trust.' It is that kind of 'steel in the spine' faith that is needed to meditate. I have no explanation for meditation except that it is sheer gift. It is the greatest gift that has come into my life and I have no doubt that it is the greatest preparation for death that I could ever find.

John Main talked often about the word 'mantra'. It is a Sanskrit word and etymologically a compound word: 'man' in Sanskrit means 'the mind' and 'tra' in Sanskrit means 'to cleanse'. So it is that process of cleansing the mind, so to speak; polishing the mirror, to use one of Father John's metaphors. Because the eye is meant to be at the service of the inner self and not the master, we go to the ground of our being and then we are no longer tyrannised by rationalisation or the movements of our sensibility or emotions. Everything is in a state of quiet. It is not a passivity. It is not a form of quietism. Saying the mantra is a very active passivity. As John Main often said. We are not just in a state of reverie or in a state of sleep. We are alert and attentive at the time of the work and the work is saying the word.

What he awakened above all in me was the importance of meditation, the importance of being faithful to the mantra, whatever the obstacles. And there were many, especially from my ego. I used to wonder, was this the only way? Is this really prayer? Or my head would go into a spin, or sometimes I would experience great peace and feel I was doing really well. He would say gently, let all that go. He was always emphasising the gentleness of saying the word. I wish I had the eloquence to express all that I really heard him saying. The only expectation he led me to have is that I would be faithful to the daily half hours of saying the word.

In regard to his teaching, the thing that struck me basically was his own inner conviction that radiated from his presence. It came especially through the intensity of his body; there was an inner intensity, an inner groundedness, and that came through in his eyes and in the tonality of his voice and the gentle movement of his arms and limbs. There was a great dignity and presence in his bodily movements. He was very true to the spirit of St Benedict, as a man 'who dwelt within himself'. I am sure it was not easy for him with the nature he had been given. And yet his depth of faith led him to the burning conviction of the importance of dying to one's self. He had a great appreciation of the paschal mystery, the mystery of Easter. His letters in the book *Letters from the Heart*, in my view, are very profound spiritual documents. You can read any letter again and again and something new strikes you each time. And the more you meditate the more you see the profundity of what he has written. I always read his books with a sense of profound excitement. There is always a sense of new adventure. Even though you may read his books many times, new insights seem to jump out of the pages. I find the same thing in listening to his taped talks. I have played them hundreds and hundreds of times yet for some of them I say, 'Did I hear this before?' There is always the element of surprise in his talks, the element of a new discovery, a new adventure. Perhaps this is one of the fruits of meditation, that we are continually making new discoveries.

BERNARD DEEGAN

When John Main visited Manchester in 1975 to give a talk on meditation, I was working in our Servite parish there. After giving the talk John came to the Servite Priory where he had been invited to stay the night. During a chat I had with him over a meal he said one thing which, somehow, has always stayed in my mind. 'Whenever I am invited to a seminary to give a retreat or a talk,' he said, 'I always ask to be shown the seminary timetable. Almost always I have noticed that no mention is ever made in the timetable of silent prayer. If the devil himself had drawn up that timetable he couldn't have done a better job on it!' It is the last sentence, for some reason, that I remember! It is typical of his forthrightness and sure grasp of the importance of meditation. This was the first time I had met John. His manner of speaking and his bearing all gave the impression of a commanding person. I suppose that is inevitable in a person who understood meditation as clearly as he did.

GERTRUDE MCLAUGHLIN

> There are nine and sixty ways of constructing tribal
>   lays,
> And – every – single – one – of – them – is – right!

This thought of Rudyard Kipling comes to mind, on another level, as one reflects on Dom John Main's use of scripture in his printed works. There are at least 'nine and sixty' ways one could approach it. Every one of them would be enlightening and rewarding.

To persons asking what should be read in order to help in their prayer Father John Main gives the direct and brief answer, 'Nothing.' However he then hastens to add, 'We recommend the slow and careful reading of scripture as an essential part of a mature Christian life.'[1] There is little originality in this advice. However it carries with it a special weight as Father John's written works reveal to what extent sacred scripture is the source both of his own thought and of his teaching.

As with persons who are truly familiar with the scriptures and live by them, one does not find in Father John's works a multitude of citations, but a few that have been experienced profoundly. These appear over and over again. Each repetition gives a new meaning, a new aspect, a new depth to the basic notion. This paucity reveals to us something of Father John's own thoughts and reflection. It is also a useful tool for his work as teacher. The same verses repeated come to be deeply imprinted and finally remembered. One finds there an echo of monastic *lectio divina.* The same verse is to be held in the mind throughout the day, murmured in periods of work and quiet until its full meaning is both grasped and savoured.

One must distinguish between the direct quotations which he uses with chapter and verse clearly indicated, and the indirect that are much more frequent. These reveal that scripture has been assimilated to the extent that it becomes his natural turn of thought, his way of expression. It would be a rewarding exercise to trace each of these to its origin. Father John often has a surprising and felicitous amalgam of citations, especially from Paul, that is enlightening.

A final characteristic is that Father John works almost exclusively with the New Testament. In fact 'Father John's Bible' is a New Testament in the New English version. It is surprising that he uses the Old Testament so seldom, especially since he does so with rare discernment.[2] Even more surprising is the scarcity of citations from the Psalms. One would expect that a monk for whom the daily recitation of the office is a centre of life, would find much to sustain his teaching. Father John does though quote several times 'Be still and know and I am God' (Ps. 46:10), which is basic to his teaching.

Father John in his person is a biblical man. He stands among us as a prophet returning us to our roots while at the same time pointing the way ahead. He saw the work the Lord gave him to do as the revitalising of prayer for all committed Christians: monks, priests, religious, lay persons. He taught one way of prayer with curt directness, starting with what one may consider the exteriors: position, silence, the repetition of the mantra. These were the conditions he suggested to any one who chose to pray, to meditate, with him. Like the prophet his teaching was often questioned and misunderstood, but his conviction of the truth of the message that possessed him was so strong that he continued to proclaim it. One feels here an echo of Jeremiah, 'his word was imprisoned in my body, like a fire blazing in my heart' (Jer. 20:9) or of St Paul, 'it would be misery for me not to preach the gospel'. Again like the prophet he seemed to have one message that, from experience, he believed in profoundly and that he repeated – sure and clear – to all comers. He knew: 'If the flute or harp does not give distinct notes, how will anyone know what is played; if a trumpet call is not clear, who will prepare for battle' (1 Cor. 14:7–8). He made certain that his listeners would hear his message distinctly and follow without hesitation.

From the response of Abraham answering the call of God to the early Christian community crying out 'Maranatha, come, Lord Jesus!' faith is the origin and basis of spiritual life. There is a triple dimension to all faith. There is first the intellectual recognition and assent – *credo Deum*[3] – I believe God; then a loving trust – *credo Deo* – I believe in God; finally the total commitment – *credo in Deum* – I give myself to God, the finality and surrender to a person and not to an idea. Father John teaches this as he reflects on John 5:24, 'give heed . . . trust . . . pass to life'. St Paul in Romans 1:17 says, 'a way that starts from faith and leads to faith'.

It is an absolute demand, the demand of faith.[4] One of his most frequent quotations presents this truth again, 'God's way . . . a way that starts from faith and ends in faith' (Rom. 1:17). He uses it as essential to the way of prayer he is teaching: 'The act of faith that meditation demands is ever-deepening. It is a journey that begins in faith and will end in faith and it is an entirely free choice whether one follows it or not.'[5] He reflects on this truth again:

> For St Paul, the whole Christian life was shaped by faith: the way began in faith and ended in faith . . . faith is, fundamentally, the experience of our being grounded in God, rooted in him with absolute sureness and with a confidence that is always deepening because the depth of God can never be measured by humankind.[6]

This is the faith that 'spans our lives' and that is almost synonymous with love. 'To be filled with faith is no less than to be filled with the power and love of Jesus – which is the self-same love with which he is loved by the Father.'[7] In many ways Father John's works are a many-faceted reflection on the faith that Jesus exacted of his followers and that Paul sees as the gift brought by Jesus, 'faith active in love' (Gal. 5:6).

The second deeply-rooted biblical concept that is basic to Father John's teaching is poverty. As with faith he presents it over and over again from various points of view. His teaching on it is so rich, so much in keeping with the whole New Testament, his insights so rewarding that one wishes he had developed the subject for itself rather than presented it incidentally in works devoted to prayer. This is the poverty of the beatitudes according to Matthew and as Father John further explains, 'It is the poor in spirit who find that the kingdom is not a place but an experience of the person who is one with love.'[8] This poverty is both a point of departure and a point of arrival: 'the absolute simplicity and deepening poverty of our meditation. We left self behind in order to find our own enduring reality, to find ourselves one with the Father.'[9] It is personified in Mary, 'the poverty of spirit that is itself a purity of heart.'[10] We find here the teaching of many commentators of the New Testament who find in the first beatitude the summing up of all the others which are really aspects of the total poverty of spirit.

From Cassian Father John borrows the expression 'grand poverty'. Although this may seem a contradiction in terms, it is the thought developed by St Thomas Aquinas who sees Christian poverty as magnanimity, 'our generous and magnanimous poverty of spirit',[11] as Father John describes this method of prayer. It requires detachment only as an effect of a greater attachment: 'the condition of detachment is really a concentration upon the Reality that contains and perfects all things'.[12] This poverty is both 'inner and outer',[13] it is an *ascesis*[14] that finds in prayer its fulfilment 'at the deepest level of our being where we acknowledge and experience our complete poverty and complete dependence upon the sustaining love of God'.[15] Finally poverty, according to Father John, is simplicity, childlikeness, silence, unity, far removed from the negative image of renunciation. 'The spirit of poverty in the deepest sense is an affirmation of our own infinite value. We are valued subjects of God's love.'[16]

Father John's fundamental work is to carry out the renewal initiated by Vatican II. He sees it as the renewal of monastic life by a return to the tradition of prayer. However the renewal does not end with the monks, but spreads to an ever-widening circle of associates: Benedictine oblates, guests, those who share the prayer life of the monastery and, potentially, all persons.[17] He bases this prayer on two essentials, biblical elements, faith and poverty. At the end of a talk on monastic prayer he presented to a group of lay people he stated: 'I suggest you now forget most of what I have said except the two words "simplicity" and "faith" – and both of these are summed up in the practice of one word that will allow you to be led by the Spirit.'[18]

One of Father John's favourite quotations is 'We do not even know how we ought to pray' (Rom. 8:25); it is an acknowledgement of our innate poverty, so that our prayer is never our own, 'but through our inarticulate groans the Spirit is pleading for us'. The expression of this poverty is the mantra, which he calls 'the sacrament of our poverty in prayer'.[19] In his teaching, prayer and poverty are so closely associated that rarely is one referred to without the other. The supreme expression of this relationship is that we must give up the notion of 'our prayer'. He writes, 'There is only one prayer and this is the prayer of Jesus . . . the stream of love that flows between him and the Father that *is* the Spirit. "Our prayer" is simply our entering into this stream of divine love.'[20]

All of Father John's works are alive with a sense of wonder at the splendour of the Christian calling:

> God's experience of himself in the Spirit: the love of the Father for the Son and the reciprocal love of the Son for the Father. The simple and indescribable wonder of the Christian life is that each of us and all of us together are called to enter this self-same experience 'in the Spirit'.[21]

He shows how one can become aware of this calling. 'It is sharing in the very being of God that is the experience of our prayer.'[22] This leaving of self to find it in God 'is the great poverty of Christ . . . It demands only faith . . . Our ultimate self-knowledge, which is the Spirit of Christ united to our spirit, means discovering ourselves in God.'[23] It is in this reflection on the divine indwelling, on the union of the person with God in the love of the Trinity, that the profound contemplative life of Father John is evident. The words of Jesus and St Paul take on a lived and experienced expression. The reader is caught up in the depths of his faith.

Father John's gifts to those who know his writings are many. Among the richest of these is a new reading of scripture, a reading done in the simplicity of faith that takes the word in its full meaning and leads it to its most daring conclusions. He leads us beyond ourselves:

> If we Christians have a fault, it is that we are so blind to the extraordinary riches that are ours, achieved for us, given to us by Jesus. We possess the mind of Christ – Christ who knows the Father and who knows us. This is what each of us is invited to discover from our own experience.[24]

Notes

1 Main, John, *Letters from the Heart* (1982).
2 ibid.
3 Main, John, *Word into Silence* (1980); cf. *Letters*.
4 Main, John, *Moment of Christ* (1984); cf. *Letters*.
5 *Letters*.
6 ibid.
7 ibid.
8 ibid.
9 ibid.
10 Main, John, *The Other-Centredness of Mary* (1983).
11 *Letters*.
12 *Other-Centredness*; cf. *Letters*.
13 *Word into Silence*.
14 *Letters*.
15 *Word into Silence*.
16 Main, John, *Christian Meditation: The Gethsemani Talks* (1977).
17 *Word into Silence*.
18 Main, John, *Monastic Prayer and Modern Man* (1983).
19 *Word into Silence*.
20 *Letters*.
21 ibid.

22   ibid.
23   ibid.
24   *Moment of Christ.*

THOMAS RYAN

About two years before meeting Father John Main I drove a thousand miles to talk to one of my former college priest professors, because I had heard he was adapting transcendental meditation to a context of Christian faith. I did not know much about transcendental meditation other than that it discouraged rational thinking and the use of images. That was all I needed to know to become interested, because both had dried up like a desert creek bed in my efforts at regular communication with God.

My former professor introduced me to imageless prayer and the use of a Christian mantra. I returned to my work as a campus minister at Ohio State University and began meditating.

A year later my community, the Paulist Fathers, was looking for someone to direct the Catholic campus ministry at McGill University in Montreal. I had an active desire to live in another country and learn another language so I raised my hand.

I arrived in August 1977, less than a month before Father John and Brother Laurence. We all spent the first few months getting our bearings and by the time I met them they were installed in the house on Vendome Street. I was referred there by Father John Wickham sj at the Ignatian Centre, whom I had gone to see in my quest for a spiritual director in this new assignment.

During our second session together Father Wickham got around to asking me how I prayed. When he heard me describe an imageless, wordless form of meditation, he recognised that prayer in the Ignatian method was not my inclination. 'I think you should go and see Father John Main,' he said. 'He's just opening a new house of prayer in the diocese and teaches a form of meditation like the one you're practising.' He gave me a phone number and I have been grateful ever since to this Jesuit who served as a disinterested broker between a Paulist and a Benedictine.

I soon called upon Father John. It was clear to me from our first conversation that he was the teacher and spiritual guide I was looking for. Since I was already meditating we were immediately on the same wavelength. He helped me to appreciate what I was doing as not just an adapted form of transcendental meditation but as a practice properly belonging to the Christian prayer tradition too. By introducing me to the teaching of John Cassian and the Cloud of Unknowing, he enabled me to see that in meditating I was on home, not foreign, ground.

Our talks focused on breathing, distractions, commitment to meditation, and the inadvisability of changing one's mantra more than once (he felt that a change of mantra could be called for in certain cases, but that it should not be done more than once and should be effected during a period in one's life when other things were stable).

There was one communication in particular that was pivotal for me. I was pleading what I thought was a very convincing argument: the life of a campus minister is too hectic and unpredictable to maintain faithfulness to the second meditation each day. Students walked in unannounced, mass preceded supper, evening courses at the Newman Centre or in the dorms followed supper – there just wasn't time!

He listened patiently and attentively until I had said my piece. He knew I was applying pressure and hoping to extract an admission that, okay, in my case, once a day would do. I was, after all, celebrating the Eucharist in that pre-supper slot.

He began sympathetically and I thought I could see a verdict in my favour forthcoming. He granted that, yes, the life of an active priest was considerably different from the more controlled world of the monastery, and he knew a second meditation in the latter part of the day was like looking for stable footing on the high seas.

I could feel a 'but' coming – and when it came it had all the unflinching firmness of an uppercut to the jaw that stops the rude challenger dead in his tracks.

'But if you wish to advance on this path it is *absolutely*

224

necessary that you be faithful to your second meditation. Look again where your time is going and make some decisions that reflect your priorities.'

It was a showdown: the path of expediency versus the path of radical commitment. Had he blinked I would today be the lesser for it. My own plea was sincere and in good faith. I was genuinely convinced that a second meditation in my schedule was unworkable.

Anything less than his unflinching response would have left me secure in my own position of compromise. But the Gibraltar-like conviction of his words stood me up straight and sent me back home with the sense that I had to take another look at the pattern of my late afternoon activities and see if everything was as important and unmovable as I was making it out to be.

When I sat down and really looked at it, I saw that he was right. We *make* time for what is important to us. I made some changes and have been meditating twice daily ever since.

Recently I was thinking about the influence of John Main's teaching on my life. The death of someone close to us often makes us take a hard look at the priorities which determine where our time and energy go. In 1986 I was deeply shaken by the death of a friend whose passing made me keenly aware that we each have only a limited time with which to respond to the gift of life on this planet. I found myself walking in the woods sorting out my priorities and reviewing my commitments.

As I did so, it became very clear to me that the most important thing I do each day is meditate. The reason is simple and straightforward: I am created in order to know, love, and serve God. Where in my day do I turn the full, focused light of my consciousness towards God? In meditation. It is most of all there that I simply am before the One who is, in loving attention. From this deepening bond of love flows the energy and motivation for service.

When I examined John Main's teaching and the place of meditation in my life, I saw that it has been valuable in several other ways as well:

- as an anchoring influence, providing a steady rudder in all sorts of waters;
- as a path of gradual surrender which leads me to cede more and more of the terrain of my own wants to God, and invites me to grow in the willingness to accept what God gives and to want only what God wants;
- as an experience of the meaning of life as loving attention;
- as an answer to my desire to encounter God in wordless silence;
- as an instrument that sharpens my 'taste' for God;
- as an experiencing of 'oneing' that increases my longing for a fuller, direct experience of the joy and delight of God's presence.

As Teresa of Avila said: 'I want to see God!'

The words of John of the Cross in 'The Ascent of Mount Carmel' exhort us to the renunciation of every conceivable appetite of sense and intellect. Why? Because the pleasure we experience in them creates the illusion of joy and – because it is illusory – 'harms the soul'. True joy is only in the emptying, in the darkness where the soul encounters the Beloved. This emptiness, this darkness is the soul's purification from illusion. 'There is nothing worthy of a person's joy,' writes John of the Cross, 'save the service of God and the procurement of God's honour and glory in all things. Outside of that joy, all is illusion.'

John of the Cross's teaching is yet another confirmation that meditation is the path, for the way of meditation is a way of emptying oneself in the darkness of one's illusions. It is a way of transformation which is gradually effected in us not through time alone, nor experience alone, but through the love at the root of our existence – the creating and recreating Spirit who has been in secret communion with our spirit all the while teaching our hearts to formulate the ultimate name: Abba.

It is in the solitude of meditation, freely chosen and entered into, that the truth of my own poverty, of my own absolute dependency, and of my own giftedness as a receiver are revealed. Here I come home to my true self, free of illusion.

The necessary condition for the unveiling of my illusions is the solitude of the heart, the home of my true self. Here I see myself as I really am: totally dispossessed, naked and poor, receiving *all*, my being and everything else besides, from God.

In the solitude of the heart I discover that secret mystery unveiled by the Spirit: my true self in God, and God in my true self. Meditation represents the commitment to return again and again to that sacred place and be 'at home' there.

GREGORY J. RYAN

Contemplation in a World of Action, a collection of Thomas Merton's essays published in 1971, three years after his death, has renewal for its theme: personal renewal, monastic renewal, and renewal in the Church. It was the underlying theoretical framework of Merton's book that suggested this comparison with John Main's monastic vision and practice, as well as a look at how both monks contributed to what has come to be called the New Monasticism.

Thomas Merton and John Main lived in very different monastic settings. Merton spent his entire twenty-seven years as a monk enclosed in a large, established Trappist monastery in the rolling hills of Kentucky. John Main embarked on a journey in 1977 from his monastery in London to found a small Benedictine monastery in the centre of Montreal. While these outward appearances might suggest great inward differences, in fact their outlooks were strikingly similar.

Thomas Merton wrote incessantly on a wide range of topics, which could be arranged alphabetically from Asceticism to Zen. Abbot John Eudes Bamberger pointed out during a radio broadcast that Merton was, first and foremost, a monk/artist,[1] much of whose writing was impressionistic, frequently employing a wide-angle lens for effect. He warns that Merton's style often calls for a special understanding on the part of the reader. Since Merton is so complex, he cannot always be taken at face value. John Main, on the other hand, wrote less than Merton, and his teaching was much more specific. He was primarily a monk/teacher, though he was not a teacher in the sense of 'schoolteacher'. Rather, he was a teacher of what a monk is called to be: a person whose primary goal is seeking God – whether inside or outside the cloister. His manner of teaching falls into the time-honoured monastic tradition of the teacher-disciple relationship. His books and tapes constitute an extension of this relationship, and his books purposely retain the flavour of the original spoken word.

It should be noted from the outset that neither Thomas Merton nor John Main *lived* at the theoretical level. Each one lived from the depths of his heart, and it is precisely this characteristic which presents a model for all women and men of our time. It is for this reason that Merton's influence and poularity continue to rise. It is for this reason that John Main's monastic community has grown to include monks and nuns, lay residents and guests, oblate members from various religious affiliations, and meditators around the world who follow his teaching on prayer.

Both monks would agree that the sickness that afflicts our world today is a morally bankrupt materialism gone mad, a kind of societal 'heart disease'. They would agree too that the cure is to be found through a rediscovery of the spiritual dimension of life: a complete recovery of what it is that makes us human. The prescription for this recovery is prayer.

Merton and Main viewed the monk's calling to be what is the essential calling of each one of us: a 'wholehearted openness to love'.[2] It is just this love which is so 'vital for the redemption of our society'.[3] How may this openness in our personal lives be achieved by the daily practice of meditation? How does this openness lead to community? How has the way of meditation contributed to the growth and development of the Benedictine Priory of Montreal? Finally, does a community rooted in meditation naturally appeal to 'the world'? Since meditation is a practice that has universal implications, it offers very real possibilities for the integration of East and West, for ecumenism among the Christian churches, and for dialogue with the un-churched.

Significantly, it is openness that leads to what Merton called 'a real personal communication with others who are recognised as *like-minded*, who are "other monks".'[4] This open, extended, revitalised community of monks and 'other monks' is what is meant by the term 'New Monasticism'.

John Main once wrote that his own experience had taught him 'that to know God we have first to know ourselves and that we can only fully know ourselves in the moment of prayer'.[5] This self-knowledge has nothing to do with selfishness or self-interest. It springs from a desire to forget ourselves, to be able to go out and meet the other. Whether the other is God or our neighbour, first we must know who *we* are.

Pointing out that knowledge is too often found only in our heads, Merton blamed Descartes for laying a curse on the life of prayer by making it into an intellectual exercise:

> What has to be rediscovered is the inner discipline of the 'heart,' that is to say, of the 'whole man'[6] – a discipline that reaches down into the inmost ground and opens out to the invisible, intangible, but nevertheless mysteriously sensible reality of God's presence, of his love, and of his activity in our hearts.[7]

It is here, in the heart, that we find our true self. And it is prayer that nourishes it and calls it forth. This process is both natural and guaranteed, since 'God is the source of Reality. What we discover, from our own experience, is that there is nothing real outside God. Only illusion exists outside the real centre.'[8] John Main's way to the experience of this Reality was the daily practice of meditation.

Meditation helps us to root ourselves in Reality and to find the hidden meaning of 'losing ourselves'. Paradoxically, the loss is pure gain, since we find that all we have lost is our limitations. Merton put it this way: 'The real purpose of meditation – or at least that which recommends itself for modern man – is the exploration and discovery of new dimensions of freedom, illumination and love'.[9]

Entry into this freedom has been won for everyone by the life, death and resurrection of Jesus Christ, whose Spirit of love pours forth eternally from our hearts. The question which faces each of us is 'How do we live out of this freedom?' One way, the way John Main practised and taught, is the way of Christian meditation.

Meditation is a way of prayer that has been handed down through the ages, from teacher to disciple, since before the time of the Desert Fathers. It is a way of silence, stillness and simplicity. The simplicity of it rests on the attentive and faithful recitation of a single prayer-word or mantra:

> This simple, practical wisdom of the East moved westwards in the monastic tradition, and entered Europe through the influence of John Cassian, who was St Benedict's teacher of prayer . . . Cassian's teaching is fully within the tradition of the teaching of Jesus 'not to go babbling on like the heathens do', not to make of God a convenient shoulder to cry on and in our *talking things over with him* to lose sight of the wonder and otherness of his love – the essential mystery of his being.[10]

John Main carried on this tradition by teaching others how to enter into this mystery. He recommended the recitation of the New Testament prayer-word 'Maranatha' for the times of meditation. Without focusing on the meaning of it, the mantra allows us to turn our attention 'beyond ourselves – a way of unhooking us from our own thoughts and concerns'.[11]

This is no mere theory. The simplicity of meditation is the key to seeing our existence as it *is* – without illusions. Echoing Merton's sentiment that the contemplative life is first of all a *life*, John Main says that 'this can sound very abstract until you approach it from the model of your own experience of love: in your marriage, your family, your friendships . . . Prayer is concerned with the reality and actuality of persons.'[12] We do not need books or courses or elaborate training. We need only experience.

As a safeguard against the seductive appeals of diverse techniques of prayer, John Main spoke of his conviction that:

> the central message of the New Testament is that there is really only one prayer and that this prayer is the prayer of Christ. It is a prayer that continues in our hearts day and night. I can describe it only as the stream of love that flows constantly between Jesus and his Father. This stream of love is the Holy Spirit . . . Again it is our conviction that it is the most important task for any human life that we should become as open as possible to this stream of love.[13]

This is the purpose of being faithful to the recitation of the mantra: to be open to that stream and to allow it to flow in our hearts without any attempt on our part to channel it.

From the very first days of the Meditation Centre he had started at Ealing Abbey in London before founding the Montreal community, John Main was insistent upon referring to this way of prayer as meditation. It was his way of indirectly settling any confusion or misunderstanding about prayer in general. In one of the many newsletters sent out from the monastery, he touched on this subject:

> This confusion was often first exposed in a misunderstanding of the word *meditation* itself. We knew, of course, that we were using it in its original, monastic sense of imageless prayer. And we knew that this meaning clashed with the more general meaning meditation had, in Christian circles, of discursive prayer with a great emphasis on the use of the imagination. On the other hand, the majority of our contemporaries, especially the younger generation, understood by meditation exactly what we meant.[14]

What he meant was this: Sit down and sit still. Gently close your eyes and silently, interiorly recite your mantra from the beginning of your meditation to the end. Without paying any attention to its meaning, listen to it as four distinct syllables: 'Ma-ra-na-tha'. Do this for half an hour every morning and every evening. This daily meditation will open your heart and allow your true self to emerge.

One of the remarkable things about discovering our true self is that we are naturally prompted to share this discovery with others. Father John often said that we are each on a pilgrimage but that pilgrims do not travel alone. The natural outgrowth of personal openness is community:

> The real spirit of openness is to renew life in the Spirit, life in love. A greater love and understanding of people is no obstacle to a true growth in contemplation, for contemplation is rooted and grounded in charity. A more generous sharing of the values of the contemplative life will increase our love instead of diminishing it.[15]

Laurence Freeman tells us that 'Many years before he became a monk, Father John used to speak to friends about starting a "new kind of community" that would answer the deep need for fellowship, oneness in mind and heart, that all people, not just religious feel . . . He called it a community of love.'[16] In actuality, it would be a community with monks at the core, joined by many other men and women with varying degrees of commitment, as their individual life-situations allowed. The monks themselves would find the monastery to be 'the place where they are called to live in freedom, to develop it and to communicate it to others'.[17]

The new monastery founded by John Main and Laurence Freeman was not bound by long-established customs, so it sank its roots deep into the spirit of primitive Benedictine monasticism to find its direction. Because of the genius of St Benedict, whose Rule is timeless, the new priory turned out to be a possible model for the future of monasticism.

The monks in this monastery would not live in isolation from others for a basic reason, one recognised years before by Thomas Merton: 'the monastic community owes other men a share in [its] quiet and solitude'.[18]

From the time of making the first arrangements with the bishops of Montreal, who had invited John Main to make a new foundation, it was understood that the monks would have one primary task: 'to be there to meditate with whoever came'.[19] And come they did. Right from the beginning, guests and visitors arrived at the doorstep.

Father John realised that he and Father Laurence had 'stumbled upon – or had been led to – two elements in [their] situation that could point the way forward to the monasticism of the future'.[20] The first element was the richness of the Christian tradition of meditation. It became John Main's life's work to spread the good news that meditation is the way to uncover the hidden Treasure that lies beneath the surface of our lives. He realised that the second element was 'the other side of the equation [which] converted self-discovery into other-centredness'.[21] This twofold teaching is what brought others to the monastery to share in the community's three (and later, four) periods of meditation, which had been integrated into the Liturgy of the Hours and the celebration of the Eucharist. The community's times of shared silent meditation witnessed to the awe-inspiring Presence found in us and among us.

On each Monday and Tuesday evening Father John addressed between forty and a hundred people who came to listen to his teaching and to meditate together. Many of these meditators would later start groups of their own, patterned after these sessions: Gather in a quiet place. Listen to a short talk on the tradition of meditation. Meditate together for about twenty-five minutes. This would be followed by time for questions or comments. Though Father John was dazzlingly eloquent and obviously an experienced, authentic master of prayer, his message was of the utmost humility and simplicity: 'Forget just about everything you have heard this evening. All you need do is say your mantra.'

Just as he believed it would, the community developed in ways that could not have been predicted. The lay group who came over from the meditation centre in England to help get the new house in Montreal in order rented an apartment near the monastery so that they could participate in the daily routine. Women guests were offered hospitality at a neighbouring convent. It soon became apparent that larger quarters would be needed. A Montreal family provided a generous, unexpected gift of a large house offering the necessary space and seclusion for prayer, in a quiet section in the heart of Montreal. Here the monastery would be readily available to anyone who sought what it had to offer.[22]

> One who begins [this spiritual journey] alone will be joined by others and in that mystery of communion the Church is reborn, rekindled in many quiet corners of the earth . . . The kingdom, realised in the innocence of a community persevering in prayer, may not conquer the world but it can love the world and redeem it by its love.[23]

Monks, visitors, guests and weekly groups – all formed a network around the unifying force of meditation. Later a permanent women's community developed, located in a house across the street from the monastery under the direction of Benedictine sisters experienced in the formation of religious. Many lay people and religious who felt called to a more formal commitment to the monastery and its work became oblate members of the community, a phenomenon as old as Benedictine monasticism.

Benedict wrote his Rule for religious, but its spirit may be lived by anyone. One oblate, Derek Smith, traced the history of oblates in western monastic tradition and pointed out that 'oblates of St Benedict are clearly conceived to be an organic part of the Benedictine *familia*'.[24] Whenever monasteries have given themselves to a life of prayer, they have been recognised and sought out by others for the:

> true familial fraternity they very often cannot find in the world. It appears that whenever monastic institutions have changed their priorities such that the life of simple prayer is supplanted by elaborate liturgy, by preoccupation with teaching in schools, by preoccupation with the cultivation of land and wealth, and even by the subordination of prayer to commendable works of mercy, the active monastic participation by lay people has waned.[25]

Some four hundred oblates from around the world now attached to the monastery are evidence that 'there is a marked trend' for oblature 'in communities which are open and receptive, and in which the "return to sources" advocated by Vatican II' has taken place.[26]

John Main appreciated the commitment of the oblates in sharing the spiritual pilgrimage of meditation with the monks. He realised that this was entered into with some degree of sacrifice and inconvenience and saw this shared commitment as an integral part of life at the monastery. 'Rooted . . . by their twice-daily meditation, [oblates] would come to share in their own experience of St Benedict's vision of the harmony of prayer and work.'[27]

The spiritual relationship is something of a two-way street. Oblature 'seems to present marvellous and large opportunities for the life of intensive Christian meditation and prayer; it is a rich inheritor of, *and contributor to*, the life of evangelical humility and simplicity envisioned by our holy Father Benedict, a man of God for all times'.[28] Father John and Father Laurence have credited oblates of the monastery with taking imaginative initiatives in spreading the teaching of meditation in their churches, workplaces, and communities around the world.

While individuals may find a home for themselves at the monastery, the monastic community is not turned in upon itself. 'A monastery is a *centre of prayer* only to the degree that it is a community of love: the prayer is an openness to the love, the monastery is the communication of the love to all within it and to all who encounter it.'[29] Community opens its heart to embrace everyone who encounters it. This loving relationship inevitably leads to communion with all:

> The tradition that we follow as Benedictine monks calls us both to understand and to experience our prayer as silent communion within our own heart. Union brings us to communion, that is to oneness with God and to oneness with all. It is a communion that is indescribably enriching, because it takes us right out of ourselves, beyond ourselves into union with all, with the All, with God. Unity, union, communion is the threefold growth of a Christian.[30]

The monastery of today offers a sign to the rest of the world. '[In] our faith-less society perhaps it is a monastery's pre-eminent service to be a place where faith is lived, honoured, and communicated. It is a place where very ordinary men . . . prove that faith is possible and necessary.'[31] As we have already seen, John Main's vision was not narrowly sectarian. He saw that meditation creates a vortex of love; all those who come into contact with meditation are irresistibly drawn into that love.

Father John's public teaching on meditation started at Merton's Abbey of Gethsemani where he was invited in 1976 to address the community on contemplative prayer.[32] During his stay there he celebrated what he described as the most loving mass of his life in Merton's hermitage. He had a profound appreciation for the trails Merton had blazed in the areas of monastic renewal, ecumenism, and East–West dialogue.

Merton's interest in the East was no faddish dabbling. During his Asian journey in 1968 Merton had plans (which never materialised) to visit a Hindu monk named Bramachari whose acquaintance he had made while he was a student at

Columbia University in the 1930s (see *Seven Storey Mountain*). Merton had been impressed by the young monk's holiness and ordinariness. This one detail in the catalogue of Merton's many eastern contacts illustrates his long-standing conviction that the West could learn much from the East. *The Asian Journal, Zen and the Birds of Appetite, Mystics and Zen Masters*, and his personal favourite *The Way of Chuang Tzu*, further testify to this. One of the high points of his stay in India was his audience with the Dalai Lama, which was extended to three sessions – from the originally planned two – due to the fruitfulness of the discussions.

There are interesting parallels to this in John Main's spiritual journey. He had spent some years in the British Colonial Service before becoming a monk. One day while carrying out his duties in Malaya, he met a Hindu swami named Satyananda, the founder of the Pure Life Society in Kuala Lumpur. Struck by the monk's holiness, Father John asked if the swami would teach him how to pray. The Hindu taught him to meditate using the mantra 'Jesus'. Father John would often state that meditating with this holy man of God for one half hour was worth more than all the books he had read about prayer. The swami's message was simple: If you want to meditate, your must do so every morning and every evening and you must faithfully recite your mantra from the beginning to the end of your meditation.

Except for a desert period that began when his novice master directed him not to, John Main continued to meditate daily for the rest of his life. Later, as a mature monk, he re-read Augustine Baker's *Holy Wisdom*, the Cloud of Unknowing, and the works of John Cassian (as Benedict directs his followers to do in his Rule), and was delighted to find that what he had learned from Swami Satyananda fell into line with the ancient Christian tradition of meditation.

Merton believed that since monks are privileged to be able to develop a prayer life in complete freedom, they 'should also, at least in some cases, be able to teach the ways of prayer to others living outside the cloister, besides providing them with a place of quiet and rest and interior renewal'.[33] John Main realised this too. 'It is true, then, to say that the new relationship of monks to the world will include a teaching function.'[34] He welcomed the changes in modern monasticism as a wonderful opportunity:

> This is the challenge to the Church and particularly to monasticism today; not to write monographs on prayer but to produce men committed to a life of prayer in the fullness of the tradition. The wonderful thing about the monastic life when it is really lived like this is that it cannot help but communicate its experience to all around it and to lead all who come into contact with it to participate in this mystery . . . [This] condition of wholehearted openness to love is the condition to which you and I and every human being is called.[35]

This challenge is not just for monks, but for the whole Church and for all people.

For some years following Vatican Council II many contemplative communities experienced various identity crises. Merton wrote that monasteries should 'consider how, and to what extent, they can be "open to the world" without losing their identity as contemplatives'. Instead of turning away from the world with the excuse of being 'contemplative' Merton focused on the positive service monasteries might offer in solidarity with all people, *precisely because* they were contemplative. He recognised that 'the only Christian communities that still retain some meaning for these people [in the world] are the contemplative communities'.[36] The monastery should be a centre where deep communication takes place with people from all walks of life. 'If our monasteries are truly centres of deeply experienced monastic life, those who are most alive in the outside world will spontaneously come to share our silence and discuss with us their own fruitful insights . . . But it all depends on solitude and prayer.'[37]

Shortly after the Montreal community was founded, the Dalai Lama was welcomed to Montreal at an Interfaith Prayer Service. When it was over John Main invited the Dalai Lama back to the monastery to meditate with the community. The invitation was enthusiastically accepted. In the silence of the meditation room, the still eloquence of eastern and western masters gave way to a loving Presence. As Laurence Freeman recalls, 'Now a Buddhist leader had come to share in the depth and silence of a Christian contemplative path, and the unity thus experienced was the more inspiring for all precisely because of that.'[38] The divisions often expressed in words had given way to communion in the one Word.

Another pioneer in the integration of East and West and a Benedictine monk is Bede Griffiths, who presently leads the Shantivanam ashram founded by Henri LeSaux osb, commonly known by his adopted Indian name, Abishiktananda. Once while Father Bede was travelling in the United States Father John visited him at Mount Saviour Monastery in Elmira, New York. The two monks discussed the present state of the world and the future role of monasticism in it. '[We shared] Father Bede's own belief that the contemplative life in the West would be revived through networks of small ashramic-type monasteries located in the main population centres as a living witness to the journey from self to God.'[39] Following Father John's death in 1982, Father Bede remarked that in his experience 'John Main is the best spiritual guide in the Church today.'

To demonstrate that 'faith is possible and necessary',[40] a new vocabulary is being developed at the Montreal Priory that might appeal to non-believers as well as believers. Some members of the community have brought meditation into the secular marketplace, teaching business people to meditate, thus bringing unity and harmony into lives otherwise scattered and shattered by frantic, demanding schedules. Co-workers meet in silence before or after work to ground their day in the experience of meditation.

One of the first oblates of the community was the Anglican Bishop Henry Hill who lived in the monastery for some years before resuming his official work of dialogue with the Orthodox churches. On one occasion Father John welcomed to the monastery 'the whole House of Bishops of the Anglican Church in Canada headed by Archbishop Ted Scott, the Primate'.[41]

In 1982 artists, poets, sculptors and musicians met one weekend at the monastery for discussions and meditation. An artists' studio has since been established near the monastery; the members meditate together – or alone – before beginning their work in the space they share.[42]

Father John addressed a thousand participants at the Palliative Care International Conference in Montreal in October 1982, just two months before his own death. Standing before these health-care specialists he introduced himself simply as a Benedictine monk and then went on to share with them his belief that, since all humans die, we must each prepare for death by 'dying to self' each day. The preparation he suggested was the daily practice of meditation.

Thomas Merton frequently wrote and spoke about the importance of silent communication among all people to realise the oneness that we already share – even though we may not be consciously aware of this oneness. 'The unique and precious dimension that the monastic life can contribute to ecumenical experience is the deepening of unity that comes not only from talking together but from being silent together.'[43] In communities such as the one in Montreal people of many faiths and diverse backgrounds come together to experience this oneness.

Reflecting on the radical nature of our humanity redeemed by Christ and the part monasticism can play in helping others experience their humanity at its deepest level, John Main had this to say: 'the monk's message to the world' – and, by extension, the message we each proclaim – 'is that everything falls apart into chaos when the centre is lost; and his message is that Christ is the universal centre, the centre of each person and of the world'.[44] Daily meditation brings us into the experience of this Reality.

Meditation helps nourish the threefold growth of which John Main spoke: unity, union, and communion. Unity can be seen as the harmony that is re-established in our own personal lives through the practice of daily meditation. Union can be found wherever people gather in community to experience this harmony together. Communion is realised in our own hearts and in the hearts of all we meet, as we share in the life, love and joy of our God.

In the quiet of his monastery Thomas Merton explored the possibilities open to contemplative life as it is lived in monasteries today. Through the publication of his books, through contacts with visitors and through correspondence with church leaders around the world, he was able to contribute in good measure to these developments. The seeds lying dormant in Merton's ideas about monasticism have germinated, flowered and borne fruit in the New Monasticism, in communities throughout America and Europe. Through John Main's clear and simple teaching, many people from all walks of life are finding a way to share in the work and fruits of this renewal of monasticism through their practice of meditation.

Notes

1   *Monasticism as Rebellion* presented 8, 15, 21 December 1986, Canadian Broadcasting Corporation.
2   Main, John, *Monastic Prayer and Modern Man* (1983).
3   Main, John, *The Present Christ* (1985).
4   Merton, Thomas, *Contemplation in a World of Action* (1973), hereafter *CWA*.
5   Main, John, *Letters from the Heart* (1982).
6   No attempt has been made to update gender-exclusive expressions. Although they sometimes used male-referenced terms, both monks were aware of male/female equality/mutuality.
7   *CWA*.
8   Main, John, *Moment of Christ* (1984).
9   *CWA*.
10 *Monastic Prayer and Modern Man*.
11 *Moment of Christ*.
12 *Monastic Prayer and Modern Man*.
13 *Moment of Christ*.
14 *Letters from the Heart*.
15 *CWA*.
16 *Monastic Prayer and Modern Man*.
17 *The Present Christ*.
18 *CWA*.
19 *Letters from the Heart*.
20 ibid.
21 ibid.
22 More detailed information about the history of the monastery may be found in John Main's *Letters from the Heart* and Neil McKenty's biography of Father John, *In the Stillness Dancing*.
23 *The Present Christ*.
24 Smith, Derek, 'Oblates in western monasticism', *Monastic Studies* 13, Autumn 1982.
25 ibid.

26 ibid.
27 *Letters from the Heart.*
28 Smith, 'Oblates in western monasticism'. Italics added.
29 *Monastic Prayer and Modern Man.*
30 *Moment of Christ.*
31 *Letters from the Heart.*
32 These talks were published in 1977 as *Christian Meditation: The Gethsemani Talks* (2nd edn, 1983).
33 *CWA.*
34 *Letters from the Heart.*
35 *Monastic Prayer and Modern Man.*
36 *CWA.*
37 ibid.
38 *The Present Christ.*
39 *Letters from the Heart.*
40 ibid.
41 *The Present Christ.*
42 ibid.
43 *CWA.*
44 *Letters from the Heart.*

JOHN WINGFIELD

In my six years in the seminary I can honestly say we were never taught much degree of spirituality. We were certainly never taught how to pray. To me that was and still is a scandal. Since then I have been urging seminary staff and professors to devote a year, rather like a novitiate, to a concentrated spiritual formation for would-be priests. The problem is that with this lack of priestly spiritual formation we get a spiritual vacuum in today's parishes.

What changed my life dramatically was a retreat given by Dom John Main to my seminary in 1977. Father John rocked our comfortable little seminary boat and probably upset a few people along the way. Firstly he asked the Rector for a copy of the daily retreat timetable to find out if daily periods of silence had been scheduled for the retreatants. When he found out that in fact there were no periods of silence, he told us 'the devil couldn't have written a better timetable'.

Needless to say periods for silent meditation, at his insistence, were built into the schedule.

Then he landed another bombshell by refusing the tradition of giving the seminary retreat in the cold, antiquated and uncomfortable chapel. He asked for and received permission to hold the retreat in a carpeted conference room with comfortable chairs that was far more suitable not only for giving talks but also for meditation. At this point we were wondering what sort of tiger we had by the tail in this particular retreat director.

After his first conference Father John gave us a choice of staying for twenty-five minutes of silent meditation or leaving. I must confess that I joined the majority of seminarians in leaving. The prospect of twenty-five minutes of silence was just a little too daunting for us future priests. In addition I was highly suspicious of any fancy new ideas of how to pray. However at breakfast the next day one of the few seminarians who had stayed said he enjoyed the meditation and that I should attend the next session. 'What a load of nonsense these new ideas are,' I replied. He said, 'Well, John, you can't say it's a load of nonsense until you go and try it.' That seemed to make sense, and here I am still 'on the pilgrimage'. Having entered the experience of it and listened to Father John all the pieces of the jigsaw fell into place and I suddenly knew I had discovered a way of prayer that made sense and was authentic.

Why has meditation changed my life? It has much to do with what I consider the greatest book of theology in the world, *The Little Prince* by Antoine de Saint-Exupéry. And the great secret in that book and the most profound statement that has ever been made in the world is this: 'You see with the heart; what is essential is invisible to the eye.' How true this is with meditation. In meditation we get beyond trivial surface things, beyond the superficial levels of self-awareness, beyond thoughts, feelings and experiences, down into the depth of the spirit within. We enter the mystery of God directly and personally and when we do this we realise that indeed 'what is essential is invisible to the eye'.

John Main taught with great urgency. He saw the vision of a renewed Church. He once said, 'We have had a biblical renewal, we have had a liturgical renewal, what we need now is a renewal in prayer.' I am in total agreement. This is the greatest need in the Church and the world today. Father John led the way. It is now up to us to follow and share his teaching with others – today.

11

The Work is Completed

It costs so much to be a full human being that there are very few who have the enlightenment or the courage to pay the price. (Morris West)

His death was the most important time of my knowing Father John. It was his consummate gift to us all. His death showed me the vital importance of love in human relationships. Here was a man dying, an integrated man, a monk. As he came into a deeper and deeper solitude and silence, he simultaneously became closer in human friendship and love with others. (Polly Schofield)

In this final chapter some close friends comment on Father John's death. In his introduction Father Laurence Freeman has pointed out that Father John felt he would not live to old age (p. 17). 'When he saw that his death was coming . . . he felt himself drawn ever more fully into the point of concentrated light, which dilated and absorbed him more completely at each time of prayer.'

There is a saying that 'when a man dies he clutches in his hands only that which he has given away in his lifetime'. The gift of meditation that Father John gave away and continues to give away to so many is the incomparable gift he clutched in his hands as he approached his Master.

POLLY SCHOFIELD

PAUL   Would you like to talk about Father John's last illness and death?

POLLY   A year before his death there is another picture that will always stay with me. As you know, he was not all that well in 1981. One freezing Saturday as I was cleaning in the meditation room, I saw him with a snow blower passing beneath the window. His beard was like Father Christmas, hanging with icicles. He had no gloves on and he was pushing this machine with total, absolute concentration – as if it was the last thing he had to do in this life. He was all there, and I thought to myself, 'My goodness, he looks as if he is doing it for the last time.' He was.

The first inkling of the seriousness of his sickness came to me one day in Iona as the community was gathering for the office. We heard a cry of pain. Several of us rushed out to see what was wrong. Incredibly Father John was smiling, 'It's nothing, it's nothing.' But apparently his foot tripped on the threshold of a door.

The last time he came to tea is another indelible memory. He was already very sick and was wearing his habit, which was significant to me. Usually he came in civvies. I opened the door and he just stood there with such incredible pain in his face, looking at me. I didn't know whether to hold him up or help him to go home. He just stood there and said, 'See, I have come.' There really wasn't much else to say. He just came for his final visit.

In the last stages of his sickness I offered to read to him each day. He said he would like that. I would bring up tea to him and read to him.

PAUL   What kind of reading?

POLLY   An assortment of things, particularly Julian of Norwich. One day during reading I could not pronounce 'ignominious'. He tried to teach me. There was Father John lying in bed, in pain, and there was me sitting in a chair trying to say ig-no-min-ious. Eventually I got it. That was the kind of person he was . . . dying but at the same time teaching and thinking of others.

PAUL   Did he talk to you about death?

POLLY   Oh yes, he talked about death and about life. His

245

death was the most important time of my knowing
Father John. It was his consummate gift to us all.
His death showed me the vital importance of love
in human relationships. Here was a man dying, an
integrated man, a monk. As he came into a deeper
and deeper solitude and silence, he simultaneously
became closer in human friendship and love with
others. It was an incredible paradox to watch. He
would love you so intensely in the present moment.
I find it very difficult to express, except that out of
his silence, his love for others burst forth. His love
and his humanness is shown in the story Father Laurence tells about him a month before his death. Father
John fell out of bed. Laurence rushed in and in the
process of lifting him on to his bed, said to him, 'Some
day we'll laugh at all this.' Father John quipped back,
'Why don't we laugh at it now.' But he was like that,
he never took himself too seriously.

By Christmas time when he was very ill I heard it
was getting very painful for Father John to change
his pyjamas. I felt I ought to go out and buy him
some nightshirts. To make a long story short, Father
John was dying and my great Christmas present was
two nightshirts. He wore those nightshirts till he died.
Towards the end as he was becoming more and more
detached from things, whatever happened he took
with the greatest calm and the greatest love. But the
fascinating thing is that he did not detach himself
from human relationships. The friendships became
deeper in proportion to his union with God. He
became closer to the people around him. I can't put
this any more simply.

No one knew Father John better, and loved him
more than Father Laurence. Father Laurence looked
after Father John totally in those last days, with the
greatest love, as disciple, as son, as 'everything'. In
addition he had the burden of running the Priory,
with all that entails. When I saw his total commitment and loving discipleship, I could only think,
'Well, this is love in action.' It will never cease to

inspire me. No one knew Father John's death was so imminent. Towards the end we were feeding him through a straw. It was so quick. It was so drastic. Yet he didn't lose consciousness. He was drugged, but he was always there – always present.

If Father John's life and teaching could be summed up in one word, as I understood it, it would be 'reciprocity' – a relationship of love – the continuous giving and the returning of oneself in love. This reciprocity is reflected in the whole of creation being given and simultaneously returned to the Father in Christ. Father John left those of us who knew him with an ineradicable sense of 'reciprocity', joy and gratitude, and wonder at the gift of life.

BALFOUR M. MOUNT

We approached the imposing exterior of the McConnell Estate with fascination and expectation. I had read of John Main's work in the *Montreal Gazette* and with a simple phone call had arranged to meet him for afternoon tea. I was accompanied by the Director of Pastoral Care for our Royal Victoria Palliative Care Service, a programme developed to improve the care of the terminally ill.

We were ushered into the formal sitting-room of the Priory with its panelled walls, comfortable furniture and crammed bookshelves. At the far end of this imposing room was a solarium filled with an intriguing array of very healthy plants. A sense of calm and orderliness pervaded the scene.

Within minutes the doors swung open and in strode Father John. Physical stature, bearing, personal appearance and the articulate speech of a disciplined mind combined to leave a lasting impression. Tea was discreetly delivered and, taking our seats in front of the fireplace, we began to explore the dimensions of each other's work. We described to Father John our health care programmes developed for the dying and their families and our attempt to deliver whole person care. We had come, as stated, to explore with him whether Christian meditation might have a place in the lives of our patients, their families or indeed the staff. We added with some hesitation that we might be interested in exploring the potential of meditation in our own personal lives.

Throughout our visit Father John acted with a formality that was courteous yet somewhat reserved. While he was attentive to the conversation, there was no evidence of enthusiasm. Our visit of forty-five minutes ended with no clear plans to pursue the dialogue.

Many months later one of our colourful colleagues in the Palliative Care Service developed a malignant brain tumour. Don was an irascible rogue who had lived many lives! He had been student, vagabond, hippy, philosopher and bon vivant. Describing himself as 'a world-famous unpublished philosopher', Don was a nursing assistant and valued member of our team. Now he lay as a patient on our ward with a sign carefully posted over his bed, 'Waiting for Godot'.

My real and lasting contact with John Main came through Don. During the final months of his illness Don became an oblate in the Benedictine community, and I was impressed by the faithfulness and interest with which Father John nurtured his involvement. Father John's visits to the bedside, while always quiet, were none the less stately if not epic, giving the strength of his presence. Don, with his eye for a 'happening' was, I believe, as delighted by the 'theatre' of these encounters as he was refreshed by their spiritual content.

Following Don's death, we were pleased to hear that Father John had agreed to conduct his funeral service to be held in a local church. Those in attendance represented a curious grab-bag of humanity representing the various lives Don had led. Jaded young intellectuals, representatives of the street and drug set, philosophers, students, businessmen and health care professionals, all there to do honour to a man they loved.

Having been asked to be one of the readers at the funeral service, I met the other participants in the vestry office just prior to the service. To my surprise, Father John was not there. He had been replaced by a youthful individual who informed me that he was Father Laurence and that he would be replacing Father John. After the service I realised that Father John would not have arranged for a replacement under ordinary circumstances. Feeling that something might lie behind this, I drove to the Priory on my way home.

A concerned member of the community met me at the door. 'I'm so glad you have come. Father John is upstairs and really in quite a bit of pain.' Without further remarks I was led to his quarters on the second floor. Recognising that it is sometimes difficult to assess the amount of distress being experienced by an Englishman (and even on occasion a tough Irishman), I surmised that it was significant, given the evident relief on his face when he saw me! His warm grasp of my hand and welcoming comment, 'I'm so glad you are here,' spoke volumes. He immediately told me of the low back pain which he attributed to an old disc problem. 'No,' he commented, following my brief examination, he did not know any local neuro-surgeons and if I could line one up for him, that would be greatly appreciated. With a brief phone call he was booked to see a senior colleague at the Montreal Neurological Hospital.

Late on the day of his appointment my phone rang and a rather puzzled if not disconcerted colleague put it to me as politely as possible that I might have mentioned to him that Father John had a known malignancy which had spread to his spine. I was taken aback and at the same time had to smile at the fact that, although Father John had talked about his distress and given me his history in an apparently candid manner, this reserved, very private man had just happened to neglect to mention that he had in recent months been under treatment for cancer. In talking to him about this later, he pointed out with sincerity and humility that he really did not want others to know about his critical state since he feared it would complicate his relationships and draw attention to himself and away from his work. From that point, the Palliative Care Service home care team became involved, always keeping at a distance dictated by Father John.

Weeks later Father John delivered a keynote address in the closing Plenary Session of the International Congress on Terminal Care, entitled 'Death: the Inner Journey'. This reflective, insightful contribution was meaningful to many. Only later did we learn that he had been in considerable pain throughout his speech.

Our involvement as a team became more direct with home visits by physician and nursing colleagues who monitored his medications and taught those closest to Father John how to give bed baths and assist with his daily care as he became weaker. While our nursing team was ready to take an active role in his care, it was clear that Father Laurence and his fellow community members wished to be the primary caregivers.

The final days of Father John's life were spent quietly at the Priory, his activity limited. The Christmas season had just passed and, as the end drew near, I made daily or twice daily visits to monitor his pain control. Sue Britton, our sensitive, observant and highly-experienced nurse, later commented that she had only seen one other person die in a way similar to Father John. In pressing her for further details, she cited two elements in his dying which seemed distinctive, first the presence of a highly-disciplined yet dynamic struggle and active questioning about his approaching death; and second a willingness to let go through the quiet process of continual meditation.

During the evening of his death, Father Laurence and I discussed by phone the morphine dose he would need for comfort. A short time later a concerned phone call from one of the members of the community took me to the Priory without delay. It seemed that Father John had just died. As I entered the room and took in the tableau of grief, community and love that surrounded Father John, I knelt by his bed and felt for his pulse. It was present and strong. It was clear that what we were seeing was not approaching death but deep relaxation due to the dose of narcotic he had just received. Quietly I took Laurence aside and commented with a wry smile, 'It's all very well, my friend – he will indeed be terribly missed. The point is, though, that right now he is just having a good deep sleep due to his medication.' Laurence caught the loving humour in the situation and the need to explain the circumstances to the grieving friends at the bedside. Gently Laurence told those assembled that Father John was still with us and only enjoying a deep sleep. He then suggested they went downstairs for a cup of tea while he and I stayed at the bedside. As they left he turned to me, his eyes twinkling, and said, 'You know, there was a little Monty Python there, Father John would have loved that.'

For the rest of the night those close to Father John took turns at his bedside. In the early hours of the morning I went home, only to be summoned back by the news that this time Father John had indeed died. No humour now, only faces lined with a deep sense of loss. Those who wished to, again took turns keeping a quiet vigil by his bedside.

Not until I read Neil McKenty's biography did I meet Douglas Main's Irish wit and the full power of his spontaneity. More recently our contact has continued to grow through the twice-daily meditations that are now part of my life.

SUE BRITTON

In December 1982 I was asked to instruct members of the Priory in how to handle a bed patient, Dom John Main, and also how to handle pain management. In my second visit I noticed in particular how very, very different Dom John Main was to other patients of mine who were dying. While he was experiencing some physical pain, nevertheless he seemed to have sublimated the pain to a higher level. I attributed this to his disciplined life of meditation. The other observation was that he was not 'hanging on' but was 'letting go'. Through it all Father Laurence was very dedicated to his care. This memory of Dom John's 'letting go' has been a lasting one and proved to me that dying does not have to be a long drawn out affair with much suffering. His death has helped me immeasurably in my palliative care role to prepare others for death.

WALTER LALLEMAND

Shortly before he died in Bangkok in early December 1968, Thomas Merton, that great contemplative monk and author of many books on prayer, wrote, 'Life is a long journey and it is all within.' Perhaps this phrase of Merton's synthesises to me much that could be said of Dom Main who succumbed to cancer in late December 1982. He was ever as I came to know him 'a man within'. This striking 'within-ness' and its transforming power of Spirit over body is held in a notable memory recall of mine, which, even as I write these lines some years later, remains evergreen.

It was a Tuesday morning in October, two months before his death, and a small group of priests had assembled for their regular Tuesday meditation. Some of us had sensed that all was not well with Father John. He had been undergoing medical treatment for some time. None the less for that session, which indeed proved to be our last with him, he led us in prayer. Prior to the half-hour meditation in silence, as was his wont he proceeded to speak on some aspect of St Paul using a phrase or two from one of the letters. What I remember most of that last talk was the precision and clarity of his thought, the 'aliveness' of his words, their lucidity and depth. This focus was truly heightened in me when, after meditation, we assembled for coffee.

Here he seemed a different man, so very tired, indeed very sick. His sparkle of humour was absent, and in our attempt to converse he had little to say. Somehow we could all sense the physical malaise. We did not tarry long, and soon brought the coffee break to a conclusion. Looking back, then and until he died, Father John was living out those words of Paul in Corinthians: 'We do not lose heart, because our inner being is renewed each day, though our body is being destroyed at the same time.'

The day before he died I visited the Priory, said a final prayer over him and gave a blessing. He seemed unconscious yet peaceful. After I whispered my presence in his ear, I then uttered in his ear the simple prayer 'Maranatha' – only this time, more of a prayer of petition; that God would bring John into that great silence where he would for ever be 'grandly poor' yet fully alive in the 'Is-ness of God'.

In the concelebrated funeral mass at the Priory, as a new year dawned, we mourned his passing as friend and teacher of prayer. And yet our mourning was tinged with joy and gratitude to the God of all 'within-ness' for his graces on Dom John Main's life and for the latter's influence on our own.

CAMILLE CAMPBELL CND

My spiritual life took a 360 degree turn when I first heard Father John Main speak on meditation. It was in the summer of 1978, and Father John had been invited to give a series of talks on prayer at a renewal planned by our community for the English-speaking sisters of Canada and the United States.

Here, I thought, was another man who would say what I had heard so often before, and who would have the delightful gift of putting me into a well-deserved sleep. The memory of him walking into a noisy, crowded auditorium is still vivid in my mind; this tall, perfectly composed man who commanded quiet and attention even before he began to speak. Within minutes he startled me into a realisation of the seriousness of my call to Christian prayer, a call that he saw as a universal one. John Main spoke with conviction, with urgency and with calmness, and his message was one of silence, of stillness and of simplicity. But, you may say, is there anything new here? The message is always new if one has ears to hear, and at that time in my life I received the gift of hearing, and with it the equally precious gift of responding to what I heard. Father John gave us the message of meditation, and he also gave us a way – the way of the mantra. For me this way opened up avenues of freedom. I was finally relieved of the burdens which had weighed down my prayer, my thoughts and my imagination.

My enthusiasm knew no bounds. I was energised to begin immediately, and visions of an instant contemplative kept racing through my mind. After all, Father John told us in his own dynamic manner that all you have to do is find a comfortable position, sit quite still, and repeat the word Maranatha in four distinct syllables. This, he said, should be done for half an hour in the morning and half an hour in the evening. What could be easier? To me it all seemed so simple. But in the years since I heard those talks the way has not been so simple or easy. The journey, in fact, has been filled with struggles of faith, of giving up, of returning. Regardless of the pain and the struggle, however, there is for me no other option but to continue.

For three years I had no further contact with Father John

except through his books and tapes. In the summer of 1982 Father John journeyed east to Nova Scotia to give a retreat on meditation. It was my good fortune to make this retreat, an experience which was to lead me on to a year of prayer in the monastery. I began that retreat with a feeling that all was well within my little kingdom. Then Father John struck again, like a bolt of lightning. His words have always had the effect of making a direct hit on my heart. Towards the close of that retreat Father John reminded us that the only way to learn to meditate was to meditate. We may ask a friend how cold the water is before jumping in for a swim, but we can only experience the coldness when we jump in ourselves. Here was another invitation from God to go further into the journey to himself. Before the retreat was over I asked Father John about the possibility of spending a year in prayer at the monastery.

This was a frightening step for me to take, and the questions I expected him to ask me were never asked. Instead he tried his best to discourage me, and took pains to impress upon me the fact that it would be a very difficult year. As he looked through me, he asked me only one question, 'What kind of work can you do?' I was deflated, but also challenged, and I proceeded to give him an exaggerated list of my talents, trying desperately to impress him. Then he looked at me with a slight smile and said, 'I think you'll do, yes, I think you'll do.' As I look back I wonder if he knew then, in some mysterious way, of the sorrow, the pain and the parting that lay ahead for him and for the community in that year. As for me, I looked forward to a year of learning about God and to a welcomed respite after thirty years in the classroom.

That YES has been a turning point in my life. That YES has blessed me with a year that will be for ever a source of strength for me. That YES gave me the privilege of experiencing the death of a man who taught me how to accept the gift of life, the gift to be myself. He taught me the art of living, and that lesson I am trying to learn more deeply each day as I 'sit quite still'.

When I arrived at the Priory in September of that year Father John met me, sitting in a wheelchair. The realisation that he was a very sick man did not come to me until Novem-

254

ber. This was a man I hardly knew, but as time went on I saw that he was living in constant pain while continuing to give of himself to others. The avenues of freedom opened up within me when I first heard Father John speak now began to take shape as I grew into the life of the Priory. I began to understand that his teaching was leading me into what he called 'liberty of spirit'. Meditation is a way to that liberty, it gives us the freedom to take off our masks and simply to be. It is a way of being free from the frustration of not being in contact with our inner selves. This is what I learned from listening to, watching and caring for Father John. As his illness grew more intense he grew more deeply into this freedom. The ultimate freedom, the freedom of desire for life itself, is the lesson that Christ taught us, and it is the lesson I saw repeated in the life and death of Father John. He died a teacher and he taught up to his very last moments. The things he taught I will for ever strive to live.

It has been years since I left the Priory, years of change, years that have made greater demands on my resources than I have ever experienced. Without my year of prayer at the Priory, this time would have been much more difficult, perhaps even impossible for my frail nature. Meditation has been the anchor in my life, it has been a beacon of peace in the troubled waters. I have so often said to those who know me, 'What would I do without my half hour in the morning and in the evening?' These are the moments of stillness that make possible the impossible. They have taught me to live in the reality of the present moment, a present moment for which I am so deeply grateful because in 1978 I received a gift, the gift of hearing Father John's message.

PATRICK MURRAY

In hearing the essence of the gospel of the paschal mystery – the death and the resurrection of Christ – I look at the mystery of John Main's own suffering. I remember looking at him in his wheelchair. One day I was up in his room. He was lying there in silence. It was in the morning, about 9.30. I asked him how he was and how he had slept. He said to me, 'The pain in my back is excruciating.' I can still hear the tonality of the word 'excruciating' as he lay there. That would have been September, about three months before he died, and yet right to the end, to use his own expression, 'he kept on keeping on'.

DOREEN ROMANDINI

Every Saturday after midday meditation we used to have a picnic in the garden at the monastery. It was a sort of 'family' day – Polly and Mark Schofield would be there with their three boys; often there would be a couple of people who had recently made contact with the community – a leisure time together. Everything would be carried up to the garden from the kitchen: glasses on big trays, water pitchers, huge bowls of salad and bread; little tables were brought out from the garage; sometimes it was a barbecue. I remember the last such event that Father John attended. We had all gone up ahead and he came later with Father Laurence. It was obvious as he climbed up the path that he was in pain. He looked very pale. He was wearing his straw hat to shade his eyes from the sun. He did not join in the revelry around the barbecue but sat in a chair off to the side in the shade. At one point I looked over and he was alone. It was the first time that I had seen him looking sad (or maybe it was wistful). I shyly went over to say hallo. I think we talked a little about his hat but most of the time we were silent. He was watching the group around the barbecue. Although I was not totally aware of it at the time, looking back over the scene several times in the past few years, I think he was really saying goodbye. It was as if part of him was already somewhere else. He was blessing us, detaching himself from us.

I remember an encounter with him before making my oblation. I had already talked with Father John about it and he had written me a note confirming that it would be at the next oblate meeting. The meeting came and went and I was not contacted about it. I was a little concerned and after one of the group nights I approached Father John and asked if I was still a candidate. He assured me that there had been an oversight and that I would definitely be informed about the next meeting. I was overjoyed and carried away by his warmth and assurance. I left the house feeling rather tipsy, I think, because when I went out on the porch, which was covered by a wonderful blanket of fresh snow that had fallen during the meeting, I slipped down the stairs but was laughing out loud and thinking how happy I was that he really did want me.

I remember the time I sat in while he took the children's meditation group on a Saturday morning. He put his hand in his pocket and pulled out a comb, which very soon became a magic comb and the children began to tell stories about the wonderful things they could do with it.

I remember the day he said he had a surprise for me – something wrapped up! 'You must come into the library,' he said. There it was, a brand new, multi-function dictaphone machine! From then on we would transcribe his talks and get them ready for publication. It was a special moment in the story of his work reaching out to so many.

My few direct encounters with Father John were all special moments like this. The most ordinary day to day events became important events in your life when you were with him. Not many words were spoken but something happened – you knew the Spirit was with you.

I remember the last days before Father John died and we began meditating right outside his room, throughout the day. The last night a large group gathered and we sang Compline together. His door was open and of course he prayed with us. Father Laurence gave the blessing and then went into the room and blessed Father John. I knew we were saying goodbye.

Christian Meditation Centres

Australia

Monastery of the Holy Spirit
24 Murray Road, Croydon
Melbourne
Victoria 3136
Tel No: 03–725 2052

Canada

The Benedictine Priory
1475 Pine Avenue West
Montreal H3G 1B3
Tel No: 514–281 0659

India

Christian Meditation Centre
1/1429 Bilatikulam Road
Calicut 673006
Kerala
Tel No: 60395

Ireland

Christian Meditation Centre
62 Park Avenue
Sandymount
Dublin 4
Tel No: 693466

New Zealand

Christian Meditation Centre
St Peter's Church
7 Harrison Road
Mount Wellington
Auckland

Philippines

Christian Meditation Centre
10 Grant Street, Greenhills
Metro Manila
PO Box 468
Tel No: 7221814

Singapore

Holy Family Meditation Centre
Church of the Holy Family
6 Chapel Road
Singapore 1542
Tel No: 3440046

Thailand

Christian Meditation Group
51/1 Sedsiri Road
Bangkok 10400
Tel No: 2713295

United Kingdom

Christian Meditation Centre
29 Campden Hill Road
London W8 7DX
Tel No: 071–937 0014

Christian Meditation Centre
St Mary's Park
Melbourn Rd
Royston Herts SG8 7DB
Tel No: 0763–246110

United States

Hesed Community
3745 Elston Avenue
Oakland, San Francisco
CA 94602
Tel No: 415–482 5573

Christian Meditation Centre
822 So. Springinsguth Road
Schaumburg
60193 Illinois
Tel No: 708–529 4429

Christian Meditation Centre
1 East 29th Street
New York
NY 10016
Tel No: 212–684 6770

Books and Cassette Tapes

Books by John Main

Christian Meditation: The Gethsemani Talks. 2nd edn, Benedictine Priory, Montreal, 1983. In 1977 Dom John was invited to give these conferences on Christian Meditation at the Abbey of Gethsemani. They have been the introduction to a deeper life of prayer for many since. The first talk gives an account of Father John's own initiation and the subsequent experiences that led him into a Benedictine monastery where he began his work as a teacher of prayer. In the second talk he speaks of how meditation helps us personally to verify the reality of our faith, participating in reality rather than by theorising. In the third talk Dom John answers questions on prayer and meditation.

The Christian Mysteries: prayer and sacrament. Benedictine Priory, Montreal, 1979; reprinted 1982. Every moment of love and worship has a meaning itself, a transcendent purpose. This is the insight underlying the sections in this book dealing with Baptism (the Mystery of Conversion), Marriage (the Mystery of Communion), Anointing (the Mystery of Wholeness), Environment for Worship (the Mystery of Sacred Space), Eucharist (the Mystery of Koinonia), and Penance (the Mystery of Poverty). This book is of special value to those seeking to bring their inner spiritual journey and their outward life of worship into a deeper unity.

Community of Love. Darton, Longman and Todd, 1990. John Main's deepest vision of life was as a community of love. In this community we experience wholeness, in ourselves, with others and with the society in which we live. For him the practice of meditation reveals a centre which unifies all the many dimensions of our personal and communal experience. (This volume includes *Community of Love*, first published in 1984, and *Death: the inner journey, The Hunger for Prayer, Monastic Prayer and Modern Man, The Other-Centredness of Mary,* all first published in 1983.)

The Heart of Creation. Darton, Longman and Todd, 1988; Cross-road, New York, 1988. This book includes John Main's treatment of themes which are important to everyone concerned with deepening their spiritual life: our need for a spiritual discipline and how to cope with its challenge; how to see the fruits of prayer in daily life; solitude and community for those living in the world; how meditation deepens our relationship with Christ; the contemplative experience as the meeting-point of religious.

Letters from the Heart: Christian monasticism and the renewal of community. Crossroad, New York, 1982; reprinted 1984. This is an inspiring source of teaching and encouragement to those on or beginning the way of meditation. The twelve letters were sent out to oblates and friends of the Benedictine Priory and form a living record of the renewal of monastic life in a modern urban setting. Each letter is prefaced by a commentary on the development of the community and its work. In the introduction Dom John reflects on an experiential theology of Christian meditation and describes the needs facing the Church and religious life today. These burning 'letters from the heart' convey the richness of our being in Christ and of the way a new monastic community is responding to it.

Moment of Christ. Darton, Longman and Todd, 1984; Crossroad, New York, 1984. Dom John talks in this book about the many aspects of meditation: the way of the mantra, leaving distractions behind, fullness of life in love and silence. These short direct teachings emphasise simplicity, transcending self-consciousness and moving beyond techniques of prayer. A handbook for everyone on the pilgrimage. (Also in German.)

The Present Christ. Darton, Longman and Todd, 1985; Crossroad, New York, 1985. These twelve spiritual letters represent the culmination of John Main's teaching in this form. Covering many aspects of the spiritual life and its connection with contemporary society, this book is a rich source of inspiration and insight. The final letter, written shortly before Father John's death, is a moving reflection on the final things and the mystery of resurrection. The introduction by Father Laurence Freeman traces the story of the community during the years these letters were written.

The Way of Unknowing. Darton, Longman and Todd, 1989; Cross-road, New York, 1989. This is a book to be read in conjunction with the experience of prayer. It is not about meditation; it is for meditation. It is a book dominated by the spirit of Christ – for the author believed that it was his first task to stand aside and to reveal the teachings of the Lord.

Word into Silence.   Darton, Longman and Todd, 1980; Paulist Press, New York, 1981. This book is a powerful general introduction to Christian meditation: the essentials of Christian thought underlying the practice of meditation and twelve short sections meant to prepare for a period of meditation. Father John's preface urges the necessity of deep prayer for revitalisation of Christian life and community. There is a short list of suggested reading. This source of inspiration by people seeking a deepening of their spiritual journey is drawn from the cassette series *Christian Meditation*. (Also in Portuguese.)

Other publications

The Joy of Being: Daily readings with John Main,   selected by Clare Hallward. Darton, Longman and Todd, 1987. Clare Hallward's selection of short extracts from John Main's published and unpublished writings is a pocket-size volume of great inspiration. Arranged thematically, it suggests the practice of the short 'sayings' of the Desert Fathers, as Laurence Freeman points out in his introduction.

In the Stillness Dancing: the journey of John Main,   by Neil McKenty. Darton, Longman and Todd, 1986; Crossroad, New York, 1987. This very readable biography of John Main traces his human development through childhood, the war, diplomatic service and law to his truest identity as monk and spiritual teacher. Well-researched, the story of his life is described in connection with the mature teaching for which John Main has been acclaimed by Bede Griffiths as 'the best spiritual teacher in the Church today'. There is a photo section and bibliography.

Cassette tapes by John Main

These are available from the Benedictine Priory, Montreal.

Awakening: retreat talks.   Set of 5 cassettes in vinyl case. This is a series of five cassettes of talks given to a missionary community on the contemplative experience as the grounding reality of every form of Christian life. The topics dealt with include Conversion, Leadership, Jesus as Teacher, The Vows, Climate for Prayer. The talks can profitably be used as a basic resource around which to structure a personal retreat. These tapes reveal another dimension of John Main's authenticity as a teacher.

Being on the Way. Set of 6 cassettes in vinyl case. These talks further enhance the collection of talks by Dom John Main. He speaks here to those who have already begun to meditate on a daily basis and are seeking to continue this journey. The value and purpose of this set is to help and encourage all those who have begun and want to persevere on this spiritual journey, with the help of a teacher.

Christian Meditation: the essential teaching. Set of 3 in vinyl case. This set of tapes contains the essential teaching Dom John communicated by word and example.

1 *An Introduction to Christian Meditation* gives a foundational description of practice and tradition of meditation in the Christian tradition (60 minutes).
2 *Meditation: the Christian experience* shows the underlying depth of thought that supports the tradition (60 minutes).
3 *Twelve Talks for Meditators* with music, is intended to prepare individuals and groups for a period of meditation (90 minutes). (Also in French.)

The Christian Mysteries: prayer and sacrament. Set of 2 cassettes. 120 minutes. These tapes are based on the book *The Christian Mysteries*. The talks were originally delivered to a group of liturgists and priests meeting in the Archdiocese of Montreal. As the spoken word they have proved of great value to many, especially those working with groups or communities in diocesan and liturgical renewal. They are an inspiration to anyone seeking to bring their religious life and their spiritual life into a deeper unity. Baptism, Marriage, Anointing, Environment for Worship, Eucharist and Penance – these sacramental mysteries are seen in the light of meditation.

Communitas. 5 sets. This is a cassette series of the talks given weekly at the Priory. Dom John Main spoke to those just beginning, and to those on the spiritual pilgrimage. They capture the spontaneity, intensity, and urgency of Dom John's teaching on meditation. These cassettes are widely used by oblates of the Priory, by individual meditators, and by meditation groups which follow this teaching in daily meditation. They are a powerful encouragement to persevere in the spiritual journey. There are 20 talks in each Communitas set.

In the Beginning. Set of 6 cassettes in vinyl case. These cassettes are part of the collection recorded at the Priory. Dom John Main speaks here to those who are beginning to meditate as part of their spiritual journey. These cassettes are used both by individual meditators and meditation groups which follow this teaching around the world. The purpose of this set is to encourage people to begin and then to keep on beginning.

The Last Conferences of Dom John Main OSB. Set of 6 cassettes in vinyl case. John Main's teaching continued through his last illness. These twelve talks to the groups meeting in the Montreal Priory each week were his last. They focus his message, his wisdom and compassion in words that open the minds and hearts of his listeners to the vision he was about to enter fully.

Word Made Flesh. Set of 10 cassettes in vinyl case. These talks were recorded at the Priory by Dom John Main. Each cassette has both an introductory talk and one addressed to those who have been meditating for some time. At the end of each talk are two short segments of music composed and recorded by Russill Paul which would be helpful to those using these cassettes for group meditation.

Other cassette tapes

The Life and Teaching of Dom John Main, by Laurence Freeman OSB. Set of 2 cassettes in vinyl case. Dom Laurence Freeman gave these talks at the Dublin School of Prayer in July 1986. John Main was his teacher of both the monastic life and meditation. In 1977 he accompanied John Main to establish the Benedictine Priory which has since become a centre for a worldwide community of meditators. Father Laurence shows how Father John's life and personality are a parable of his teaching.